Holy Scripture in
the Qumran Commentaries
and Pauline Letters

Holy Scripture in the Qumran Commentaries and Pauline Letters

TIMOTHY H. LIM

CLARENDON PRESS · OXFORD
1997

Oxford University Press, Great Clarendon Street, Oxford OX2 6DP
Oxford New York
Athens Auckland Bangkok Bogota Bombay
Buenos Aires Calcutta Cape Town Dar es Salaam
Delhi Florence Hong Kong Istanbul Karachi
Kuala Lumpur Madras Madrid Melbourne
Mexico City Nairobi Paris Singapore
Taipei Tokyo Toronto Warsaw
and associated companies in
Berlin Ibadan

Oxford is a trade mark of Oxford University Press

Published in the United States
by Oxford University Press Inc., New York

© Timothy H. Lim 1997

All rights reserved. No part of this publication may be reproduced,
stored in a retrieval system, or transmitted, in any form or by any means,
without the prior permission in writing of Oxford University Press.
Within the UK, exceptions are allowed in respect of any fair dealing for the
purpose of research or private study, or criticism or review, as permitted
under the Copyright, Designs and Patents Act, 1988, or in the case of
reprographic reproduction in accordance with the terms of the licences
issued by the Copyright Licensing Agency. Enquiries concerning
reproduction outside these terms and in other countries should be
sent to the Rights Department, Oxford University Press,
at the address above

British Library Cataloguing in Publication Data
Data available

Library of Congress Cataloging in Publication Data
Holy Scripture in the Qumran commentaries
and Pauline letters / Timothy H. Lim.
Revision of the author's thesis (doctoral)
University of Oxford, 1991.
Includes bibliographical references.
1. Bible.   O.T.—Criticism, interpretation, etc., Jewish.
2. Dead Sea Scrolls—Criticism, interpretation, etc.
3. Bible. O.T.—Relation to Epistles of Paul.   4. Bible. N.T. Epistles of
Paul—Criticism, interpretation, etc.   I. Title.
BM487.L54   1997   221.6'09'015—dc21   97-10994
ISBN 0-19-826206-x

1 3 5 7 9 10 8 6 4 2

Typeset by Regent Typesetting, London
Printed in Great Britain on acid-free paper by
Biddles Ltd., Guildford and King's Lynn

PREFACE

This book is a thoroughly revised dissertation that was submitted to the Faculty of Oriental Studies of the University of Oxford in 1991 for the degree of Doctor of Philosophy. Revision has taken the form of corrections, additions and reformulations in light of suggestions made by the examiners, publication referees, and other colleagues. I have also taken into consideration as many of the newly released Qumran scrolls as were available in preliminary or official publications and studies. Thanks are due to Geza Vermes and John Ashton, who acted as my supervisors, and Sebastian Brock and Philip Alexander, who examined the thesis at the viva.

Over the years, I have discussed many of the topics covered in this book at numerous conferences and seminars in the UK, USA, Canada, and Israel, including the Oxford Forum for Qumran Research, New Testament Seminar, Theology Faculty of the University of Oxford, St Andrews University Biblical Study Seminar, University of Chicago, Oriental Institute Symposium, the University of Michigan (Ann Arbor) Near Eastern Studies Seminar, McMaster University Department of Religious Studies Seminar, and Hebrew University of Jerusalem Comparative Religions Seminar. I should like to thank all those who invited me and responded to my work.

I should also like to thank Emanuel Tov for his advice and instruction on text-critical matters when I spent 1989-90 at the Hebrew University as Lady Davis Doctoral Fellow in the Department of Bible. The late Jonas Greenfield, to his blessed memory, not only taught me as a doctoral student, but subsequently alerted me to scholarly discussions on PYadin 19. My good friend Peretz Segal has been a conversation-partner for many years on a whole range of matters, and Leonard Greenspoon took time out of his own sabbatical to read and comment on the dissertation.

My present colleagues in the Department of Hebrew and Old Testament Studies and Department of New Testament, Language, Literature and Theology at the Faculty of Divinity of the University of Edinburgh have heard me read parts of the book in seminars

Preface

and lectures over the past few years. Their questions and responses have been useful in clarifying my thinking on certain issues.

Financial support was provided by: Overseas Research Scheme Award (1986–9); the Social Sciences and Humanities Research Council of Canada for doctoral (1988–90) and postdoctoral fellowships (1993); Lady Davis Fellowship Trust for a doctoral fellowship at the Hebrew University of Jerusalem (1989–90); Kennicott, Pusey and Ellerton Fund for a Grant (1988–9) and the Kennicott Hebrew Fellowship (1991–3); and Wolfson College, Oxford (1990–1), Oxford Centre for Hebrew and Jewish Studies (1991–3), and St. Hugh's College, Oxford (1991–3) for Junior Research Fellowships.

I should also like to acknowledge the courteous and professional editorial work of the Arts and Reference Division of Oxford University Press, especially Hilary O'Shea, Enid Barker, Liz Alsop, and Sylvia Jaffrey.

A heartfelt thanks is offered to my parents, Benjamin and Josephine Lim, and my in-laws, Zelick and Barbara Perler, for their encouragement and support over the years.

My son, Jonathan Christopher, and daughter, Alison Emily, have been a source of constant joy for their father.

This book is dedicated to my dear wife Laura.

T. H. L.

CONTENTS

Contents

ABBREVIATIONS

ABD	D. N. Freedman (ed.), *Anchor Bible Dictionary*, 6 vols. (New York: Doubleday, 1992)
AJ	Josephus, *Antiquitates Judaicae*
ANRW	*Aufstieg und Niedergang der römischen Welt* (Berlin: Walter de Gruyter, 1972-)
AO	*Archiv Orientálni*
ARN	*'Abot de Rabbi Nathan*
BA	*Biblical Archaeologist*
BAGD	W. Bauer, W. F. Arndt, F. W. Gingrich, and F. W. Danker, *A Greek–English Lexicon of the New Testament and Other Early Christian Literature* (Chicago: University of Chicago Press, 1979)
Barn.	*Barnabas*
BASOR	*Bulletin of the American Schools of Oriental Research*
BDB	F. Brown, S. R. Driver, and C. A. Briggs, *A Hebrew and English Lexicon of the Old Testament* (Oxford: Clarendon Press, 1906)
Ber.	*Berakot*
BGU	*Berliner Griechische Urkunden (Ägyptische Urkunden aus den Kgl. Museen zu Berlin, 1895-)*
BHS	*Biblia Hebraica Stuttgartensia*, ed. K. Elliger, W. Rudolph, *et al.* (Stuttgart: Deutsche Bibelgesellschaft, 1966–7)
Bib.	*Biblica*
BIOSCS	*Bulletin of the International Organization for Septuagint and Cognate Studies*
BJ	Josephus, *Bellum Judaicum*
BJRL	*Bulletin of the John Rylands Library*
b. Meg.	Babylonian Talmud, *Megillah*
BO	*Bibliotheca orientalis*
BSac	*Bibliotheca Sacra*
b. Sanh.	Babylonian Talmud, *Sanhedrin*
BSOAS	*Bulletin of the School of Oriental and African Studies*
CA	Josephus, *Contra Apionem*

Abbreviations

CBQ	*Catholic Bible Quarterly*
CD	Cairo Damascus (Document)
CHB	*Cambridge History of the Bible*, i. *From the Beginnings to Jerome* (1970), ii. *The West from the Fathers to the Reformation* (1969), iii. *The West from the Reformation to the Present Day* (1963) (Cambridge: Cambridge University Press)
1 Clem.	*1 Clement*
CS	*Cahiers Sioniens*
Did.	*Didache*
DJD	*Discoveries in the Judaean Desert*, 13 vols. (Oxford: Clarendon Press, 1955–94). See Select Bibliography.
DSD	*Dead Sea Discoveries*
DSSE	Geza Vermes, *Dead Sea Scrolls in English*, 3rd edn. (London: Penguin Books, 1987)
EI	*Eretz-Israel*
ESBNT	Joseph A. Fitzmyer, *Essays on the Semitic Background of the New Testament* (London: Chapman, 1971)
Eus. *HE*	Eusebius, *Historia Ecclesiastica*
FYR	Devorah Dimant and Uriel Rappaport, *The Dead Sea Scrolls: Forty Years of Research* (Leiden: E. J. Brill, 1992)
Gen. Rab.	*Genesis Rabbah*
GKC	*Gesenius' Hebrew Grammar*, ed. and rev. E. Kautzsch and A. E. Cowley (Oxford: Clarendon Press, 1910)
HDSS	Elisha Qimron, *The Hebrew of the Dead Sea Scrolls*, Harvard Semitic Studies (Atlanta: Scholars Press, 1986)
8ḤevXIIgr	Minor Prophets Scroll, from Nahal Ḥever
HJP	*History of the Jewish People in the Age of Jesus Christ*
HR	*History of Religions*
HTR	*Harvard Theological Review*
HUCA	*Hebrew Union College Annual*
IDBS	K. Krim (ed.), *Interpreter's Dictionary of the Bible Supplementary Volume* (Nashville: Abingdon, 1976)
IEJ	*Israel Exploration Journal*

Int.	*Interpretation*
IOS	*Israel Oriental Studies*
JAOS	*Journal of the American Oriental Society*
JBL	*Journal of Biblical Literature*
JJS	*Journal of Jewish Studies*
JNES	*Journal of Near Eastern Studies*
JQR	*Jewish Quarterly Review*
JSNT	*Journal for the Study of the New Testament*
JSS	*Journal of Semitic Studies*
JTS	*Journal of Theological Studies*
JWSTP	Michael Stone (ed.), *Jewish Writings of the Second Temple Period* (Assen: Van Gorcum, 1984)
KB	Ludwig Köhler and Walter Baumgartner, *Lexicon in Veteris Testamenti Libros* (Leiden: E. J. Brill, 1974)
LXX	Septuagint
m.	Mishnah
Madrid	J. Trebolle Barrera and L. Vegas Montaner (eds.), *The Madrid Qumran Congress: Proceedings of the International Congress on the Dead Sea Scrolls, Madrid, 18–21 March 1991*, 2 vols. (Leiden: E. J. Brill, 1992)
Mikra	M. J. Mulder (ed.), *Mikra, Text, Translation, Reading and Interpretation of the Hebrew Bible in Ancient Judaism and Early Christianity* (Assen: Van Gorcum, 1988)
MT	Masoretic Text
NovT	*Novum Testamentum*
NTS	*New Testament Studies*
OS	*Oudtestamentische Studiën*
PAM	Palestine Archaeology Museum
PEQ	*Palestine Exploration Quarterly*
PYadin	Papyrus Yadin
Qoh.	Qohelet
1Q22	Qumran, Cave 1, no. 22
1QH	Qumran, Cave 1, *Hôdāyôt* (*Thanksgiving Hymns*)
1QIsa[a]	Qumran, Cave 1, Isaiah, first copy
1QpHab	Qumran, Cave 1, pesher on Habakkuk
1QpMic	Qumran, Cave 1, pesher on Micah
1QpPs	Qumran, Cave 1, Psalms

1QpZeph	Qumran, Cave 1, pesher on Zephaniah
1QS	Qumran, Cave 1, *Serek hayyaḥad* (Rule of the Community)
1QSa	Qumran, Cave 1, Rule of the Congregation
1QSb	Qumran, Cave 1, Rule of Blessing
2QDeut^c	Qumran, Cave 2, Deuteronomy, 3rd copy
2QEx^b	Qumran, Cave 2, Exodus, 2nd copy
3QpIsa	Qumran, Cave 3, pesher on Isaiah
4Q158	Qumran, Cave 4, no. 158
4Q177	Qumran, Cave 4, no. 177
4Q252	Qumran, Cave 4, no. 252
4Q285	Qumran, Cave 4, no. 285
4Q365^a	Qumran, Cave 4, no. 365, 1st copy
4QCatena^a	Qumran, Cave 4, no. 177
4QDeut^{j-l}	Qumran, Cave 4, Deuteronomy, 10th–12th copies
4QDeut^n	Qumran, Cave 4, Deuteronomy, no. 41, 14th copy
4QExod^b	Qumran, Cave 4, Exodus, 2nd copy
4QExod–Lev^f	Qumran, Cave 4, Exodus–Leviticus
4QFlor	Qumran, Cave 4, *Florilegium*
4QJer^b	Qumran, Cave 4, Jeremiah, 2nd copy
4QMMT	Qumran, Cave 4, *Miqsat Ma'aseh Torah*
4QpaleoExod^m	Qumran, Cave 4, Exodus, no. 22
4QpHos^{a-b}	Qumran, Cave 4, pesher on Hosea, 1st and 2nd copies
4QpIsa^{a-e}	Qumran, Cave 4, pesher on Isaiah, 1st–5th copies
4QpNah	Qumran, Cave 4, pesher on Nahum
4QpPs^{a-b}	Qumran, Cave 4, pesher on Psalms, 1st and 2nd copies
4QpUnid	Qumran, Cave 4, unidentified pesher
4QpZeph	Qumran, Cave 4, pesher on Zephaniah
4QS^{a-j}	Qumran, Cave 4, *Serek hayyaḥad* (Rule of the Community), 1st–10th copies
4QSam^a	Qumran, Cave 4, Samuel, 1st copy
4QTanh	Qumran, Cave 4, no. 176
4QTest	Qumran, Cave 4, no. 175
4QTLev ar^b	Qumran, Cave 4, no. 213
11Q19	Qumran, Cave 11, no. 19
11QMelch	Qumran, Cave 11, Melchizedek text
11QPs^a	Qumran, Cave 11, Psalms

11QTS	Qumran, Cave 11, Temple Scroll
QHBT	F. M. Cross and S. Talmon (eds.), *Qumran and the History of the Biblical Text* (Cambridge, Mass.: Harvard University Press, 1975)
Qoh.	Qohelet
RB	*Revue biblique*
RQ	*Revue de Qumran*
RSPT	*Revue des sciences philosophiques et théologiques*
RTP	*Revue de théologie et de philosophie*
SDB	*Supplément de Dictionnaire de la Bible* (11 vols. to date; Paris: Letouzey et Ané, 1928-)
SE	*Studia evangelica*
SP	Samaritan Pentateuch
SP	*Studia patristica*
SR	*Studies in Religion/Sciences religieuses*
SSCW	G. J. Brooke and B. Lindars (eds.), *Septuagint, Scrolls and Cognate Writings* (Atlanta: Scholars Press, 1992)
ST	*Studia theologica*
Syr.	Syriac
TAPA	*Transactions of the American Philological Association*
Tg. Onk.	*Targum Onkelos*
t. Yad.	Tosepta, *Yadayim*
TR	*Theologische Realenzyklopädie*
VT	*Vetus Testamentum*
VTS	*Vetus Testamentum, Supplements*
WUNT	Wissenschaftliche Untersuchungen zum Neuen Testament
y. Meg.	Jerusalem Talmud, *Megillah*
ZAW	*Zeitschrift für die alttestamentliche Wissenschaft*
ZNW	*Zeitschrift für die neutestamentliche Wissenschaft*
ZTK	*Zeitschrift für Theologie und Kirche*

A NOTE ON CONVENTIONS

Brackets

In the main text brackets are used conventionally so that

( ) set something off parenthetically; and

[ ] indicate an authorial intervention in a modern source.

In the quotations from ancient sources, whether in the original Hebrew, Greek, or Aramaic, or in English translation or transliteration the following conventions are used:

[ ] indicate mutilated text. The brackets may enclose words or letters of editorial reconstruction or restoration, or may be empty where no reconstruction has been offered.

Vacat indicates an empty space in the manuscript itself.

⟨ ⟩ indicate the editorial correction of a mistake in the ancient manuscript.

( ) enclose authorial supplements or comments

Hebrew

Note that the punctuation in a sentence runs from left to right according to the conventional order for English although the Hebrew itself reads from right to left.

PART I
Prolegomena

1

Holy Scripture and Post-Biblical Exegeses

Jewish and Christian scriptural interpretations that date to the centuries between the Bible and the Mishnah, approximately 200 BCE to 200 CE, have often been described as 'post-Biblical exegeses', even though, strictly speaking, every interpretation of the Bible after the closing of the canon up to the present day may also be described as post-Biblical. By restricting the post-Biblical period to the 400 years around the turning of the era, the implication seems to be that writings falling within these chronological parameters occupy a notable position and exhibit distinctive characteristics of interpretation which may be described as post-Biblical. But how are the writings of this limited post-Biblical period different from those of the eighteen hundred years that follow it?

The adjective 'post-Biblical' contains another curiosity, the notion of the canon: it assumes that there already existed a group of writings that may be identified as 'the Bible' for which the post-Biblical exegeses serve as interpretative traditions. Was there already a canon of the Bible? While there remains debate about precisely when the canon was fixed, few, even those of the conservative persuasion, would push that date back before the middle of the second century BCE.[1] Other scholars have argued that the fixation of the canon took place at the so-called 'council' of Yavneh (90 CE) or later.[2] Is it not anachronistic, then, to speak

---

[1] See Roger Beckwith, *The Old Testament Canon of the New Testament Church and its Background in Early Judaism* (London: SPCK, 1985), ch. 4, who argues that the closing of the canon occurred at *c.*160 BCE, and Sid Z. Leiman, *The Canonization of Hebrew Scripture: The Talmudic and Midrashic Evidence*, Transaction 47 (Hamden, Conn.: Connecticut Academy of Arts and Science, 1976), 131–5, who dates the closing of the canon in most Jewish circles at *c.*150 BCE.

[2] Albert C. Sundberg, *The Old Testament of the Early Church* (Cambridge, Mass.:

of these writings as belonging to the post-Biblical period or even the period 'between the Bible and the Mishnah'[3] when some of them date to an age prior to the presumed closing of the canon?

Questions of terminology aside,[4] it may also be asked how post-biblical exegeses[5] distinguish themselves, in technique and hermeneutical principles, from their immediate successors, the rabbinic and patristic writings,[6] and their predecessors, the later biblical books. This question is difficult to answer, since most generalizations offered here would merely disclose the degree to which the broad range of exegeses has not been accounted for. What has become clearer in the last decade or so is how certain exegetical traditions dating to the period before the destruction of the Temple (pre-70) can also be found in writings of the rabbinic period.[7] Few features are distinctive to the post-biblical period. There is moreover a greater recognition of how this interpretative process can be traced back to the bible itself. The phrase coined for

Harvard University Press, 1964), 101–5 (Alexandrian canon; law and prophets closed, but writings without fixed collection); John Barton, *Oracles of God: Perceptions of Ancient Prophecy in Israel after the Exile* (London: Darton, Longman & Todd, 1986), and 'Canon' in R. J. Coggins and J. L. Houlden (eds.), *Dictionary of Biblical Interpretation* (London: SCM Press, 1990), 102 (only Torah closed by New Testament times).

[3] e.g. Jacob Weingreen, *From Bible to Mishna* (Manchester: Manchester University Press, 1976).

[4] Scholarly disagreements about the closing date of the canon centre upon the interpretation of a number of key passages (e.g. Luke 24: 44, 'Moses, prophets and psalms'; cf. Albert C. Sundberg, 'Reexamining the Formation of the Old Testament Canon', *Int.* 42 (1988), 78–82), for which the Qumran scrolls will provide important evidence (see now 4QMMT and the apparent tripartite division into the books of Moses, the Prophets and David and Eugene Ulrich's comments in 'Pluriformity in the Biblical Text, Text Groups, and Question of Canon', in *Madrid*, i. 34). Alternatively this could mean that David was considered a prophet (cf. 11QPs[a] 27. 2–11 and Acts 2: 30).

[5] The terms 'bible'/'biblical', 'Bible'/'Biblical' are used respectively for the pre- and post-canonical periods, but the capitalized form is used when both periods are in view.

[6] The attitude of the Greek fathers, in particular Origen, to the LXX has been discussed by Marguerite Harl, 'La Septante et la pluralité textuelle des écritures: Le Témoignage des pères grecs', in *Naissance de la méthode critique: Colloque du centenaire de l'École biblique et archéologique française de Jérusalem* (Paris: Cerf, 1992), 231–43.

[7] Cf. e.g. the reasons given for cursing Canaan and not Ham (since he had already been blessed by God; Gen. 9: 1) in *Gen. Rab.* 36. 4–5, 7, and the partially reconstructed text of 4Q252 col. 2, ll. 5–8 (see my 'The Chronology of the Flood Story in a Qumran Text (4Q252)', *JJS* 43 (1992), 294).

this latter phenomenon in which the bible is seen to be interpreting itself is 'inner biblical exegesis'.[8]

If works of this post-biblical period are seen to be falling within exegetical trajectories, as recent research suggests,[9] it may be asked whether they occupy any special place within the whole history of Bible interpretation. Have they been artificially isolated from the long history of Bible interpretation for the practical purpose of studying and teaching a manageable unit? Or are there inherent features that distinguish them from subsequent interpretative writings?

Theologically, the significance of the New Testament is obvious; it not only constitutes the primary witness to Jesus of Nazareth, the central figure of Christianity, but also evidences that the writings of the Early Church themselves, especially the letters of Paul, were very soon raised to the status of sacred scripture.[10] From the viewpoint of Bible interpretation, however, it is increasingly recognized that the New Testament's exegeses of the Old Testament, the Christological interpretation being a notable exception,[11] may be seen within the continuum of Jewish Bible interpretation that stretches from the post-exilic biblical books of the Persian and Hellenistic periods to the medieval rabbinic sources of the Mishnah, Talmudim, and Midrashim.[12]

What, then, makes the literature of this period so special? In many ways, full answers to this question will have to await further comparative studies. There are, however, individual points that may be made. First, the writings that date to the centuries around

---

[8] Although anticipated by several others, above all Nahum Sarna, 'Ps. 89: A Study of Inner Biblical Exegesis', in A. Altmann (ed.), *Biblical and Other Studies* (Cambridge, Mass.: Harvard University Press, 1963), 29–46, the most comprehensive discussion of this phenomenon is found in Michael Fishbane, *Biblical Interpretation in Ancient Israel* (Oxford: Clarendon Press, 1985).

[9] *Contra* David Instone Brewer, *Techniques and Assumptions in Jewish Exegesis before 70 C.E.* (Tübingen: J. C. B. Mohr, 1992), who argues unconvincingly for a disjunction between pre- and post-70 exegeses.

[10] The earliest indication of which is in 2 Pet. 3: 15–16 where the Pauline letters were said to be difficult to understand and the unlearned distort them as they do the rest of the scriptures (τὰς λοιπὰς γραφὰς).

[11] Attempts to find a slain messiah in the Qumran scrolls (4Q285) have not been successful (see counter-arguments by Geza Vermes, Timothy H. Lim, and Robert Gordon, 'Oxford Forum for Qumran Research Seminar on the Rule of War from Cave 4 (4Q285)', *JJS* 43 (1992), 85–90).

[12] See e.g. Martin McNamara, *Palestinian Judaism and the New Testament* (Wilmington, Del.: Michael Glazier, 1983).

the turning of the era have a chronological priority. These works stand at the head of a long queue of interpretations on the Bible.[13] That is to say, the continuous exposition of Israelite law and teaching up to this day began in this period. To be sure, this process of interpretation was already under way in the biblical books themselves, but the post-biblical consciousness, as manifested above all in the act of citing biblical texts,[14] can be clearly seen to be emerging for the first time in such exegetical compositions as the Qumran pesharim and Pauline letters. Broadly speaking, their own stance seems to be one of exposition—the commentary of a written text—although, as will be discussed, this does not entirely convey their hermeneutical position.

Second, the boundaries of 'the Bible' have yet to be determined. In fact a book such as Daniel, which was later included in the canon, was likely to have been composed after the non-canonical works of the Wisdom of Ben Sira[15] or the Enochic literature.[16] In this period, the issue is about the exegetes' attitude to authoritative,[17] rather than canonical, texts.[18] Third, the textual form of individual biblical books has yet to be fixed. The diversity of textual types is characteristic of this period and the standardization (or selection[19]) of the proto-Masoretic Text probably occurred some time around 100 CE.[20]

By suggesting that these post-biblical writings, such as the Qumran scrolls, are at the front of the exegetical queue, it is assumed that there already existed a corpus of texts of such nature and status as to deserve special consideration and attention,

---

[13] Cf. Moshe Goshen-Gottstein, 'Scriptural Authority (Judaism)', *ABD* v. 1018, describes this age as 'the twilight period between biblical and post-biblical literature'.

[14] Cf. the use of שֶׁנֶּאֱמַר and γέγραπται in the New Testament and Mishnah (Joseph A. Fitzmyer, 'The Use of Explicit Old Testament Quotations in the New Testament', in *ESBNT*, 3–58, and Bruce Metzger, 'The Formulas Introducing Quotations of Scripture in the New Testament and the Mishna', *JBL* 70 (1951), 297–307).

[15] W. C. van Unnik (ed.), *La Littérature juive entre Tenach et Mischna* (Leiden: E. J. Brill, 1974), 4, dismisses this anomaly as a '*Schönheitsfehler sans importance*'.

[16] The books of *Enoch* were, however, included in the Ethiopian canon (cf. Edward Ullendorff, *Ethiopia and the Bible* (Oxford: Oxford University Press, 1967), 34–5, and Beckwith, *Old Testament Canon*, 480–1).

[17] See James Barr, *Holy Scripture. Canon, Authority, Criticism* (Oxford: Clarendon Press, 1983), 1–22.

[18] Cf. the use of 1 *Enoch* 1: 9 in Jude 14 as proof-text: προεφήτευσεν δὲ καὶ τούτοις ἕβδομος ἀπὸ Ἀδὰμ Ἑνὼχ λέγων.

[19] So Ulrich, 'Pluriformity', 27–9.

[20] All the biblical scrolls from Wadi Muraba'at are proto-Masoretic.

and whose authoritative contents may be described, in the non-canonical sense, as 'bible' or 'holy scripture'. There must have been something there for the exegetical queue to form in the first place. In modern discussions about the canon, this loosely defined corpus is often described as consisting of the Torah or Pentateuch, probably most of the Prophets and some of the Writings (cf. prologue to Ben Sira).[21]

The relationship between the authoritative texts and their interpretations, however, is more complicated than the exegetical queue can express. Some of the interpretations, to be sure, showed a prima facie distinction between the biblical text that is cited and the comments that surround it. Compared to later biblical books that incorporate earlier material in their composition (e.g. prophetic sayings of Jeremiah in Daniel or in Zechariah; Genesis–Kings in Chronicles[22]), the former may be distinguished from the latter as bible interpretation is from biblical writing.[23] In certain works, however, such as those belonging to the 'rewritten bible' genre, the line between the sacred text and its exposition is blurred. *Jubilees*, the Temple Scroll, Liber Antiquitatum Biblicarum, for instance, rewrite the biblical text and rework the material into a new composition.[24] The Temple Scroll, which harmonizes biblical laws from the Pentateuch, has even been described as 'the Torah of the Lord', 'the Qumranic Torah', or 'the sixth book of the Torah' of the Essenes.[25] Their approach to the authoritative writings is similar to

[21] Cf. the discussions of Sundberg, *Old Testament of the Early Church*, and Beckwith, *Old Testament Canon*.

[22] An alternative view by A. G. Auld, *Kings without Privilege: David and Moses in the Story of the Bible's Kings* (Edinburgh: T. & T. Clark, 1994), argues for a common source used by Sam.–Kgs. and Chr.

[23] Cf. Joseph Blenkinsopp, *A History of Prophecy in Israel: From the Settlement in the Land to the Hellenistic Period* (Philadelphia: Westminster Press, 1983), 255–7, who contrasts the incorporation of earlier oracles into the prophecy of Zechariah with the commentary form of the pesharim.

[24] While these rewritten bibles do assume the existence and authority of scripture (so Philip S. Alexander, 'Retelling the Old Testament', in D. A. Carson and H. G. M. Williamson (eds.), *It is Written: Scripture citing Scripture: Essays in Honour of Barnabas Lindars* (Cambridge: Cambridge University Press, 1988), 116–17), they are distinguished from works with explicit citations in the subsumation of the biblical text (Michael Fishbane, 'Inner Biblical Exegesis: Types and Strategies of Interpretation in Ancient Israel', in Geoffrey H. Hartman and Sanford Budick (eds.), *Midrash and Literature* (New Haven: Yale University Press, 1986), 19–40).

[25] So Yigael Yadin, *The Temple Scroll*, Eng. trans. (Jerusalem: Israel Exploration Society, 1983), i. 390–2, and Ben Zion Wacholder, *The Dawn of Qumran* (Cincinnati: Hebrew Union College Press, 1983), ch. 1, and Hartmut Stegemann,

the incorporation of earlier biblical material by the chronicler or deuteronomist.[26]

By contrast, the exegetical works that quote biblical texts verbatim (e.g. the Qumran pesharim, Damascus Document, certain writings of Josephus, the Matthean Gospel, Pauline letters) manifestly exhibit their post-biblical perspective. The biblical quotation, frequently preceded by a short phrase (e.g. 'it is written' or 'as God said through Isaiah the Prophet, son of Amoz . . .', CD 4. 14), is separated from the comment that interprets it. In several works, the best-known of which are the Qumran commentaries, the interpretation is further differentiated from the lemma by an introductory formula (e.g. 'the interpretation of the verse is'). Here more than elsewhere, it would seem, the distinction between the biblical text and its interpretation is strictly maintained. Yet is it entirely so? It has been argued, for example, that the biblical lemma, cited by, say, Matthew, has been conformed to the Gospel writer's interpretation.[27] If this were so, are the exegetes who adapt and reformulate their verbatim biblical quotations not also in fact rewriting their biblical text?

PRESENT TASKS AND AIMS

The foregoing discussion has been leading up to the subject of the present book, an examination of the attitude to holy scripture in works that stand at the head of this exegetical queue. Did the pesherists and Paul consider the biblical texts that they quoted to be holy in the sense of being the inviolable word of God, or did they also rework their scriptural passages in a manner similar to the rewritten bibles' paraphrasing and recasting of the biblical material? Phrased differently, the formula of citation plus commentary[28] at

'The Institutions of Israel in the *Temple Scroll*', in *FYR*, 156–85, and 'Is the Temple Scroll a Sixth Book of the Torah—Lost for 2,500 years?', in H. Shanks (ed.), *Understanding the Dead Sea Scrolls* (New York: Random House, 1992), 126–36.

[26] Cf. Shemaryahu Talmon, 'The Textual Study of the Bible: A New Outlook', in *QHBT*, 378–81.

[27] So Krister Stendahl, *The School of Matthew and its Use of the Old Testament* (Lund: C. W. K. Gleerup, 1954), but see his more cautious remarks in the Preface to the 2nd edn. (1968).

[28] True, explicit citations, especially in the Pauline letters, take on a variety of forms (e.g. lists of biblical passages juxtaposed to one another; biblical phrases interspersed within passage), but they can be broadly described as constituting a lemma and comment.

first glance appears to distinguish clearly between the scriptural text that is quoted (*oratio recta*) and the comments of the pesherists and Paul. The lemma, so it would seem, was lifted out of an extant biblical scroll or recalled from memory rather than reworded in a paraphrase. The commentary likewise appears to be the interpretation of the lemma rather than the interweaving of biblical texts and exegesis in a paraphrase.

Yet, are the lines between the biblical lemmata and exegetical commentary clearly drawn? If it can be shown that the pesherists and Paul did in fact modify the words of their biblical quotation, are not the lines between biblical quotation and commentary now blurred? And, are not the pesherists and Paul to some extent also rewriting their biblical text? It will be the task of the following chapters to locate the position of the Qumran pesharim and Pauline letters within the continuum of biblical composition, rewritten bible, and bible interpretation. To what extent can the Qumran commentators and Paul be seen to be rewriting their scriptural quotations and thus also be described as biblical authors?

Investigation will begin with the technical question of textual adaptation of biblical quotations before proceeding to lay bare the underlying hermeneutical engine that drives this exegetical machinery. Why did they feel free to modify their biblical quotations? It is surely paradoxical, if nothing else, that the citation of biblical texts, which is evidently an appeal to a recognized authority whose message is being conveyed, should also become the very instrument for change and innovation. At first glance, the act of quoting a text, as opposed to its wholesale take-over by paraphrase, seems to point to an external source that is being faithfully passed on and whose authority is being averred. Yet the intrusion of textual modifications into the biblical lemmata suggests that the locus of authority and hermeneutical centre lie elsewhere. The very words of the bible were not considered to be immutable like some mathematical formula, the alteration of even one of whose components invalidates the entire equation, but were treated as malleable clay in the hands of an expert and authoritative interpreter. It will be one of the tasks of the present study to locate the hermeneutical centre of the Qumran exegetes and Paul and identify their source of authority.

Hitherto, it has simply been assumed that the Qumranians and Paul modified their biblical quotations for their interpretation. The ability to demonstrate this phenomenon, however, has been severely constrained by recent findings of post-Qumran textual criticism[29] and the diversity of textual types. While scholarly debates regarding the degree of this diversity, the method of textual characterization, and the categorization of the data remain, it is undeniable that the Qumran biblical scrolls attest to a greater diversity than was previously known. These issues will be discussed in Chapter 2.

What is important to note here is the application of post-Qumran textual criticism to exegesis: divergence from the MT, LXX, or SP by itself is no decisive reason for supposing that a reading was exegetically created. The variant may already have been found in the text which the exegete had before him, his *Vorlage*: he simply interpreted that which was there. In fact, the entire manner by which a reading is compared to a standard, say the medieval Leningrad Codex B 19[A] (L), and its deviation described as an exegetical variant is questionable: against which textual standard should these 'variants' be measured? More specifically, did, say, the Qumran exegete have a text of Habakkuk that was identical with Codex L which he then modified? Or again, did Paul cite and reformulate Greek texts from the 'Septuagint'[30]? The evidence of the Qumran scrolls clearly demands a fresh approach to these exegetical questions.

By an examination of the Qumran pesharim and Pauline letters separately and a comparison of their exegetical methods and hermeneutical principles, the present book intends to contribute to the mutual illumination of the two. In previous studies, the Qumran pesharim have been investigated for the light that they shed on the New Testament writings, most notably on the Gospel of Matthew and the letters of Paul. The exegetical method of Paul has even been described as a 'midrash pesher'.[31] As far as one can ascertain, no previous work has studied Pauline exegesis for the illumination of the Pesharim: Are there any aspects of the Qumran commentaries that may be described as 'Pauline exegesis'?[32]

---

[29] The hyphenated term 'post-Qumran' is a convenient abbreviation of textual criticism of the Bible that has been shaped significantly, though not exclusively, by biblical scrolls found at Khirbet Qumran (see Emanuel Tov, ביקורת נוסח המקרא (Jerusalem: Bialik, 1989), rev. and trans. as *Textual Criticism of the Hebrew Bible* (Minneapolis: Fortress Press, 1992)). [30] See Ch. 2 for issues of definition.
[31] E. Earle Ellis, *Paul's Use of the Old Testament* (London: Oliver & Boyd, 1957).
[32] D. Flusser's well-known study of Pauline writings for the illumination of

There are five sections and eleven chapters in this book. Chapter 2, which completes this first Part, the Prolegomena, will discuss the relevance of the Qumran scrolls and the new perspectives of investigation that this evidence demands. Part II consists of two chapters that will treat literalistic features of ancient exegesis. Here, the aim is to show how issues raised in this book about the Qumran pesharim and Pauline letters address neglected aspects of ancient bible interpretation. Part III consists of three chapters on the exegetical techniques and hermeneutical principles of the pesharim, and Part IV three chapters on Paul's use of the biblical quotations. Finally, Part V will compare the hermeneutical principles of the two together.

A final word about the discrepancy in number when comparing several Qumran exegetes with Paul. Romans, 1 and 2 Corinthians, and Galatians, often described as the Capital Letters, are the only genuine writings of Paul that cite biblical texts. They, together with 1 Thessalonians, Philippians, and Philemon, were written by one man.[33] By contrast, the sixteen Qumran commentaries (1QpHab, 4QpNah, 1QpPs, 4QpPs[a], 4QpPs[b], 1QpMic, 1QpZeph, 4QpZeph, 4QpHos[a], 4QpHos[b], 3QpIsa,[34] 4QpIsa[a], 4QpIsa[b], 4QpIsa[c], 4QpIsa[d], 4QpIsa[e]) were composed presumably by as many individuals. There is an apparent imbalance in the comparative scale with Paul on one side and all sixteen Qumran exegetes on the other. While the present book will give due attention to the individual characteristics of each pesher, the decision to compare all the Qumran commentators with Paul was made on practical grounds. It is somewhat misleading to think of the commentaries enumerated above as sixteen separate works, since several are badly mutilated and are fragments more than they are scrolls. From the point of view of exegetical techniques, there is simply not enough comparative material to be found in any one pesher, the Habakkuk Pesher (1QpHab) being the only possible exception.

Qumran theology being one such model ('The Dead Sea Sect and Pre-Pauline Christianity', in C. Rabin and Y. Yadin (eds.), *Scripta Hierosolymitana 4* (Jerusalem: Magnes Press, 1958), 215–66).

[33] A source theory of the Pauline letters is proposed by J. C. O'Neill in *Paul's Letter to the Romans* (Harmondsworth: Penguin, 1975).

[34] The eschatological orientation, indicated by [ם]פשׁ[ה] המשׁ[י] in l. 6, is characteristic of pesherite texts (e.g. to 1QpMic, fr. 10. 6–7). Cf. Maurya Horgan, *Pesharim: Qumran Interpretations of Biblical Books* (Washington: Catholic Biblical Association of America, 1979), 1 and 260–1.

2

Post-Qumran Perspectives on Exegesis

The scrolls found in the caves near the archaeological site of Khirbet Qumran have often been hailed as the greatest manuscript discovery in Palestine and Israel in the twentieth century. After some fifty years of intensive research, and particularly since all of them are now accessible, it may be asked just how these scrolls have shaped the study of Bible interpretation in the Second Temple period.

On one level, the contribution of the Qumran scrolls is obvious. The Hebrew and Aramaic scrolls retrieved from the caves have enlarged the field of Bible interpretation by increasing the number of exegetical exemplars that date to this period.[1] Counted among them are compositions hitherto preserved only in languages different from their supposed original (e.g. Jubilees[2] and Tobit[3]), a broad range of formerly unknown exegeses (e.g. Genesis Apocryphon, Pesharim) and works that harmonized and supplemented the Torah (e.g. Temple Scroll, Reworked Pentateuch[4]) or whose arguments about legal matters is reminiscent of the previously known halakhic disputes between the Sadducees and Pharisees in the Mishnah (4QMMT: 'Some precepts of the torah'[5]).

The identification of the community or communities that owned these exegetical scrolls is a matter of continuing debate, but despite

---

[1] The recent carbon-14 tests of several Qumran scrolls carried out by scientists of the Zurich laboratory, while restricted in sample size, have generally confirmed the dates deduced from palaeographic analyses (see G. Bonani *et al.*, 'Radiocarbon Dating of the Dead Sea Scrolls', *'Atiqot*, 20 (1991), 27–32).

[2] James VanderKam and Jozef Milik in *DJD* xiii. 1–175.

[3] Joseph A. Fitzmyer, 'Preliminary Publication of pap4QTob[a] ar, Fragment 2', *Bib.* 75/2 (1994), 220–4.

[4] Emanuel Tov and Sidnie White in *DJD* xiii. 187–352.

[5] Elisha Qimron and John Strugnell, *DJD* x.

telling criticisms of the theory in recent years and, in view of the lack of a better alternative, the Qumran-Essene identification remains the working hypothesis of the overwhelming majority of scholars.[6] This will also be assumed in the present book. It is actually misleading to speak of *the* Qumran-Essene theory, since there are in fact several versions, each one postulating one or more distinctive features (e.g. the Babylonian origin,[7] six wicked priests, daughter sect of the Essenes,[8] and Sadducean halakha[9]) but sharing the common identification of the Essenes with the Qumranians.

This is not the place to argue for a theory of the Qumran-Essene community. Suffice it to say that the interpretation of the bible was a central concern, if not a preoccupation, attested as it is by the exegetical works found in the adjoining caves and the corresponding descriptions in the Rules and classical sources. Over a history of approximately 220 years or so (*c.*150 BCE to 70 CE), the developing community, or, more appropriately, communities, devoted themselves to the study of scripture and its exposition was guided by several leaders, the most important of whom was the Teacher of Righteousness.[10] More will be said about this in the ensuing

[6] For a review of two competing theories, the Jerusalem Hypothesis and Groningen Hypothesis, see my article, 'The Qumran Scrolls: Two Hypotheses', *SR* 21 (1992), 455–66.

[7] Jerome Murphy-O'Connor, 'The Essenes and their History', *RB* 81 (1974), 215–44, and Philip R. Davies, *The Damascus Covenant: An Interpretation of the 'Damascus Document'* (Sheffield: JSOT Press, 1983).

[8] Florentino García Martínez, 'Qumran Origins and Early History: A Groningen Hypothesis', *Folia Orientalia*, 25 (1988), 113–36, and id. and A. S. van der Woude, 'A "Groningen" Hypothesis of Qumran Origins and Early History', *RQ* 14 (1990), 521–42. See my 'The Wicked Priests of the Groningen Hypothesis', *JBL* 112 (1993), 415–25.

[9] A shared halakhic stance (notably about the red heifer and poured liquid) between the Qumran community and the Sadducees has recently been emphasized by Lawrence H. Schiffman, '*Miqsat Ma'aseh Ha-Torah* and the *Temple Scroll*', *RQ* 14 (1990), 435–57, and *Reclaiming the Dead Sea Scrolls* (Philadelphia: Jewish Publication Society, 1994), but this is not irreconcilable with a Qumran-Essene theory (Joseph Baumgarten, 'The Disqualification of Priest in 4Q Fragments of the "Damascus Document", a Specimen of the Recovery of pre-Rabbinic Halakha', in *Madrid*, ii. 503–6, and Y. Sussman, 'חקר תולדות ההלכה מגילת מדבר יהודה :הרהורים *Tarbiz*, 59/1–2 (1989–90), 11–76; a ,תלמודיים ראשונים לאור מגילת "מקצת משעי התורה"' translation with selected notes appears in DJD x. 179–200.

[10] Shemaryahu Talmon, *The World of Qumran from Within* (Jerusalem: Magnes Press; Leiden: E. J. Brill, 1989), 7–8, observes that the descriptors 'sect' and 'sectarian' presuppose knowledge of the mother community, for which see now García Martínez, 'Qumran Origins and Early History', and E. P. Sanders, *Judaism: Practice and Belief 63 BCE–66 CE* (London: SCM Press, 1992), pt. 2, 'Common Judaism'.

chapters. What is important to point out here is that the scrolls, when viewed within the context of the Qumran-Essene community, contribute substantially to Bible interpretation of the Second Temple period by portraying a group that searched the scriptures and by providing some of the results of this exegetical endeavour. Of course, not all of the scrolls discovered in the caves were composed by the Qumranians, but all of them do testify to the community's exegetical concern.

BIBLICAL SCROLLS AND TEXTUAL CRITICISM

Unlike the exegetical compositions, the biblical scrolls found at Qumran have not enjoyed the same recognition of relevance for Bible interpretation, even though they too should have fundamentally modified the manner in which exegesis is viewed. The reasons for this neglect are attributable in part to the indirect nature of the evidence and the division of the Qumran scrolls into the categories of 'biblical' and 'non-biblical'.

Compared to the immediate impact of even one exegetical work upon exegesis,[11] the biblical scrolls as such do not have a direct, let alone obvious, relevance: a text of, say, Isaiah is just that—a biblical text; it is not an exposition of Isaiah and on the face of it has a limited contribution to make to the interpretation of the prophecy. When it is integrated into the study of ancient exegesis its relevance becomes apparent: how do the readings of this Isaiah scroll compare with another biblical scroll or the scriptural quotations of an exegetical text. Do they share readings that vary from one of the traditional standards of the MT and LXX? If so, can these readings be described as exegetical variants?

A single biblical scroll may become highly relevant for Bible interpretation in another way. Depending upon its textual characteristics, a biblical scroll could become an important witness of the extent to which the biblical texts diverged from one another in the Second Temple period. Thus, a text of, say, Samuel (4QSam^a) that follows neither the MT nor LXX, but has affinities to both and some additional material is an important landmark which all subsequent textual theories will have to account for. The view taken of the textual situation will then indirectly influence scholarly

---

[11] See e.g. my analysis of the chronography of the flood story in 4Q252 fr. 1 ('The Chronology of the Flood Story in a Qumran Text (4Q252)', *JJS* 43 (1992), 288-98).

judgements in characterizing the textual type of quotations from a biblical book and in determining the exegetical significance of specific readings attested in them.

Another reason for the neglect of the biblical scrolls is in the specialization of scholarly interests, so that, in general, textual critics handle the biblical scrolls while exegetes examine the interpretative works. Like all generalizations, there are exceptions in this one and few Qumran scholars are exclusively one or the other, but this rule of thumb was operative in the original division of editorial assignments and it continues to serve a practical purpose today. It is interesting to note also that scholars who publish anthologies of Dead Sea Scrolls, whether in their original Hebrew and Aramaic (e.g. by E. Lohse and A. M. Habermann) or translation into a European language (e.g. by G. Vermes, E. Lohse, J. Maier, J. Carmignac, L. Moraldi, and F. García Martínez), for the most part select only non-biblical texts. The biblical texts, which together make up the 'Qumran bible', have not hitherto been collected and published.[12] The underlying assumption of the extant anthologies seems to be that biblical texts belong to the purview of the specialist and textual critic, whereas non-biblical scrolls and fragments are the concern of the broader group of exegetes, historians, theologians, and other interested readers.

Concomitant with the above reasons are the issues of access to the unpublished material and the development of post-Qumran textual criticism. Since all the Qumran scrolls are now available to the scholarly world, there is no need to dwell on this point, except to say that the restriction of access in the past must have contributed to the reservation of most scholars in expressing an opinion about the local texts theory that emerged from the initial study of the Qumran biblical scrolls.[13] Equally important to the past restriction is the development of post-Qumran textual criticism. A great deal of basic editorial work and ground-breaking studies on individual biblical scrolls had to be conducted before scholars could even begin to discuss fundamental issues of textual criticism.

---

[12] Hermann Lichtenberger of the Institut für antikes Judentum und hellenistische Religionsgeschichte, Universität Tübingen, has announced a project of *Biblia Qumranica*.

[13] The refusal to engage in scholarly debate when not everyone had access to the unpublished material goes some way to answer Shemaryahu Talmon's complaint ('The Textual Study of the Bible—A New Outlook', in *QHBT*, 321–4) that few, apart from Israeli scholars, were willing to debate Frank Cross and his school.

Essentially, the significance of the Qumran biblical scrolls for bible interpretation is in the method of ascertaining an exegetical variant: given the plurality of text-types in the Second Temple period and the number of variants attested in them, how can one know that a reading that diverges from the standards of the MT, LXX, and SP originated with the ancient exegete? Did the Qumran commentator and Paul modify the biblical lemma to conform it to their interpretation, or did they simply adopt it from one biblical text or more that already contained these 'variants'?

This is a question of which came first, the variant or the interpretation. In the latter case, the ancient exegete does not modify his biblical lemma, but comes upon a reading in one of his biblical scrolls. That is to say, the comment was made after an extant reading. In the former case, it is the reverse process: the ancient exegete knew what he wanted to say in the first place and he modified the biblical text to make it correspond more closely to his views. Why he did so, given the elasticity of exegesis in this period and the different techniques available by which a comment could be brought nearer to the source, need not detain us, since the modification of a biblical lemma appears to be one of the exegetical techniques available to the ancient interpreter.

The manner by which scholars argue for exegetical variants in the pesharim and Pauline letters is based upon several specific assumptions about the textual nature of their biblical quotations, which will be examined below. What needs to be discussed here are those broader issues of textual criticism that pertain to the identification of exegetical variants.

Diversity of Text-Types

Theories that seek to explain the overall textual situation in the Second Temple period have a limited significance for exegesis, since they take account of biblical scrolls rather than the biblical quotations embedded in exegetical works. They do, however, inform the scholar and the broader textual outline that they provide serves as a useful guideline for his textual judgement.

The main relevance for exegesis of text-critical theories arising out of the discovery of the Qumran biblical scrolls is to be found in the issue of diversity rather than in questions of provenance of text-types or the original text (variously described as the archetype or *Urtext*). The concern of the exegete is not primarily with questions of how, say, the text of Habakkuk was transmitted or whether at the compositional (as opposed to the scribal transmission) stage the prophecy included the hymn of the third chapter. Rather, the one who studies the commentary on Habakkuk confines himself to the evaluation of the readings in the biblical lemmata. In the context of the overall textual situation, how are the readings that diverge from the standards of the MT or LXX to be weighed? Are they exegetical variants, assuming that the original readings were identical with the MT or LXX, or are they readings, divergent though they may be from the medieval standard, already found in the biblical scroll that he was using? Sharpened in this way, the point is not about the transmission of the Habakkuk text generally, but concerns the apparently divergent reading embedded in the commentary.

The reading may be legitimately described as 'divergent' or 'a variant' in the sense that when compared to the standard of the MT (or LXX) it is not identical with it but varies from it. This is a textual characterization, for heuristic purposes only, and not a statement of its original form nor an assertion of any exegetical modification. Phrased differently, a textual characterization describes the *proximity*[14] of a biblical text to certain standards, usually the MT, LXX, and SP; it does not assume that that biblical text, however close it might be to one of the standards, is identical with it.[15]

For the sake of greater clarity and a better appreciation of the nuances, let us take the biblical quotations embedded in 1QpHab for illustration. Supposing that the original biblical text of Habakkuk, the *Vorlage* (that is the putative, unadulterated form

[14] Thanks to Emanuel Tov for discussing this distinction with me. See now his *Textual Criticism of the Hebrew Bible* (Minneapolis: Fortress Press, 1992), 163, and 'Some Notes on a Generation of Qumran Studies (by Frank M. Cross). A Reply', in *Madrid*, i. 18.

[15] The conventional use of critical editions to represent the MT (BHS), LXX (Göttingen, Brooke-Mclean, and Rahlfs) and SP (von Gall) should not mislead one to suppose uniformity in these traditions. Harry Orlinsky, 'Prolegomenon', in Christian D. Ginsburg's *Introduction to the Massoretico-Critical Edition of the Hebrew Bible* (New York: KTAV, 1966), long ago pointed out that there never existed one single MT text, since the tradition continued to fluctuate. The issue is one of the degree of divergence from each other which, in the case of the medieval texts of the Masoretes, has been reduced to orthography, synonyms, and short phrases (Benjamin Kennicott, *Vetus Testamentum Hebraicum cum variis lectionibus* (Oxford: Clarendon, 1780), and Johannes Bernardus de Rossi, *Variae Lectiones Veteris Testamenti* (Parmae: Regio Typographeo, 1784, 1785, and 1788), i–iii).

that the exegete had before him), was recoverable from the Habakkuk Pesher and that this biblical text was shown to agree more frequently with the MT than LXX, the textual characterization of 'proto-Masoretic Text' would then refer to its proximity to the MT and not its identity with Codex L of BHS. In fact, the description of 'proto-Masoretic Text', strictly speaking, requires that the Habakkuk text, as it is reconstituted from 1QpHab, agrees with the MT against *not only* the LXX, but all other traditions (e.g. 8HevXIIgr, Vulgate, Syriac, Targum). How one characterizes a text, given that the textual traditions share a common base, will be further discussed below.

What is more important to note here is that the putative *Vorlage* of the Habakkuk text of 1QpHab refers to a stage prior to that of the Qumran exegete. It may be significant for the overall textual situation in the Second Temple period, but hitherto has no relevance for the Qumran commentator's handling of the biblical text. Only when this supposed *Vorlage* is compared to the form of the biblical lemmata as it appears in 1QpHab can exegetical adjustments be detected: are there any differences between the *Vorlage* and the biblical quotations? The actual textual characterization of the Habakkuk text in 1QpHab is much more difficult than the description of it here, since the *Vorlage* (if there be only one) is inextricably bound up with exegetical alterations, nevertheless this hypothetical case illustrates well the different stages of the *Vorlage* and biblical quotation that must be clearly maintained.

To return to the question of how theories that describe the textual situation in the Second Temple period help the scholar in his identification of exegetical variants: in most instances of textual divergence, it is impossible to prove that a variant was exegetically created, since the *Vorlage* is indistinguishable from the biblical quotations. There are a few cases, discussed in the following chapters, where exegetical modification is probable and likely, but apart from these the scholar will have to use his judgement. Like all subjective evaluations, however, textual judgement is susceptible to untenable presuppositions and biases. One way of keeping subjectivity in check is to have an eye on the broader picture of the textual situation while working on the details. This is the chief benefit of the text-critical theories.

Post-Qumran Textual Theories

The theory of local texts proposed by Frank Moore Cross[16] and the multiple-texts theory of Emanuel Tov[17] attempt to describe the textual situation of the Second Temple period in the light of the discovery of Qumran biblical scrolls that are either close to the MT (e.g. 1QIsa[b]), LXX (e.g. 4QJer[b], 4QExod[b18]), and SP (e.g. 4QpaleoExod[m], 4QExod-Lev[f19]) or show similarities *and* significant differences from all of them (e.g. 4QSam[a]).[20] For Cross, the Qumran biblical scrolls, both in the plurality of text-types that they reflect and the manifest affinities that they share with each other, may be classified according to three text-types that are to be associated with the localities of Egypt, Palestine, and Babylon. By contrast, Tov argues that the Qumran evidence cannot simply be accounted for by this schema in which a biblical scroll is characterized by its relationship to the MT, LXX, and SP, but that a fundamental rethinking of the tri- or bipartite model, a vestige of pre-Qumran textual criticism, has to take place. His 'new theory' is described as a multiple-texts theory, where the number of textual traditions is theoretically speaking infinite, even if a majority of them could be grouped together.[21]

---

[16] *The Ancient Library of Qumran*, 3rd edn. (Sheffield: Sheffield Academic Press, 1995), 168–94; 'The History of the Biblical Text in the Light of Discoveries in the Judaean Desert', in *QHBT*, 177–95; 'The Contribution of the Qumran Discoveries to the Study of the Biblical Text', in *QHBT*, 278–92; 'The Evolution of a Theory of Local Texts', in *QHBT*, 306–20; and 'Some Notes on a Generation of Qumran Studies' in *Madrid*, i. 1–14.

[17] This theory was developed in a number of publications (from 'The Textual Character of 11QpaleoLev' (Heb.), *Shnaton*, 3 (1978–9), 238–44 ff.) the most important of which is 'A Modern Textual Outlook Based on the Qumran Scrolls', *HUCA* 53 (1982), 11–27, and the latest formulations are found in '*Textual Criticism*, 160–3, and 'A Reply', 18.

[18] Frank Moore Cross in *DJD* xii. 79–85.

[19] Ibid. 133–44.

[20] Their theories were anticipated by W. F. Albright, 'New Light on Early Recensions of the Hebrew Bible', *BASOR* 140 (1955), 27–33, and Talmon, 'Textual Study', respectively. Talmon's emphases upon sociological aspects of textual diversity of *Gruppentexte* may also be considered alongside the above two (so Eugene Ulrich, 'Horizons of Old Testament Textual Research at the Thirtieth Anniversary of Qumran Cave 4', *CBQ* 46 (1984), 613–36), but the significance for exegesis is the same as Tov's multiple-texts theory.

[21] Tov, *Textual Criticism*, 114–17, now describes five groups of texts: (1) texts written in the Qumran practice; (2) proto-Masoretic texts; (3) pre-Samaritan texts; (4) texts close to the presumed Hebrew source of LXX; and (5) non-aligned or independent texts. While the grouping of texts is a development of his earlier formulations, an analysis of his latest description shows that the number of textual

At the heart of Cross and Tov's disagreements about the number of textual types[22] are two interrelated, though distinguishable, issues which may, for convenience, be called textual characterization and classification. How does one characterize a text? How many agreements and disagreements must there be before a text is described as, say, septuagintal? Inherent within this description of 'septuagintal' is the assumption that it may be classified as belonging to the septuagintal text-type or group just as other texts are categorized as 'proto-Masoretic' or 'pre-Samaritan'. In other words, textual characterization is the process of describing how readings of one text agree and disagree with another text, whereas textual classification is the assessment of these results in the description of the text as belonging to one or more of these standard versions.

Recently discussions have attempted to address the problem of textual characterization and classification. Cross has correctly observed that the difference between the theory of local texts and the multiple-texts theory is a matter of perspective.[23] Some, like himself, are 'clumpers'; they prefer to see 'bad genes', 'corrupt readings', or *Leitfehler*[24] found in texts as evidence for extant relationships in a textual family. Whereas Tov, is a 'splitter', one who emphasizes differences between the same comparative texts and prefers to draw distinctions where others would point to their similarities.

True though this observation may be,[25] the different perspectives of Cross and Tov only account for certain aspects of the problem. Unlike, say, the proverbial glass of water where one person sees it

traditions remains the same: four groups (including the controversial one based on putative Qumran orthography) + N (non-aligned texts), where N = an undefined number of different texts.

[22] Tov does not use this term, but reserves it for Qumran scrolls that have a *typological* relationship to a textual tradition (e.g. 4QJer[b] to LXX). Others use 'type' more loosely to mean 'a kind of'.

[23] 'Some Notes', 6–9.

[24] Tov, 'The Contribution of the Qumran Scrolls to the Understanding of the LXX', in *SSCW*, 24–5; 'A Reply', 18; and *Textual Criticism*, 163, translates this term as 'indicative errors', whereas Paul Maas, 'Textual Criticism', in M. Cary (ed.), *The Oxford Classical Dictionary* (Oxford: Clarendon Press, 1949), 888–9, uses the term *errores significativi* or 'significant errors'.

[25] Similar issues are raised by Shaye Cohen's discussion of 'separators' and 'unifiers' ('The Modern Study of Ancient Judaism', in S. J. D. Cohen and Edward L. Greenstein (eds.), *The State of Jewish Studies* (Detroit: Wayne State University, 1990), 55–74).

as half-empty and the other half-full, the classification of a text in a supposed tripartite stemma[26] is not simply a matter of emphasizing one aspect over the other (the water instead of the empty space, the filiation over the separative elements, or vice versa). Where should, for instance, a text such as 4QSam[a] be located? Because it agrees with both the *Vorlagen* of the LXX and MT, it may be supposed that the Qumran scroll ought to be placed between these two textual standards, with an accompanying explanation of its sharing bad genes with the former.

But what of those passages in 4QSam[a] not found in the LXX or MT (e.g. the well-known Jabesh-Gilead episode of 1 Sam. 11[27])? A two-dimensional stemmatic model (vertical and horizontal axes) could not adequately account for them. A three-dimensional model, however, with 4QSam[a] between the LXX and MT but also projecting forward (to represent this supplementary material), could do so, but this model would no longer be a conventional tripartite division of the textual tradition.[28] A significant portion, given Tov's statistics that 40 per cent are proto-Masoretic Texts,[29] of the Qumran biblical scrolls may be classified according to the traditional two-dimensional stemma, but if a theoretical model is to achieve any advance it should account for all the evidence.

It would seem best to liberate the Qumran biblical scrolls from the two-dimensional, stemmatic straitjacket of pre-Qumran textual

---

[26] For extra-pentateuchal books, the tripartite division is maintained by analogy. Cross argues, for instance, that Samuel had the *Vorlage* of the LXX in Egypt (cf. Sebastian Brock, 'The Recensions of the Septuagint Version of 1 Samuel' (Oxford D.Phil. thesis, 1966), esp. ch. 2), 4QSam scrolls in Palestine, and the proto-MT in Babylon.

[27] It would seem that Josephus' narrative, in *AJ* 6. 5. 1 (68), is based upon a biblical text, such as 4QSam[a], that explained Nahash's apparently unprovoked attack on the inhabitants of Jabesh-Gilead (cf. F. M. Cross, 'The Oldest Manuscripts from Qumran', in *QHBT*, 147–76; 'The Ammonite Oppression of the Tribes of Gad and Reuben: Missing Verses from 1 Samuel 11 found in 4QSamuel[a]', in H. Tadmor and M. Weinfeld (eds.), *History, Historiography and Interpretation* (Jerusalem: Magnes Press, 1983), 151–8; and Eugene Ulrich, *The Qumran Text of Samuel and Josephus* (Missoula, Mont.: Scholars Press, 1978)).

[28] Many thanks to Sebastian Brock for several discussions on this matter. Cf. Michael Weitzman's critique of the classical stemma of Paul Maas and discussion of three-dimensional models ('The Analysis of Open Traditions', *Studies in Bibliography*, 38 (1985), 84–120).

[29] 'Groups of Biblical Texts found at Qumran', in D. Dimant and L. H. Schiffman (eds.), *Time to Prepare the Way in the Wilderness: Papers on the Qumran Scrolls* (Leiden: E. J. Brill, 1995), 101. An earlier estimate of proto-MT texts was higher, at 60% (*Textual Criticism*, 115).

criticism and allow them to express the full range of their textual diversity. The emerging picture of the textual situation in the Second Temple period includes both texts that cluster around the proto-Masoretic, septuagintal, and pre-Samaritan text-types and others that cannot be classified by any one of these standards.

The implication for exegesis is clear: the Qumran pesharim and Pauline letters are dated to a period when the textual situation is fluid and more than the three traditional textual traditions of the MT, LXX, and SP should be posited.

Classification of Texts

In considering post-Qumran textual theories, issues of textual characterization and classification relevant to exegesis were raised: how are texts to be classified? How many agreements and disagreements must there be with, say, the LXX before the text is described as septuagintal? The issue of judging the character of a text is important not only for textual criticism but also for exegesis, since all who study variants supposedly created by the interpreter must evaluate, instinctively or reflectively, the overall textual character of the underlying biblical texts (or in the case of the pesharim the scriptural prophecies as reconstituted from the lemmata) to be proto-Masoretic, septuagintal, pre-Samaritan, or non-aligned (or independent). Underlying this assessment is the assumption that the variation did not originally belong to the *Vorlage* but was subsequently produced by the ancient interpreter.

By what criteria are texts classified? Text-critics often pronounce that this or that text is 'septuagintal', 'proto-Masoretic', or 'pre-Samaritan', but few discuss the reasoning behind their textual judgement. Here, it would seem, more than in other areas of textual criticism, can the procedure be described as 'artistic' and the appeal to authority most convenient. It is true that textual criticism is an art rather than a science and the judgements of specialists who immerse themselves in the relevant texts rightly carry great weight, but no opinion is infallible nor should the basis upon which the text-critic makes his evaluation be beyond debate.[30] After all, as A. E. Housman sardonically put it, all who concern themselves with textual criticism should have a head, and not a pumpkin, on the shoulders and brains, and not pudding, in

---

[30] I raised this issue previously in 'Eschatological Orientation and the Alteration of Scripture in the Habakkuk Pesher', *JNES* 49 (1990), 189 and n. 22.

the head.[31] Partisanship of any form handcuffs the textual critic to his school, teachers, and associates.[32]

Subjective elements involved in the classification of texts are unlikely to disappear even with the application of the most rigorous and strictly controlled methods, but the appeal to common sense should be complemented by external guidelines and should not be used to cover a range of methodological sins.

How does one classify a text? In the above discussion, the notion of bad genes, corrupt readings, or significant errors was applied to the evaluation of a text's type. Thus, for example, it was argued that despite the agreements with the MT and addition of supplementary material, 4QSam[a] should be classified as a septuagintal text, since it shares a long list of bad genes (secondary readings and errors) with the *Vorlage* of the Old Greek.[33] Bad genes are a better indicator of textual grouping than good genes, apparently because an uncorrupted reading must have been shared by many other manuscripts that are no longer extant.[34] That is to say, bad genes help distinguish a group of manuscripts from the majority.

There are a number of debatable points in the application of the concept of bad genes or significant errors to textual criticism of the Bible, but they have a limited significance for exegesis and will not be discussed in detail. Suffice it to say that the descriptors 'bad', 'corrupt', or 'errors' are value judgements and assume that the uncorrupted readings are also the original readings in the putative stemma of manuscripts. Not all text-critics will agree with this theoretical framework nor with the assumption that the 'better' reading is also the original. For example, the original expressions of a modern author are not necessarily better than subsequent changes introduced by his editor.[35] Moreover, the

[31] 'The Application of Thought to Textual Criticism', in J. Diggle and F. R. D. Goodyear (eds.), *The Classical Papers of A. E. Housman* (Cambridge: Cambridge University Press, 1972), 1069.

[32] Ibid. 1060. Cf. also P. Kyle McCarter, *Textual Criticism: Recovering the Text of the Hebrew Bible* (Philadelphia: Fortress Press, 1986), 25.

[33] So Cross, 'Some Notes', 7.

[34] Tov, 'A Reply', 18–19. Tov's views are now closer to those of Cross in giving more weight to disagreements ('Contribution', 23–5). Distinct from Cross, however, he classifies 4QSam[a] in both the Septuagintal *and* the non-aligned groups. The oddity of this dual classification illustrates well the inadequacies of a two-dimensional, stemmatic model.

[35] It is clear from the discussions that bad genes are not copyist errors. See now

assertion that an uncorrupted reading must have been shared by many more texts no longer extant is not necessary; there could have been just as many texts that shared the corrupted reading, depending upon how the texts were subsequently transmitted.[36]

More germane to the analysis of the pesherite lemmata below is the issue of enumerating variant readings, whether corrupted or uncorrupted readings. In comparing the textual affinities of different biblical texts from Qumran, it is virtually meaningless to suggest that a particular text, such as 4QSam[a], shares a long list of variants with the LXX, or even to provide an absolute number in order to prove that that scroll should be described as Septuagintal, since biblical books vary in length and how much of a particular book is preserved in a Qumran scroll directly affects the extant and potential number of variants.

These difficulties may be illustrated by juxtaposing two extreme examples. 2QDeut[c] preserves one minor variant in Deuteronomy 10: 8-12 ([ללא]ה) which agrees with the LXX against the MT,[37] whereas 4QSam[a] contains on the face of it an impressive catalogue of variants,[38] agreeing and disagreeing with the proto-Lucianic text, MT, and Josephus' *Vorlage*. A comparison of these two texts, however, would require that the variants be converted to a percentage of the extant text, the *proportion* of variants to words in common with, say, the LXX standard, since 2QDeut[c] preserves a mere twenty partial or whole words[39] while 4QSam[a] numerous fragments (on more than twenty-five photographic plates) that

---

Frank Polak's use of statistics to circumvent the difficulties of identifying an original from a secondary or erroneous one ('Statistics and Textual Filiation: The Case of 4QSam[a]/LXX (with a Note on the Text of the Pentateuch)', in *SSCW*, 221).

[36] Given the number of proto-MT manuscripts at Qumran, 40% by Tov's latest reckoning and extrapolation of this figure to the textual situation in the Second Temple period, the example of 1 Sam. 1: 24 leads in the opposite direction to the conclusion put forward in 'Contribution', 24-5, 44 n. 12; 'A Reply', 19: the *corrupted* reading (בפרים שלשה) of the MT must have been shared by many more texts than the *uncorrupted* (בפרמשלש/ἐν μόσχῳ τριετίζοντι) readings of the LXX (*c*.10%) and 4QSam[a]. Cf. P. Kyle McCarter, *1 Samuel* (Garden City, NY: Doubleday, 1980), 56-7, who alternatively reads '[bpr bn] bqr mšlš'.

[37] M. Baillet in *DJD* iii. 61-2 (pl. XII, no. 12). Tov, 'Contribution', 38, correctly dismisses the editor's characterization of the text to be approaching the LXX and Vulgate.

[38] The variants for 1 Sam. 1-2 and 10 and 2 Sam. 11-24 are enumerated by Polak, 'Statistics', 225-76.

[39] Tov, 'Contribution', 38, counts them slightly differently and arrives at 12 words.

attest to substantial portions of 1 and 2 Samuel. In other words, the fact that 4QSam[a] contains a long list (the actual number is not given) of variants is due not only to the character of the text but also the chance preservation of so much of this substantial biblical book. Conversely, the 5 per cent variation of 2QDeut[c] cannot be taken as an indication of the textual affinity with the LXX standard, since the random choice of twenty words out of four verses does not constitute a large enough sample. How large a textual sample should be before it can be considered to be statistically significant remains a moot point. Ideally, textual comparison should involve equal size texts of the same portions of the bible, but the textual reality is much less straightforward.

Statistics alone cannot account for qualitative elements, and variants, as conventional wisdom has it, should be weighed and not (simply) counted. Minimally, this means that orthographical (and morphological) variants should carry little or no weight in the evaluation of a text-type. What is more, a variant such as the conjunction [ולא]ו of 2QDeut[c] is not only minor,[40] but also should not be considered in the same category as, say, the long addition of 1 Samuel 11 which, by convention, is also counted as one variant.[41] The enumeration of the number of variants, theoretically speaking, should be based upon a basic unit (i.e. a word). More will be said about this in the chapters on the pesharim.

Language and Textual Classification

In textual criticism of the Bible, to state that language should not be used as a criterion for textual classification would be merely stating the obvious, since the comparison of texts written in Hebrew and Greek is the staple of text-critical work. Even before 1947, it was not uncommon to find a comparison based upon retroversions from the Greek text of the LXX to the presumed Hebrew *Vorlage*. Such retroversions, of course, were only as good as the scholar who retranslated the text back to its supposed original, since there were many pitfalls in this procedure: as has been recognized in ancient times, the act of translation is also an act of interpretation and what was expressed in Hebrew does not have the exact same sense in Greek. A retranslation from the

[40] According to Baillet, it is also attested by 17 MSS of Kennicott, 38 MSS of Kittel, the SP, Syriac, and Vulgate.
[41] Cf. Polak, 'Statistics', 217.

extant Greek back to its supposed Hebrew *Vorlage* compounds the difficulties and increases the degree of uncertainty.[42]

With the discovery of the Qumran biblical scrolls, however, there are now texts written in Hebrew (e.g. 4QJer[b], 4QExod[b]) that are close to the presumed *Vorlage* of the Septuagint.[43] That is to say, while there may have been in the past a tendency to view the three textual traditions of the MT, LXX, and SP as aligned according to language and script, the discovery of Hebrew exemplars of septuagintal texts has meant that the character of a text must now be determined by the readings that it contains rather than the language in which it was written.[44]

The significance of this for biblical quotations written in Greek will be discussed in the chapters on Pauline exegesis. What is important to underscore here is that just because a biblical quotation is written in Greek is no reason for supposing that it is necessarily septuagintal. Paul expressed himself in the language that was understood by his Greek-speaking audience. Being polylingual, he could most likely read biblical texts in their Hebrew original, one or more of the Greek translations (including the Septuagint) or an Aramaic targum. The high view of the Septuagint in New Testament scholarship has rightly been questioned by David Gooding:

[E]xcessive veneration of the Greek translation was a development of later, post-Apostolic, times. The New Testament shows a more realistic attitude: it uses the Septuagint widely and takes over some of its interpretations. But it does not confine itself to the Septuagint, as though the Septuagint were a uniquely authoritative translation. . . . When they so prefer, the New Testament writers use other translations.[45]

When he quoted biblical passages, however, Paul could only do so in the Greek language. Sometimes he used a translation that was readily at hand; on other occasions his biblical quotation

---

[42] A judicious discussion of the difficulties is found in Emanuel Tov, *The Text-Critical Use of the Septuagint in Biblical Research* (Jerusalem: Simor, 1981), 97–179.

[43] See Tov, 'Contribution', 28–38, for a survey and analysis of the degree of proximity of these Qumran scrolls to the LXX.

[44] While there is good reason for stressing this here, given the past research on Pauline quotations, Greek on the whole is still a characteristic feature of the septuagintal text-type since the overwhelming majority of witnesses are written in this language.

[45] *Relics of Ancient Exegesis: A Study of the Miscellanies in 3 Reigns 2* (Cambridge: Cambridge University Press, 1976), 117.

corresponds to no known Greek translation. These latter Greek biblical quotations may agree with the Masoretic Text, when it differs from the Septuagint, or can reflect an existing exegetical interpretation on a biblical passage. In yet other places, especially when the Hebrew original is ambiguous or exegetically opaque and there is no extant textual support, one suspects that Paul himself may have provided his own rendering into Greek.

A REMARK ON TERMINOLOGY

Anyone who attempts to maintain a consistent set of terminology in mind as he reads previous research on the present topic and related issues will quickly become frustrated, since scholars use different words and labels in different languages at different times to describe the same phenomena. In part, the use of such a variety of terms can be explained by the period in the history of scholarship (e.g. 'recensions' and 'textual family'), the cultural and national preference (e.g. the term 'Old Greek' for the earliest recoverable form of the Septuagint; the *Urtext*), the particular task being pursued and the inherent nature of the material that defies modern compartmentalization.

Fortunately, the present exegetical study can circumvent many of these difficult, if not intractable, problems.[46] There is no need to argue for terminological definitions here, so long as that which is being discussed is clear. To add a greater degree of perspicuity to the discussion the following, therefore, should be noted as broad guidelines:

1. 'The bible', 'holy scripture', and 'holy writ' are preferred designations to the Old Testament, Hebrew Bible, TaNaK, or First Testament.

2. 'LXX' or '(the) Septuagint' refers to the entire tradition of Jewish Greek Scriptures transmitted primarily in Christian tradition. The first translation of the Hebrew Bible into Greek is 'the Old Greek'. For the biblical quotations in the Pauline letters, it will be

---

[46] See the discussions of Moshe Goshen-Gottstein, 'The Textual Criticism of the Old Testament: Rise, Decline, Rebirth', *JBL* 102 (1983), 365–99; David Gooding, 'An Appeal for a Stricter Terminology in the Textual Criticism of the Old Testament', *JSS* 21 (1976), 15–25; Leonard Greenspoon, 'The Use and Abuse of the Term "LXX" and Related Terminology in Recent Scholarship' *BIOSCS* 20 (1987), 21–9; and Ulrich, 'Pluriformity', 37–8.

argued that Paul cites from *a* Greek text which may or may not agree with the Old Greek, the LXX, or one of its subsequent revisions.

3. 'Pesher' (adjective: pesherite) primarily refers to the literary genre of continuous Qumran commentaries. A related usage is found in the description of exegesis of individual verses within a thematic context, a phenomenon frequently described as *pesher thématique* or thematic pesher. Other exegeses that resemble these, but cannot technically be so described are designated 'pesheresque'. Similarly, 'Midrash' refers to the classical rabbinic texts and 'midrashic' to exegesis that resembles them. 'Pesherist' (coined by analogy to 'midrashist') refers to the ancient exegete at Qumran.

PART II
Aspects of Ancient Bible
Interpretation

3

Wording of the Biblical Text

It was stated in the Prolegomena that the present book intends to locate the Qumran pesharim and Pauline letters within the continuum of biblical composition and Bible interpretation. One way of achieving this, it was suggested, was to assess their attitude to the sanctity of the biblical text: did the pesherists and Paul merely quote scriptural texts or did they also modify the very words of the biblical lemma to make them conform more closely to their interpretation?

Intuitively, it may be supposed that the pesherists and Paul did alter their biblical quotation, since paraphrasing and rewriting of the biblical texts are found in other works of the Second Temple period. What prevents us from making similar assumptions about the pesherite and Pauline lemmata are: (1) the technique of citation is different from the paraphrase of biblical texts; and (2) in view of the advances of post-Qumran textual criticism and the pluriformity of textual types attested in the Second Temple period, demonstrating that an exegetical change had in fact taken place is no easy task.

An exegetical alteration assumes that the original, unmodified reading is identifiable. In most passages, however, there is only the extant reading. Should this extant reading vary from one of the textual standards of the MT, LXX, or SP, it could then be suggested that it was a modification of the exegete to suit his own interpretative purposes. But it is also possible that the exegete's *Vorlage* contained this so-called 'variant' and the exegete used what was already there.

In other words, caution must always be exercised in describing an extant reading as an 'exegetical alteration' simply on the basis of its variation from the MT, LXX, or SP. Or again to reformulate the question slightly differently and more concisely: from which biblical texts did the Qumran pesherists and Paul cite their scriptural quotations and did these biblical texts already contain readings which varied from the MT, LXX, and SP? As will be shown in the ensuing chapters of Parts III and IV, the significance of post-Qumran textual criticism for exegesis requires a reinvestigation into the entire question of exegetical alterations in the pesharim and Pauline letters.

Before proceeding to them, however, a discussion of neglected aspects of ancient Bible interpretation is in order. In suggesting that the pesherite and Pauline attitude to holy scripture may be assessed by an investigation of exegetical alterations, we have assumed that ancient exegetes were indeed concerned not just with the message of the biblical text, but also with its exact wording. Was this in fact the case?

The two chapters in this part will show how attention to the wording of the biblical text was also a feature of ancient Bible interpretation and a concern of the pesherists and Paul. In some cases, the basic hermeneutical tension involved the opposing forces of preservation and application. While a central concern of ancient Bible interpretation is in making earlier traditions meaningful for subsequent generations there is often a corresponding tendency within the same texts, or in other texts representing a different exegetical trend, to preserve (if, in some instances, only by way of rhetorical posturing) not only the sense but also the actual words of scripture.

The present attention to verbal formulations of the biblical quotations in the pesharim and Pauline letters is not a modern question anachronistically imposed on these texts; it is a feature of ancient Bible interpretation that manifests itself in ancient testimonies, scribal interventions, and literalistic exegeses. Unfortunately, there has been very little discussion of this topic from the point of view of the history of Bible interpretation. Scholarly studies that survey Bible interpretation in this period for the most part emphasize the growth of the exegetical traditions and how earlier biblical texts were adapted, translated, and interpreted to suit the circumstances of the exegetes' communities.[1]

What is needed is a discussion of those aspects of ancient Bible interpretation that emphasize the faithful preservation of the

[1] See e.g. among several others, the excellent surveys and studies by Geza Vermes in 'Bible and Midrash: Early Old Testament Exegesis', in *CHB*, i. 199–231; Michael Fishbane, *Biblical Interpretation in Ancient Israel* (Oxford: Clarendon Press, 1985); and James Kugel in id. and Rowan A. Greer, *Early Biblical Interpretation* (Philadelphia: Westminster Press, 1986).

received tradition and sacred texts.[2] By situating them in the historical context of the Second Temple period, these important aspects of ancient exposition may be separated from their frequent association with modern, fundamentalist Christian debates about literalism and inerrancy. The preservation of the word of God is a feature of ancient exegesis that deserves to be studied in its own right.

TESTIMONIES AND PROHIBITIONS

Basic to any exegesis of written law codes[3] or sacred texts is the hermeneutical tension between application and preservation. An interpreter of written texts must often attempt to make the past relevant for the present (e.g. updating obsolete language, translating into vernacular, harmonizing contradictions), since new situations of succeeding generations demand a reinterpretation of the received tradition.[4] In some cases, however, he must apply the message in a way that remains (or at least appears to remain) faithful to the original formulation or intention, lest he incur the charge of innovation or, worse, distortion. This hermeneutical tension can be found in virtually any phenomenon that involves a written document and an interpretative tradition.[5] In the

[2] Previous studies that have brought together much valuable material include W. C. van Unnik, 'De la régle μήτε προσθεῖναι μήτε ἀφελεῖν dans l'histoire du canon', *VC* 3 (1949), 13–36; id., *Flavius Josephus als historischer Schriftsteller* (Heidelberg: Verlag Lambert Schneider, 1978), ch. 2, 'Die Formel "nichts wegnehmen, nichts hinzufügen" bei Josephus'; and Birger Gerhardsson, *Memory and Manuscript: Oral Tradition and Written Transmission in Rabbinic Judaism and Early Christianity* (Lund: C. W. K. Gleerup, 1961), pt. I; Moshe Weinfeld, *Deuteronomy and the Deuteronomic School* (Oxford: Clarendon Press, 1972), 260–6; H. W. Attridge, *Interpretation of Biblical History in the Antiquitates Judaicae of Flavius Josephus* (Missoula, Mont.: Scholars Press, 1976), 43–60; Shaye Cohen, *Josephus in Galilee and Rome: His Vita and Development as a Historian* (Leiden: E. J. Brill, 1979), 24–33; and L. H. Feldman, 'Use, Authority and Exegesis of Mikra in the Writings of Josephus', in *Mikra*, 466–70.

[3] e.g. Reuven Yaron, 'Acts of Last Will in Jewish Law', in *Actes à Cause de Mort*, Recueils de la Société Jean Bodin pour l'histoire comparative des institutions, 59 (Brussels: De Broeck Université, 1992), 31, states: 'The biblical provisions are *Grundnormen*, which the Rabbis, the scholars and sages of the Talmudic period, are bound to follow, from which they are not entitled to deviate. Altogether, it is a theory not difficult to formulate, but rather difficult to live up to.'

[4] Cf. Daniel Patte, *Early Jewish Hermeneutic in Palestine*, SBL and Scholars Press Dissertation Series, 22 (1975) and George J. Brooke, *Exegesis at Qumran: 4QFlorilegium in its Jewish Context* (Sheffield: JSOT Press, 1985).

[5] Cf. Carmel McCarthy, *The Tiqqune Sopherim and other Theological Corrections in the Masoretic Text of the Old Testament* (Göttingen: Vandenhoeck & Ruprecht, 1981),

following, it will be suggested that certain exegetical traditions of the Second Temple period may also be characterized by this hermeneutical tension between application and preservation.

The interpretation of the biblical texts in the Second Temple period was by no means a monolithic phenomenon, consisting as it did of a variety of techniques and exegetical approaches. Most of these exegetical works involved either some form of amplification and clarification of a biblical word, passage, or story, or harmonization and retelling of precepts, ordinances, or narrative. Often neglected within this collection of exegeses, however, are testimonies and scribal and exegetical phenomena found here and there that underscore the faithful preservation of the biblical passage in a strictly literalistic manner, probably the ones that come most readily to mind being Jesus' promise that not one iota (ἰῶτα ἕν) or a dot (μία κεραία) shall pass from the Law until all is accomplished (Matt. 5: 18), and the deuteronomic prohibition of neither adding to (לא תספו), nor subtracting anything from (לא תגרעו), the Mosaic commandments (Deut. 4: 2; 13: 1).

Non addetis, neque auferetis

From the modern standpoint, where authoritative lists of canonical writings exist for various Jewish and Christian traditions, careful attention to the actual words of those books that comprise Holy Scripture may be an obvious, if not also a natural, concern. The Bible, variously defined, has long been fixed in writing, and, for some, in inspired translation (e.g. the Septuagint, Vulgate, the Authorized Version), and the task of the modern expositor is to elucidate, with varying degrees of help from tradition and commentaries, the intended or applied meaning of these biblical texts. The expositor may stress the main points of the passage, draw out the significance of issues hinted at only *en passant*, or seek a meaning entirely unintended by the ancient authors. Whatever he may do, as for example in the rearrangement of letters and words of the biblical passage found in traditional Jewish exposition, it is understood that scripture continues to have meaning for succeeding generations.

Moreover, there is usually a separation between the written

15: 'This tradition of so-called emendations took shape in an atmosphere that was particularly conscious of the need to protect the sacred text and to interpret it suitably for succeeding generations.'

34

word of the biblical text and the commentary that accompanies it. The scriptural passage, often read out first or recalled from memory, is distinct from the exposition: however the biblical message may be incorporated into the interpretation, the original verbal formulations remain intact and retrievable for comparison.

The ancients too paid close attention to the words of their biblical texts. The editor of the book of Deuteronomy himself,[6] despite reusing and reshaping earlier parts of the Pentateuch (e.g. the Decalogue (Exod. 20: 1-17); Covenant Code (Exod. 20: 22–23: 33)[7]), pronounced warnings against tampering with the law and enjoined the Israelites from adding to (יסף), or subtracting anything from (גרע),[8] the Mosaic commandments (Deut. 4: 2; 13: 1). Given that the editor of Deuteronomy has himself reshaped earlier material, the force of this prohibition appears to be: no *further* changes should be introduced to the law.

But was anyone deterred by this warning? The Deuteronomic prohibition, of course, could have been addressing a situation where the law *was* being modified. It was necessary to forbid such activity precisely because the Israelites were adding to and subtracting from the law.

Alternatively, it is possible to understand prohibitions against changes literally[9] and to regard such compositions as *Jubilees*, the Temple Scroll, and Liber Antiquitatum Biblicarum not as retellings of the books of Genesis to 2 Samuel interspersed with passages from elsewhere, but as independent compositions that drew upon a common pool of oral and written sources. That is to say, the Deuteronomic warning was taken to heart. Compositions such as the Temple Scroll, *Jubilees*, and Liber Antiquitatum Biblicarum were not rewritten at all, but were competing accounts of the same narrative, legend, and law.

---

[6] Moshe Weinfeld, *Deuteronomy 1-11* (New York: Doubleday, 1991), 81–4, argues that this prohibition refers to the editing of Deuteronomy during the reign of Josiah and Hezekiah.

[7] See now the All Souls Deuteronomy and its conflation of the two versions of the command to observe the Sabbath (Sidnie White, 'The All Souls Deuteronomy and the Decalogue', *JBL* 109 (1990), 193-206).

[8] While this verb can also mean 'to diminish', the sense of subtraction better fits the context of this stereotype formula (cf. ἀφαιρέω).

[9] See e.g. J. C. O'Neill and his application of the prohibition to Jesus' logia: 'If the words of prophets and seers were sacred, how much more sacred were the words and deeds of the Son of God himself' ('The Lost Written Records of Jesus' Words and Deeds behind our Records', *JTS* 42 (1991), 484).

Should the Temple Scroll, for example, be described as a rewritten Deuteronomy? Yigael Yadin[10] and Ben Zion Wacholder[11] argue that the Temple Scroll is the Qumran Torah, containing as it did not only laws (substantially about the Temple) found in Deuteronomy, Leviticus, Numbers, and Exodus, but also others besides (e.g. the extra-biblical laws on polygamy, incest, and sexual intercourse; cf. CD 4. 20-5. 11; 12. 1-2). Strikingly, the Qumran Torah features God speaking in the first rather than the third person of Deuteronomic tradition (e.g. compare 11QTS 53-7, 60-6 and Deut. 12-23: 1). Hartmut Stegemann, who argues for a non-Qumranic provenance, similarly proposes that the Temple Scroll is the sixth book of the Torah of the Essenes, encompassing material left out when the Pentateuch was canonized in the fifth century.[12]

Whether the Temple Scroll, *Jubilees*, and Liber Antiquitatum Biblicarum be described as 'rewritten Bibles' or independent accounts[13] drawn from a common tradition remains an open question. The publication of Qumran texts described as 'paraphrases' (e.g. 4QPsalms of Joshua, 4QReworked Pentateuch, and 4QTemple?[14]) raises the whole issue of what a biblical text is. Before the fixation of individual books, there appeared to have been works that both shared a relationship with and remained distinct from books that were eventually included in the canon. Much more work on this area is needed before the relationship between a biblical text and its paraphrase is clarified.[15]

---

[10] *The Temple Scroll* (Jerusalem: Israel Exploration Society, 1983), i. 390-2.

[11] *The Dawn of Qumran* (Cincinnati: Hebrew Union College Press, 1983), ch. 1.

[12] *The Origins of the Temple Scroll* in VTS 40 (Leiden: E. J. Brill, 1988), 235-56; 'Is the Temple Scroll a Sixth Book of the Torah—Lost for 2,500 years?', in H. Shanks (ed.), *Understanding the Dead Sea Scrolls* (New York: Random House, 1992), 126-36. Cf. A. Graeme Auld, *Kings without Privilege: David and Moses in the Story of the Bible's Kings* (Edinburgh: T. & T. Clark, 1994), who puts forward the view that Kings and Chronicles drew from a common source.

[13] Perhaps Revelation should also be considered as a rewritten bible, since it seems to treat the prophecy of John as a new mosaic dispensation (Rev. 22: 4, 18-19; cf. Christopher Rowland, *Revelation* (London: Epworth Press, 1993), 153-9).

[14] Emanuel Tov and Sidnie White in DJD xiii. 255-334, have suggested that five fragments of 4Q365 are better described as a source of the Temple Scroll (4Q365a).

[15] Cf. Carol Newsom, 'The "Psalms of Joshua" from Cave 4', *JJS* 39 (1988), 56-73; and Emanuel Tov, 'Textual Status of 4Q364-367', in *Madrid*, i.

Rhetorical Topos or Genuine Concern?

Reconsideration of the 'rewritten Bibles', however, is but one aspect of the question that is being asked. Others include the evaluation of the warnings against changes, literalistic exegesis, and scribal practices.

How should the Deuteronomic warning be understood? To begin with, it is important to realize that the mathematical notion of 'adding to' and 'subtracting from', expressed in the Vulgate by *non addetis ad* (you shall not add to) and *neque auferetis ex* (neither shall you subtract from), is formulaic. Similar expressions, using the verbs יסף/προσθεῖναι and גרע/ἀφελεῖν or their cognates and synonyms, are found in a broad range of contexts, including the fidelity of the Septuagint translation (*Ep. Arist.* 310-11; Philo, *Mos.* 2. 34 (139); Josephus, *AJ* 12. 108-9 (13)), the drafting of a treaty (1 Macc. 8: 30), the unchangeable nature of providence (Qoh. 3. 14),[16] the literary accuracy of a narrative history (Josephus, *AJ* 1. 17 (Pr. 3), 20. 260-1; *CA* 1. 42 (8)), the immutability of prophecy (Rev. 22: 18-19; *1 Enoch* 104. 10-12), and the perfection of works of art (Aristotle, *Ethicae Nicomachaea*, 2. 6. 6-9). This formula has antecedents in the ancient Near East[17] and was also applied by the Early Church[18] to the message of the Gospel.[19]

The formula of 'adding and subtracting' was used by the ancients as a rhetorical topos. In the Letter of Aristeas (310-11), for example, the people greeted the completion of the Greek translation of Hebrew scriptures with the imprecation against anyone who should revise (διασκευάσει) the text by adding (προστιθείς), transposing (μεταφέρων), or excising (ποιούμενος ἀφαίρεσιν) anything from the present form (ταῦθ' οὕτως ἔχοντα), so that the work might be guarded from change always (ἵνα διὰ παντὸς ἀέναα καὶ μένοντα φυλάσσηται).[20] Notable here is the passing comment that this threat was made according to their custom (καθὼς ἔθος αὐτοῖς

---

[16] Cf. Kurt Galling, 'Das Rätsel der Zeit im Urteil Kohelets (Koh. 3, 1-15)', *ZTK* 58 (1961), 1-15.

[17] Weinfeld, *Deuteronomy and the Deuteronomic School*, 260-5.

[18] See J. Leipoldt and S. Morenz, *Heilige Schriften* (Leipzig, 1953), 56-62, and the discussion of the 'canonical formula' (cf. *Did.* 4. 6. 13; *Barn.* 19. 7. 11).

[19] See van Unnik's comprehensive discussion of the anonymous anti-Montanist's fear of misrepresenting the Gospel (Eus. *HE* 5. 16. 3; 'Μήτε προσθεῖναι μήτε ἀφελεῖν').

[20] Moses Hadas (ed.), *Aristeas to Philocrates (Letter of Aristeas)* (New York: Harper & Bros., 1951), 221-2.

ἐστιν). That is to say, it was customary to pronounce such warnings.

Or again, in a different context altogether, Aristotle applies his rule of the golden mean to perfect works of art: excess and deficiency destroy the perfection (τὸ εὖ). Like Pseudo-Aristeas, Aristotle supports this statement on *objets d'art* with the customary remark (εἰώθασιν ἐπιλέγειν) that nothing is to be taken from (οὔτ' ἀφελεῖν ἔστιν) nor added to them (οὔτε προσθεῖναι; *Ethicae Nicomachaea*, 2. 6. 9).

From these two passing comments alone, it is evident that the formula of 'adding and subtracting' was a common topos that transcended linguistic and cultural boundaries. When used in the context of a warning against making changes to the biblical text, however, two further questions may be raised: was it intended solely for rhetorical effect[21] or were the audience and readers expected to take heed of its counsel? And secondly, how did subsequent exegetes understand such a warning?

In the book of Deuteronomy, the explicit prohibition against adding and subtracting should be understood in the context of other admonitions to keep (לשמר), learn (ללמד), and practise (לעשות) the divine statutes and ordinances given through Moses (cf. Deut. 5: 1; 6: 1; 8: 1; 26: 16–19; and 27: 1). The notices in Deuteronomy 4: 2 and 13: 1 are simply the most literal of such exhortations, warning Israel from adding to or subtracting from the *word* (כל דבר/דבר) which Moses has commanded.[22] Furthermore, there was no expectation of fulfilling such a high standard of obedience. These admonitions were set up as ideals to which every Israelite must strive; ideals, however, that admit imperfect obedience to the commandments (Deut. 28: 58–68) and ensuing apostasy (Deut. 31: 29).[23] Should the Israelite keep to the Mosaic law, then he will live and be blessed. If he does not, then he is cursed and will perish (Deut. 30: 15–20).

The Temple Scroll also understood this prohibition in the non-

---

[21] Use of a rhetorical topos does not necessarily imply disingenuity on the part of the author or speaker (see my 'Not in Persuasive Words of Wisdom, but in the Demonstration of the Spirit and Power', *NovT* 29 (1987), 143–4 n. 20).

[22] Philo, *de Specialibus legibus*, 4. 27 (143–4), understood the Deuteronomic prohibition literally but referring to the whole law.

[23] Cf. W. D. Davies, *The Setting of the Sermon on the Mount* (Cambridge: Cambridge University Press, 1964), 170, who points out that while the Torah was considered immutable changes were allowed in the Messianic age.

literal sense. In column 54, lines 5–7, the warning against adding
to and subtracting from the Mosaic commandments is cited and
Deuteronomy 13 (on idolatry) is juxtaposed to the laws on vows
made by women (Num. 30: 1–16). Here, it would seem that even
part of the verse expressing the prohibition against adding to and
subtracting from the law was altered to suit the new situation (cf.
the plural כול הדברים).[24] The author of the Temple Scroll did not
perceive the Deuteronomic text from which he was presumably
rewriting to be fixed and immutable[25] nor did he understand the
formulaic warning literally.[26]

If the Deuteronomic warning is not to be understood literally,
then what does it signify? The formula of 'not adding to or subtracting from', whether it be drawn from wisdom tradition[27] or
elsewhere, belongs together with other exhortations to learn, keep,
and do the commandments, and it expresses an impulse to preserve the Mosaic precepts within the context of a contemporary
application of the law. Deuteronomy 5: 1–3, for example, states:

And Moses called to all Israel and said to them, 'Hear, O Israel the statutes
and precepts which I speak in your hearing today, and you shall learn
them and take care to do them. The Lord our God established a covenant
with us in Horeb. Not with our fathers did the Lord make this covenant,
but with us, we who are all of us here alive today.'

Manifestly, the tension is between learning the statutes and precepts (למדתם), carefully practising them (שמרתם לעשתם), and applying
them to contemporary life ('which I speak in your hearing this day
(היום)'; 'not with our fathers did the Lord make this covenant, but
with us, we who are all of us here alive today' (אתנו אנחנו אלה פה היום
כלנו חיים)). The Israelite is asked to receive the laws as they have
been passed on and to preserve them faithfully by dutifully practising them in the present situation.

[24] Due to אלה החקים of Num. 30: 17 (so Yadin, *Temple Scroll*, ii. 243 n. 5). Ibid.
n. 6, for variants (e.g. תשמור) attested in the versions.

[25] Cf. the characteristic substitution of אנכי for יהוה אלהיכם in 11QTS 54. 12 (Deut.
13: 4).

[26] Josephus too understood the Deuteronomic warning in a non-literal sense
(so van Unnik, *Flavius Josephus*, 26–40; Cohen, *Josephus*, 24–47; and Attridge,
Interpretation of Biblical History, 43–60), even if greater care must now be exercised
in arguing for his exegetical alterations (Eugene Ulrich, 'Josephus' Biblical Text for
the Books of Samuel', in L. H. Feldman and G. Hata (eds.), *Josephus, the Bible and
History* (Detroit: Wayne State University Press, 1989), 81–96).

[27] Weinfeld, *Deuteronomy and the Deuteronomic School*, 260–5, argues that wisdom literature influenced the Deuteronomic school.

Deuteronomy 4: 2 and 13: 1, of course, are the only two instances where the Deuteronomic warning explicitly prohibits adding to and subtracting from the Mosaic commandments. Here, the texts come closest to expressing the impulse to preserve not just the sense but also the wording of the biblical text ('everything (את כל הדבר) that I command you you shall take care to do; you shall not add to it nor take from it', 13: 1). The fact that such strict observance of the law and preservation of the biblical text[28] were not maintained or even expected to be accomplished (cf. Deut. 30) does not diminish the force of the formula: all Israel must try to keep fastidiously to the word, if not also the letter, of the law.

In sum, then, the issue is not whether the Deuteronomic prohibition be a rhetorical topos or a genuine concern, as they are juxtaposed in the title of this subsection, but that the ancient exegete expressed his impulse to preserve the words of the divine commandments with the conventional formula of leaving the biblical text intact from supplementation and excision.

EXEGETICAL, TRANSLATIONAL, AND SCRIBAL PHENOMENA

Legal Exegesis

The impulse to preserve not just the sense but also the very words of the law also surfaces in the phenomena of literalistic exegeses of the law. In the Sermon on the Mount, Jesus declares:

Do not think that I have come to abolish the law or the prophets. I did not come to abolish but to fulfil them. For truly I say to you: Until heaven and earth pass away, one iota ($\iota\hat{\omega}\tau\alpha$ $\acute{\epsilon}\nu$) or a dot ($\mu\acute{\iota}\alpha$ $\kappa\epsilon\rho\alpha\acute{\iota}\alpha$) shall not pass from the law until all is accomplished. Therefore, whoever looses one of the least of these commandments and teaches men thus, he shall be called least in the kingdom of heaven. But he who does and teaches them will be called great in the kingdom of heaven. (Matt. 5: 17-19)[29]

Referring to the first two divisions of the Bible, the Torah and the prophets, Jesus rejects the implicit charge that he had in any way annulled the demands of the scriptural commandments. Instead,

---

[28] Cf. the equation of the law with Deuteronomy ('this book of the law', Deut. 31: 26).

[29] The other briefer version in Luke 16: 16-17 emphasizes both the eternal nature of the law and its supersession by the Gospel.

he asserts that the law, even in its minutiae (an iota or dot[30]), will be observed until all is accomplished, a statement that seems to echo the Deuteronomic prohibition against adding to or subtracting from the word of the Mosaic commandments. How this plain sense[31] of the Matthean beatitudes corresponds to his practices remains a controversial issue and depends upon the particular reconstruction of the historical Jesus that is being followed. Did Jesus forbid the swearing of oaths (Matt. 5: 34)? Did he negate *lex talionis* ('the law of retaliation', Matt. 5: 39), sabbath (Matt. 12: 1) and food laws (Mark 7), and other commandments?[32] Or were these the later creations of his followers, forged out of controversies between Hellenized and Judaized groups. While a discussion of these complex issues lies far beyond the present concerns, one point needs to be made: Jesus' attitude towards the law should be seen in the context of the Early Church's practices. If Jesus abrogated the food laws, for example, why did the Early Church continue to argue about the observance of *kashrut*?[33]

More germane for the present discussion of literalistic exegesis is Jesus' emphasis upon the observance and perpetuity of the law even to its smallest letter and most insignificant stroke. Not only will the entire law remain valid, but whoever among his followers should loose or abolish (λύσῃ) even one of the least of these commandments (μίαν τῶν ἐντολῶν τούτων τῶν ἐλαχίστων) and teach men so shall be called least in the kingdom of heaven. Conversely, he who practises and teaches them strictly will be honoured. The ideals implied in the Deuteronomic prohibition have taken on new garments.[34]

Jesus was not the only one to whom a literalistic method of legal exegesis has been attached. Approximately a century after Jesus,

[30] Probably indicating something insignificant (e.g. a stroke, dot, hook, or horn of a letter (קוֹץ or כתר)).

[31] See W. D. Davies and D. C. Allison, *The Gospel According to Saint Matthew* (Edinburgh: T. & T. Clark, 1988), i. 491, for arguments against T. W. Manson's suggestion that Jesus is here criticizing the conservatism of scribes with bitter irony.

[32] See recently Geza Vermes, *Religion of Jesus the Jew* (Minneapolis: Fortress Press, 1993), 21-45.

[33] The view that takes Matt. 5: 19 as a reference to the commandments of Jesus (cf. 28: 20; Graham N. Stanton, *Gospels and Jesus* (Oxford: Oxford University Press, 1989), 74-5) would require that the demand is for the strict obedience of the dominical sayings.

[34] Cf. Robert Banks, *Jesus and the Law in the Synoptic Tradition* (Cambridge: Cambridge University Press, 1975), 218, points out that the rhetorical statement emphasizes the difficulty in setting aside the law.

Rabbi Akiba ben Joseph was known to have practised a form of exegesis that sought meaning in every word of the scriptural text. His literalistic exegesis is told in the oft-cited anecdote of Moses arriving in heaven and finding the Holy One attaching little crowns to the letters of the Torah. When asked of its significance, God explained that after many generations a man called Akiba ben Joseph would come and derive mounds of halakhot from each one of these crowns[35] (*b. Menah*, 29b). As is common with anecdotes, here a known characteristic is illustrated with humour and exaggeration.

But the exaggeration contains a kernel of truth. As Dominique Barthélemy has convincingly shown, Rabbi Akiba's exegetical method, though artificial in its isolation of individual words, was a veritable *passe-partout* that allowed him to open the precepts of the law to the amplifications of the oral tradition.[36] For example, he understood the double occurrence of the particle את in Genesis 1: 1 not simply as the superfluous untranslatable object markers for heaven and earth, but as significant pointers to the inclusion of the sun, moon, and stars and trees, herbaceous plants, and the Garden of Eden respectively. That is to say, Rabbi Akiba believed that God created not only heaven (את השמים) and earth (ואת הארץ), but also the lights in the sky and the vegetation on the earth, an exegesis that depends upon reading relevance out of what appears by the conventions of grammar to be insignificant particles (the double use of את). Such literalistic exegesis was not accepted by Akiba's contemporary Rabbi Ishmael, who argued that the law is expressed 'in the language of man', nor followed unhesitatingly by such of his disciples as Rabbi Meir.

Translation

Akiba's literalistic exegesis did, however, influence Aquila who, according to Jerome, was his student ('Akibas quem magistrum Aquilae proselyti autumant'[37]). Aquila's Greek translation of the Hebrew was literal in the extreme and left him open to the charge

---

[35] לדרוש על כל קוץ קוץ תילין תילין של הלכות.

[36] *Les Devanciers d'Aquila: Première publication intégrale du texte des fragments du Dodécaprophéton trouvés dans le Désert de Juda, précédée d'une étude sur les traductions et recensions grecques de la Bible réalisées au premier siècle de notre ère sous l'influence du rabbinat palestinien* (Leiden: E. J. Brill, 1963), 14.

[37] *Comment. in Esaiam*, 8. 11 (*Les Devanciers d'Aquila*, 3–15).

of barbarism.[38] For example, the LXX, Symmachus, and Theodotion translated Genesis 1: 1 idiomatically as ἐν ἀρχῇ ἐποίησεν ὁ Θεὸς τὸν οὐρανὸν καὶ τὴν γῆν whereas Aquila rendered it slavishly as ἐν κεφαλαίῳ ἔκτισεν ὁ θεὸς σὺν τὸν οὐρανὸν καὶ σὺν τὴν γῆν. For 'in the beginning' (בראשית), Aquila translated ἐν κεφαλαίῳ, 'at the head', derived etymologically from רואש/ראשית plus the preposition ב;[39] ברא ('he created') is literally rendered by ἔκτισεν (symbolically 'giving birth' to the heaven and earth[40]) rather than the idiomatic ἐποίησεν ('he made'); and Aquila translated את (the untranslatable accusative signifier) by σύν ('with'), adverbially construed.[41]

In the past generation, with the discovery of the Minor Prophets Scroll from Nahal Ḥever (8ḤevXIIgr)[42] and the advent of Dominique Barthélemy's study of it in *Les Devanciers d'Aquila* (1963), it is now more widely recognized[43] that Aquila's translation was not produced *de novo*. Instead, it is the culmination of a line of literalistic translation that stretches back to the period preceding the destruction of the Temple. A tradition that has been called the *kaige* ('and', the stereotype Greek translation for the Hebrew גם) recension or proto-Theodotion recension, the latter owing to its affinities to the earlier recension from which Theodotion presumably drew up his revision.[44]

Aquila's slavish translation was not unique. The Greek translations of Qohelet and Song of Songs were also of the most literal kind, a characteristic which some believe point to their Aquilanic origin.[45] *Onkelos*, the Aramaic targum of Babylonia, was also similarly literal in its rendering of the Hebrew. The identification of

---

[38] Jerome, *Epist. LVII ad Pammach*, ii, referring to the translation of Gen. 1: 1, disparages Aquila: 'dicitque . . ., quod Graece et Latina lingua omnino non recipit'. This negative evaluation should be tempered by James Barr's analysis of the logic of literalism in *The Typology of Literalism in Ancient Biblical Translations* (Göttingen: Vandenhoeck & Ruprecht, 1979), 282-4.

[39] Cf. Charles Taylor, *Fragments of the Book of Kings According to the Translation of Aquila* (Cambridge: Cambridge University Press, 1879), vi, and F. Field, *Origenis Hexaplorum* (Oxford: Clarendon Press, 1875), i. p. xxi.

[40] Similarly in Philo, *de Opificio Mundi*, 132.

[41] See the grammatical discussion in S. Jellicoe, *The Septuagint and Modern Study* (Oxford: Clarendon Press, 1968), 81.

[42] *Editio princeps* in Emanuel Tov, *DJD* viii.

[43] See Leonard Greenspoon, 'Aquila' and 'Theodotion' in *ABD*, i and vi respectively.

[44] Olivier Munnich, 'Contribution à l'étude de la première revision de la Septante', *ANRW* 20/1 (1987), 190-220, has questioned the direct link between the *kaige* recension and rabbinic exegesis.

[45] So Barthélemy, *Les Devanciers d'Aquila*, 10-30 and 158-60.

43

Onkelos with Aquila, however, may have arisen from a Babylonian misunderstanding of a reference to the Aquilanic Greek translation for their own official targum.[46]

Rendering a text literally is but one option available to the translator and such literal products do reveal something of the attitude of the translator to his text. In several penetrating articles,[47] Sebastian Brock has analysed the principles governing translational types. Where along the literary–literal continuum a translation is to be situated depends upon the translator's perception of his own role *vis-à-vis* the source text.

The expositor is someone who orients his translation to the reader; he is confident in his ability to render the sense of the text into a different language; he will attempt to resolve linguistic difficulties; and he will work with larger units to convey that which is signified by the word. The expositor conforms more closely to the modern ideals of a translator and his translation will be literary rather than literal. By contrast, the *interpres*, the literal translator, perceives his own role to be that of a more or less neutral medium: his translation is oriented towards the source text; he has a diminished role and he passes on to the translation any linguistic difficulties; he works primarily with the actual words that are used and produces a literal translation that is characterized by lexical stereotypes and etymological renderings.

The translations of Aquila, *kaige*, Qohelet, Song of Songs, and *Onkelos* are all literal products for which the Hebrew source text is translated according to the principle of *verbum e verbo* rather than *sensus de sensu*.[48] The translators were concerned not just with the sense of the passage but also with the very words that were used.[49]

---

[46] Cf. R. Yirmeyahu's logion in *b. Meg.* 3a and *y. Meg.* 71c and P. S. Alexander's discussion in 'Jewish Aramaic Translation of Hebrew Scriptures', in *Mikra*, 217–18.

[47] 'To Revise or not to Revise: Attitudes to Jewish Biblical Translation', in *SSCW*, 301–38; 'Some Aspects of Translation Technique in Antiquity', and 'Some Aspects of Greek Words in Syriac', in *Syriac Perspectives on Late Antiquity* (London: Variorum Reprints, 1984), iii and iv.

[48] Most early translations are compromises between the literal and free. The development towards literalism was partly caused by the elevation of inspired scripture (Barr, *Typology of Literalism*, 324–5).

[49] In the words of Jerome: 'ubi et verborum ordo mysterium est' (where even the order of the words is a mystery), *Epist. LVII ad Pammach.* See Brock, 'Aspects of Translation Technique', iii. 69–70.

Scribal Practices

The rabbinic tradition that produced the Masoretic exemplars of the Hebrew Bible in use today emphasize nothing if not the importance that the medievalists attached to the word of the biblical texts.[50] Great care was exercised in copying the texts accurately, counting the words[51] and spacing the verses and paragraphs, and annotating the margins with variant readings and cross-references. But what about the scribal practices before the destruction of the Temple? What were they like?

In 1961, Birger Gerhardsson published a monograph entitled *Memory and Manuscript* in which he argued that the Jewish model of teacher and student found in rabbinic literature helps explain Jesus' relationship to his disciples and the transmission of the Gospel tradition. Like the rabbis, Jesus taught his disciples orally; he made them memorize his teachings; and he inculcated in them the exegetical principles of expounding the written Torah with an authoritative exposition. The Early Church practised these oral techniques of 'memory texts', but as time passed some of these teachings were written down on notebooks and private scrolls. When the Evangelists compiled their Gospels, they had in their possession a tradition that was partly oral and partly written.

Gerhardsson's thesis was criticized by Morton Smith[52] and Jacob Neusner[53] at several points, the most important of which for the present purposes is the illegitimate retrojection of later rabbinic techniques to the time of Jesus. Gerhardsson has since replied[54] and has received qualified support from other quarters.[55]

Whether all or any later rabbinic evidence reflects the situation of an earlier period remains one of the central questions in the

[50] B. J. Roberts, *The Old Testament Text and Versions: The Hebrew Text in Transmission and the History of the Ancient Versions* (Cardiff: University of Wales, 1951), 32-9.

[51] Even if the accuracy of the scribal counting has recently been questioned by F. Anderson and A. Dean Forbes, 'What *Did* the Scribes Count?', in D. N. Freedman, F. Anderson, and A. Dean Forbes (eds.), *Studies in Hebrew and Aramaic Orthography* (Winona Lake, Ind.: Eisenbrauns, 1992), 318.

[52] 'A Comparison of Early Christian and Early Rabbinic Tradition', *JBL* 82 (1963), 169-76.

[53] *The Rabbinic Traditions about the Pharisees before 70* (Leiden: E. J. Brill, 1971), iii. 143-79.

[54] *Tradition and Transmission in Early Christianity* (Lund: Gleerup, 1964).

[55] e.g. W. D. Davies, 'Reflections about the Use of the Old Testament in the New in its Historical Context', *JQR* 74 (1983), 108-9, who feels that criticisms against Gerhardsson were exaggerated.

study of ancient Judaism. Debates about the identity of the Pharisees and Sadducees, for example, and the early development of the halakha will surely be revived as more Qumran texts (e.g. 4QMMT) are published,[56] as well as the extent to which the Qumran scribal practices and the rabbinic techniques (e.g. קרי/כתיב,[57] אל תקרי, אם למקרא,[58] תקוני הסופרים) correspond.

Thanks to several studies on the production of the scrolls, it is now evident that the Qumran scribes did take particular care in the preparation of the skin or papyrus,[59] repairing damaged and torn segments,[60] ruling the top, bottom, left, and right margins, paragraphing and correcting mistakes in the text. Some of these scribal practices do correspond to the Masoretic tradition,[61] but no generalization should be made from one scribe's practice to another.[62] While it is still premature to state the extent to which Qumran and rabbinic techniques correspond—this can be done only after all the texts have been thoroughly studied—there can be no doubt now that scribes in the Second Temple period did systematically and methodically preserve the biblical text, even if some of their techniques and results differ from those of their successors. What is more, such scribal practices reveal the importance which the ancients attached to the words of their biblical text.[63]

---

[56] See now, Elisha Qimron and John Strugnell, *DJD* x.

[57] Shemaryahu Talmon, 'Aspects of the Textual Transmission of the Bible in Light of Qumran Manuscripts', in *The World of Qumran from Within* (Jerusalem: Magnes Press; Leiden: E. J. Brill, 1989), 76–84, has discussed the development of 'double readings' as an earlier method of variant preservation.

[58] Shlomo Naeh, אין אם למסורת או :האם דרשו התנאים את כתיב התורה שלא כקריאתו המקובלת?', *Tarbiz*, 61 (1992), 401–48, has argued that this technique is not found in the tannaitic stratum of rabbinic literature.

[59] Michael O. Wise, 'Accidents and Accidence: A Scribal View of Linguistic Dating of the Aramaic Scrolls from Qumran', in T. Muraoka (ed.), *Abr-Nahrain Supplement 3* (Louvain: Peeters Press, 1992), 143–67.

[60] See e.g. the patching of col. 8, 4Qpaleo-Exod^m (P. Skehan, E. Ulrich, and J. Sanderson in *DJD* ix, pl. XI.

[61] Yadin, *Temple Scroll*, i. 9–10 (cf. Massekhet Soferim ii. 10); Skehan, Ulrich, and Sanderson, *DJD* x. 19; and Stephen Pfann, 'The Aramaic Text and Language of Daniel and Ezra in the Light of Some Manuscripts from Qumran', *Textus*, 16 (1991), 127–37.

[62] Inconsistency is found even within a manuscript (cf. the ruling of the top margins in cols. 1–7 and 8–12 in 1QpHab).

[63] Scribal practices of the ancient Near East have been discussed by A. R. Millard, 'In Praise of Ancient Scribes', *BA* 45/3 (1982), 143–54, and Michael Fishbane's discussion of Mikra as artefact in 'Use, Authority and Interpretation of Mikra at Qumran', in *Mikra*, 342–7.

CONCLUSIONS

Attention to the wording of the biblical text is a feature of ancient exegesis that does not admit facile summary. On one level, it is literalism and no more. But stopping there would ignore the complexities with which the ancient exegete worked and the dynamics that underlie the tension between preservation and renewal of biblical tradition. The self-perception of the ancient exegetes and translators determines the role which they play in making the past relevant for the present. Tendency to literalism, whether in exegesis or translation, downplays the intrusive role of the ancient interpreter and discloses a high regard for the sanctity of the words of the biblical texts; whereas the literary approach stems from confidence in the ability to transpose the sense into the terms and contexts of the targeted audience. The scribal practices too, especially in the phenomena of preparing, copying, and then correcting their texts, can similiarly be characterized by the principles that underlie exegetical and translational activity.

4

Features of Literalism

The strand of literalism discussed in Chapter 3 leads to the question of whether the pesharim and Pauline letters also paid attention to the words of the biblical quotations. At first glance, it may seem odd to be posing such a question, since pesherite and Pauline exegeses are well known for their creative handling of the biblical texts, a phenomenon that has sometimes even been described as 'midrashic exegesis' and is, if anything, non-literal. But, as has been shown above, features of literalism do appear even within a thorough reworking of the biblical texts. It is the task of this chapter to draw attention to some of these.

PESHARIM

There are three well-known features of the pesharim that show how the biblical text was important to the Qumran commentator: (1) the verse-by-verse explication of the biblical text; (2) the isolation and identification of key scriptural words; and (3) the lexical play between the biblical quotation and exposition.

Structure of the Pesharim

The commentary-form, with its sequential ordering of biblical quotations followed by corresponding interpretations, is one of the most striking features of the Qumran pesharim. Unlike some ancient interpretations that follow a specific argument, pesherite exegesis is bound to the structure of the biblical text. Column 1, line 1 of 1QpHab, for instance, cites the first verse of chapter 1 of Habakkuk's prophecy, followed by a formula (e.g. 'the interpretation of the verse'[1]), its comment, quotation of verse 2, introductory formula, another comment, and so on until the end of the second chapter (the hymn of the third chapter does not appear in the

[1] See recently Moshe Bernstein, 'Introductory Formulas for Citation and Recitation of Biblical Verses in the Qumran Pesharim', *DSD* 1 (1994), 30–70.

48

commentary). This lemmatic form attests to the importance that the pesherist attached to the structure of the biblical text. Not all types of pesharim follow the biblical text sequentially, but all those of the 'continuous' kind do enumerate verses from large sections of the biblical text. The definition of the pesher and the characteristics of its exegesis will be discussed in Chapters 5–8.

Isolation and Identification

It is not merely the structure of the biblical text that is attended to, but key words are also highlighted and particular interpretations are attached to them, exegetical procedures often referred to as atomization and actualization. In column 12, lines 3–4 of 1QpHab, for example, the commentary explains that the words 'Lebanon' and 'beasts' of Habakkuk 2: 17 may be identified with contemporary institutions and figures: 'for the "Lebanon", it is the council of the community and the "beasts" they are the simple of Judah'. The identification of 'Lebanon' with 'council of the community' requires a restoration of several omitted exegetical steps to be intelligible. 'Lebanon' is often related to the Temple of Jerusalem in ancient exegesis,[2] by virtue of the fact that wood was brought from Lebanon to build the Temple (1 Kgs. 7: 2; 10: 17, 21; and 2 Chr. 9: 16, 20). The Qumranians, who composed the 'council of the community',[3] regarded themselves to be embodying the spiritual Temple of Jerusalem. Thus, 'Lebanon' is 'the council of the community', namely the Qumran community.[4]

The figures identified with the 'beasts' are the 'simple ones of Judah'. It is not clear whether these are a subset of the larger Qumran community,[5] but they are described as 'those who observe the law'. What is important to underscore here is that it is not just the sense of Habakkuk 2: 17, with its description of the violence done to Lebanon and the destruction of the beasts, that is in view, but also the specific words, 'Lebanon' and 'beasts'.

---

[2] Elsewhere with 'nations' (and 'Kittim') and 'kings', see Robert Gordon, 'The Interpretation of "Lebanon" and 4Q285', *JJS* 43 (1992), 92–4.

[3] In the earliest layers of 1QS, however, 'council of the community' referred to the nucleus of fifteen representatives of the pioneer community (1QS 8. 1).

[4] See Geza Vermes, *Scripture and Tradition in Judaism: Haggadic Studies* (Leiden: E. J. Brill, 1961), 26–39.

[5] The term 'simple' also occurs in 4QpNah 3–4. iii. 7 as those who no longer supported the seekers-after-smooth things (M. Horgan, *Pesharim*, 53).

Between the Lemma and Comment

Finally, the lexical play between the lemma and interpretation is further evidence of the importance attached not just to the meaning but also to the words of the biblical text. In column 11, lines 8–14 of 1QpHab, Habakkuk 2: 16 is quoted (in italics), followed by an interpretation:

You have been sated with dishonour instead of glory. Drink you also and stagger. The cup of the right hand of the Lord will come round to you and (will be) *shame upon your glory.* Its interpretation concerns the wicked priest whose dishonour exceeds his glory, for he did not circumcise the foreskin of his heart and he walked in the ways of drunkenness to quench the thirst . . .

To appreciate the play on the biblical words, it is important to realize that for 'stagger' (הרעל) the MT has 'to be uncircumcised' (הערל). 1QpHab, however, did not simply substitute one reading for another,[6] since the interpretation shows that the pesherist is clearly aware of both notions of staggering ('he walked in ways of drunkenness') and uncircumcision ('he did not circumcise the foreskin of his heart').

The lexical play indicates that the Qumran pesherist knew different readings of the biblical passage of Habakkuk, for 'to stagger' is also attested in the LXX, Aquila, Syriac, and Vulgate. He may well have had different texts of Habakkuk in front of him, rather than simply remembering variant readings, as he sought to elucidate the meaning of the prophecy. What is more, his enumeration of uncircumcision of the heart and walking in ways of drunkenness as reasons for the dishonour of the wicked priest shows detailed attention to key words and not just the overall sense of the biblical text.

PAULINE LETTERS

Turning to the Pauline letters, the clearest appeal to the word rather than the sense of the biblical text is to be found in Galatians 3 and the arguments for the one seed: 'Now the promises were spoken to Abraham and to his seed. It does not say "and to seeds", referring to many, but referring to the one, "and to your seed",

---

[6] If the variants arose as a result of metathesis of ע and ר in the verbs, such an inversion was already known to the Septuagint (σαλευθητι, σεισθητι).

who is Christ' (v. 16). Here, Paul meets his opponents' interpretation by drawing attention to the literal wording of Genesis:[7] God's promise was made to Abraham and 'to your seed' (τῷ σπέρματί σου), grammatically in the singular. It does not say (οὐ λέγει) 'and to seeds' (τοῖς σπέρμασιν). This slavish rendering of σπέρμα, which has the collective sense in Genesis, allows Paul to identify Abraham's seed with Jesus Christ (Gal. 3: 16,[8] 22). The whole literalistic argument of the passage, however, is much more complex.

Context of Galatians

In his concern to define the relationship of the law to faith in Jesus Christ, an issue raised by Jews in Galatia who insisted that Gentile Christians too should observe the Mosaic commandments, Paul bases his arguments for the intermediary role of the law on the Abrahamic promise and blessing in Genesis. According to Paul, men of faith (i.e. believers in Jesus) are the true heirs of Abraham, for the original promise was made because of the Patriarch's faith (3: 6–9). Abraham's faith did not depend upon observance of the Mosaic commandments, for the law was not given for another 430 years[9] (3: 17).[10] It was rather established on his belief that God would bless him with a multitude of descendants despite his current childlessness (Gen. 15: 1–6).[11] This principle of faith shown by Abraham in believing the promise of future descendants is, according to Paul, the link with Christians ('you know then that they of the faith, these are the sons of Abraham', Gal. 3: 7), even though it could be questioned whether faith in Christ is comparable to Abraham's belief in God.[12]

To extend the blessing of Abraham to the Gentiles, Paul further

---

[7] In so far as it follows the number. A figurative sense is already implied in the Gen. use of (sowing) 'seed' for 'offspring'.

[8] ὅς ἐστιν χριστός may be a gloss, but a scribal intervention that conforms to the identification of seed and Christ in the passage.

[9] The dating of the reception of the Torah at Sinai seems to follow the Septuagint of Exod. 12: 40 (tallying with 400 years in Egypt of Gen. 15: 13; so also Acts 7: 6). In the MT of Exod. 12: 40, the Israelites spent all 430 years in Egypt.

[10] A similar argument exonerating David from polygamy is found in CD 5. 2–3.

[11] Rom. 4: 18–22 equates Abraham's faith with the hope that God will fulfil his promise despite his own and Sarah's physical conditions.

[12] In keeping with ancient Jewish exegetical practice, the whole context of the Abrahamic promise is referred to by the mere citation of one verse, 'Abraham believed God and it was reckoned to him as righteousness' (Gen. 15: 6 in Gal. 3: 6).

asserts that the Gospel had already been preached to Abraham, a Gospel that included provisions for the Gentiles. This is proved by 'all the nations (πάντα τὰ ἔθνη) shall be blessed in you', a verse that is derived primarily from Genesis 12: 3.[13] Whether Paul thought Abraham to be conscious of the significance of this blessing is an interesting question which cannot be dealt with here.[14] More importantly, the extension of the blessing in Genesis to all the nations shows that the inheritance of Gentile Christians was also pre-proclaimed in Abraham's promise ('thus they of faith will be blessed with Abraham, the man of faith', Gal. 3: 9). Through faith in Jesus, the Gentiles will receive the promise of the Spirit (3: 14; cf. 3: 2-4).

By infusing the original promise made to Abraham with the pre-proclaimed Gospel message, Paul circumvents his Judaizing opponents' insistence on Gentile observance of the Mosaic commandments. The inheritance of Christians, both Jewish and Gentile (3: 27-9), depends not upon the law but on the promise of Abraham, which takes primacy over the law temporally (3:17) and in significance (3: 19, 21, 23-6).

By contrast, those who rely on the works of the law (ὅσοι ἐξ ἔργων νόμου) are cursed, because no one is able to observe all the things written in the book of the law (3: 10-11). Here, Paul seems to be restating the Deuteronomic tension between strict legal observance and imperfect obedience discussed in the last chapter. With another twist that contradicts Habakkuk 2: 4 (at least as it is known in the MT),[15] Paul then argues that the one who is righteous through faith shall live (3: 11-12), a sense that departs from its original context of a righteous man living by his faith in God and the law.[16] Here, one who is righteoused through faith in

---

[13] Paul probably has in mind also similar verses where Abraham's seed is explicitly mentioned (Gen. 22: 18; 26: 4; and 28: 14). In view of Gal. 3: 8 it seemed convenient to him to cite τὰ ἔθνη (גוי) of Gen. 18: 18; 22: 18; and 26: 4 rather than αἱ φυλαί (משפחה) of 12: 3 and 28: 14 (contrast the analysis of N. T. Wright, *The Climax of the Covenant. Christ and the Law in Pauline Theology* (Edinburgh: T. & T. Clark, 1991), 162-8).

[14] The prophet Habakkuk himself was unaware of the mysteries that God eventually revealed to the Teacher of Righteousness (1QpHab 7. 1-5).

[15] James A. Sanders, 'Habakkuk in Qumran, Paul and the Old Testament', rev., in C. A. Evans and J. A. Sanders (eds.), *Paul and the Scriptures of Israel* (Sheffield: Sheffield Academic Press, 1993), 108-9, lists ten different renderings of this verse. Literally, the Hebrew is translated into Greek as καὶ δίκαιος ἐν πίστει αὐτοῦ ζήσεται (8HevXIIgr 17. 30).

[16] The Qumranians interpreted 'in his faith' as belief in the authoritative teach-

Jesus and not by keeping the law will live.[17] Finally, Paul argues that the crucifixion of Jesus, a curse according to the precepts of the Mosaic law (Deut. 21: 23), has a dual purpose of paradoxically redeeming Jews[18] from the curse of the law and bringing the blessing of Abraham to the Gentiles.

The Promise over the Law

Essential to a better understanding of Paul is the recognition that his letters give the reader only one side of the dialogue with his opponents[19] and that a discussion of argumentative strategies necessarily constitutes a reconstruction of the whole conversation. In Galatians, this task of reconstruction is vital, since Paul's arguments are not straightforward: the presuppositions of which the modern reader has indirect knowledge are assumed and not discussed and the arguments of the opponents, which are known only through Paul's own words, are often turned and flung back at them in rebuttal.

In Galatians, two identifiable, though intertwined, argumentative strategies are especially pertinent to the passage on Abraham's seed: (1) there is an appeal to a competing exegesis of the law; and (2) external examples are cited that bolster the exegesis.

Paul confronts the issue of Gentile observance of Mosaic commandments by an extended discourse on the intermediary role of the law (Gal. 3: 6–4: 31). This argument is based upon an exegesis of selected biblical texts that centre on inheritance and circumcision. Why he chose inheritance and its requirement of circumcision cannot now be known for certain, since he could have countered the legal obligations of the Gentile with arguments against purity laws or table fellowship (as, say, in Acts 15; cf. Gal. 2: 12–13). In any case, the whole section is framed by quotations from Genesis at the beginning (3: 6–8) and at the end (4: 21–30).

---

ings of the Teacher of Righteousness (1QpHab [7. 17]–8. 3; so Gert Jeremias, *Der Lehrer der Gerechtigkeit* (Göttingen: Vandenhoeck & Ruprecht, 1963), and Sanders, 'Habakkuk in Qumran, Paul and the Old Testament', 100.

[17] For the restoration of the old Anglo-Saxon verb 'to righteous', see E. P. Sanders, *Paul* (New York: Oxford University Press, 1991), 45–9.

[18] Suggested by the use of the 1st person plural in 3: 13. The purpose clause of 3: 14 (ἵνα εἰς) is problematic but refers cryptically to the significance of the cross in bringing the blessing of Abraham to the Gentiles.

[19] This has long been recognized in ancient epistolary theories. Artemon, editor of Aristotle's letters, regards a letter as one of two sides of a dialogue (οἷον τὸ ἕτερον μέρος τοῦ διαλόγου; Ps.-Demetrius, *On Style*, 4. 223).

The choice of inheritance as the central issue gives Paul the strategic advantage of undercutting his opponents' argument for Gentile observance of the Mosaic commandments and of asserting his own belief that the Gospel message had already been pre-proclaimed in Abraham's promise. The nature of circumcision, Paul counters, is a case that proves the primacy of the promise over the law, since Abraham's righteousness was predicated on his belief that God would, despite the current state of childlessness, provide him with descendants (3: 6–7). Here, the whole context of the Abrahamic covenant in Genesis must be kept in view: circumcision is the *result* of Abraham's belief, the sign of his covenant (Gen. 17: 9–14), *not* its prerequisite. The law, which formalized circumcision, among other practices, into a legal requirement, came 430 years later (Gal. 3: 17) and was added, on account of sin, as an interim measure until the fulfilment of Abraham's promise in the offspring (3: 19), Jesus Christ (3: 16, 22).

By addressing the issue within the context of the Abrahamic promise, Paul is able to argue specifically against the presupposition underlying circumcision and call into question generally the primacy of the law. Just as circumcision is merely the outward sign of the Abrahamic covenant, so also the law is secondary to the promise and fulfilment.

Paul's view hardens even more in Gal. 4: 21–31 when he addresses those who wish to subject themselves to the law. Referring again to the heir of Abraham, Paul now denigrates the covenant of the law established at Mt. Sinai to be that of the slave Hagar. This allegory would have been shocking to Jews of Paul's time who saw themselves as descendants of Isaac, son of Abraham's wife Sarah, and not of Sarah's slave Hagar. Gentile Christians who wish to submit themselves to the law, Paul contends, will become heirs of the slavewoman who must be cast out and have no inheritance.

But how are Jews and Gentiles[20] who obey the law sons of the slavewoman? Paul's argument involves a series of twists to common views and presupposes that the spiritual is superior to the physical. His starting-point is the biological descendancy of the Jew from Abraham which he challenges. The first twist involves tracing this physical birth ('being born according to the flesh', Gal.

---

[20] Reference to both Jewish and Gentile Christians is indicated by οἱ θέλοντες εἶναι in 4: 21 (so Richard Longenecker, *Galatians* (Dallas: Word Books, 1990), 206).

4: 23) back to Hagar and not to Sarah. In the Genesis story, Abraham had sexual intercourse with Hagar ('he went into Hagar and she conceived', Gen. 16: 4), but no physical relations with Sarah is mentioned.[21] Instead, the visitation of the Lord results in the pregnancy of Sarah and birth of Isaac (Gen. 18: 10 and 21: 1-2). In Paul's words, Isaac 'was born according to the Spirit' (Gal. 4: 29) and is a child of the promise (Gal. 4: 28).[22]

A further twist to the argument follows when Paul assumes that Gentiles too, and not just Jews, would become children of the slavewoman (4: 31) if they subjected themselves to the law (4: 21). If they followed the Mosaic commandments, Gentiles would become children of the slavewoman, like the Jews, even though they are not direct descendants of Hagar and Abraham. Here, evidently, Paul no longer operates with a plain reading of Genesis: the literal sense of 'according to the flesh' has been conflated with a negative figurative meaning.

By contrast, those who believe in Jesus Christ are like Isaac, children of the promise and born according to the Spirit. They are heirs of Abraham's promise, for they are children of Sarah the free woman (Gal. 4: 28-31). Paul strengthens this interpretation by appealing to Genesis 21: 10, 'cast out the slave and her son, for the son of the slavewoman shall certainly not inherit with the son of the freewoman' (Gal. 4: 30).[23]

Curse of the Law

Integral to Paul's view of the primacy of the Abrahamic promise is his exegesis of Deuteronomy and the curse of the law in Galatians 3: 10-14.[24] Characteristic of the letter as a whole, there are numerous twists and turns in this terse argument that those who rely on the law are cursed because they are unable to observe all the Mosaic commandments and that the crucifixion of Jesus, a

---

[21] Apart from Sarah, Philo, *de Cherubim*, 43-7, mentions Leah, Rebecca, and Zipporah as having conceived in a supernatural manner. Cf. *Gen. Rab.* 53. 6.

[22] J. Bligh, *Galatians: A Discussion of St Paul's Epistle* (London: St Paul, 1969), 398-400, rejects the *prima facie* meaning of Gal. 4: 23, 27, and 29 by an unlikely interpretation that 'he was strong in faith' (Rom. 4: 20) indicates that Abraham regained his sexual potency through faith in God's promise.

[23] Τῆς ἐλευθέρας fits the Pauline context better than υἱοῦ μου Ἰσαάκ/בני יצחק of the LXX and MT.

[24] Recent studies by Wright, *Climax of the Covenant*, ch. 7; Richard Hays, *The Faith of Jesus Christ: An Investigation of the Narrative Substructure of Galatians 3: 1-4: 11* (Chico, Calif.: Scholars Press, 1983), ch. 3.

curse according to the law, has paradoxically enabled the blessing of Abraham to reach the Gentiles.

As was discussed in the previous chapter, one of the tensions in the book of Deuteronomy is to be found in the ideal of strict adherence to the law, expressed by the prohibition against adding to and subtracting anything from the commandments (Deut. 4: 2; 13: 1), and its recognition of imperfect obedience. All Israel must learn the precepts and do them carefully, but if they fail to do so, they will be cursed (Deut. 28: 58–68). Likewise, blessings will come upon faithful Israel who observe the commandments (Deut. 28: 1–14).

Paul's argument in Galatians 3: 10–14, however, does not conform to the blessing and curse pattern of Deuteronomy, which he explicitly calls 'the book of the law' (Gal. 3: 10). Rather, it emphasizes the negative features, the consequence of a person's failed attempt to do all the things written in the law: that is, he is cursed. Those who rely on the works of the law (ὅσοι ἐξ ἔργων νόμου[25]) are under a curse (ὑπὸ κατάραν εἰσίν). The hard line that he takes on the observance of the law is supported by two scriptural passages: (1) all who do not do everything in the law are cursed (Deut. 27: 26); and (2) he who does them (i.e. those who are observant) will live by them (Lev. 18: 5[26]).

The key to understanding Paul here is to be found in the quotation of Deuteronomy 27: 26 in Galatians 3: 10: 'Cursed is everyone who does not abide by (ἐμμένει) all that which is written in the book of the law to do them (τοῦ ποιῆσαι αὐτά)'. The precise sense of 'abiding by' (ἐμμένω) is defined by doing (ποιέω) or observing[27] the law. By the law, Paul has in view here[28] the totality of everything that is written in the book of Deuteronomy (πᾶσιν τοῖς γεγραμμένοις ἐν τῷ βιβλίῳ τοῦ νόμου[29]). That is to say, everyone who does not observe *everything* in the law is cursed. The obedience demanded

---

[25] Equivalent to מעשי התורה (4QMMT) and already in Exod. 20: 18.

[26] Although negatively formulated against the rebellious house of Israel, Ezek. 20: 13 nevertheless accords with the view of Lev. 18: 5.

[27] That 'doing' means 'observing' is evident (e.g. עושי התורה, 1QpHab 8.1).

[28] Elsewhere, the law can mean much more to Paul than the book of Deuteronomy (Peter Tomson, *Paul and the Jewish Law: Halakha in the Letters of the Apostle to the Gentiles* (Assen: Van Gorcum, 1990)).

[29] Cf. the less absolute form of the MT (את דברי התורה הזאת). The LXX, ἐν πᾶσιν τοῖς λόγοις τοῦ νόμου τούτου, is less explicit than Galatians in the identification of the book of the law with Deuteronomy. Deuteronomy calls itself 'a second law' or 'repeated torah' (17: 18; 31: 26).

here is similar to the absolute requirement implied in the prohibition against adding to and subtracting anything from the Mosaic commandments (Deut. 4: 2; 13: 1).

The difference between Paul and the book of Deuteronomy, however, is in the conception of this absolute obedience. Deuteronomy, as discussed in the previous chapter, sets up the adding-subtracting prohibition as an ideal. It recognizes the difficulties of upholding such a standard and that Israel will disobey and stray. Complete obedience to the law is an ideal for which Israel must strive, but an ideal that admits of disobedience.

Paul, by contrast, insists on absolute obedience to the law. Righteousness, that is the state of complete obedience to the divine precepts, cannot be achieved: 'for it is clear that no one is righteoused by the law (ἐν νόμῳ οὐδεὶς δικαιοῦται) before God'. This is proved, Paul argues, by the fact that the righteousness of the suffering Israelite in the prophecy of Habakkuk is based upon faith: 'the righteous from faith will live' (Hab. 2: 4). Whether or not this was the original sense of Habakkuk 2: 4 is not germane. Paul, as he has quoted Habakkuk 2: 4 (ὁ δίκαιος ἐκ πίστεως ζήσεται), has interpreted 'faith' not in the observance of the law, but in God or, by extension, in Jesus Christ whom God promised to Abraham.

The stringency of Paul has another feature, the mutual exclusion of law and faith. This centres around the verse of Leviticus 18: 5 quoted in Galatians 3: 12: 'the one who does them (i.e. the Mosaic precepts and statutes) shall live by them'. Anyone who seeks righteousness through obedience to the law shall live by them.[30] In Leviticus 18: 5, the phrase 'shall live by them' (ζήσεται ἐν αὐτοῖς; וחי בהם) refers positively to the reward of observance of God's statutes (חקת) and ordinances (משפטי). For Paul, however, the same phrase has the ominous ring of judgement (cf. Rom. 2: 12–28), for he says that all who rely on the works of the law are 'under a curse' (ὑπὸ κατάραν; Gal. 3: 10) and Christ had to redeem the believers 'from the curse of the law' (ἐκ τῆς κατάρας τοῦ νόμου; Gal. 3: 13) by the paradox of himself becoming a curse on the cross. In other words, Paul has described his opponents' righteousness to be that which depends *solely* upon the observance of *all* the laws, a view of perfect obedience that neither he nor the book of Deuteronomy finds viable.

---

[30] Cf. Rom. 10: 5.

Irrevocability of the Promise to Abraham

A different strand of literalistic argumentation is found in Galatians 3: 15–18 when Paul turns to the irrevocability of the Abrahamic promise: 'Brothers, I speak according to a human example: Just as no one annuls or adds to a human will that has been ratified *so also here*' (v. 15). The phrase 'so also here', referring to the Abrahamic promise, is not found in the text, but had to be supplied in order to complete the comparison began with 'just as' (ὁμῶς).[31] The irrevocability of God's covenant/promise with Abraham is compared to the inviolability of a human will. Notable are the terms 'to annul' (ἀθετέω) and 'to add fresh clauses'[32] (ἐπιδιατάσσομαι), which resound with the mathematical notions of adding and subtracting of Deuteronomy 4: 2 and 13: 1.

The example to which Paul refers, however, is not a biblical one. It is 'according to a human example' (κατὰ ἄνθρωπον), one found in the ancient world. But which one? An auspicious line of enquiry has sought to identify the type of legal arrangement for inheritance alluded to in διαθήκη (Gal. 3: 15).[33] Accordingly, it has been argued that Paul has in mind here either Greek, Roman, or Egyptian forms of will. The main difficulty, however, is that all these wills and testaments are revocable.

More recently, Ernst Bammel has suggested that the διαθήκη referred to here is a deed of gift of someone contemplating death.[34] Basing himself on the work of Reuven Yaron,[35] Bammel argued that Paul had in mind a legal institution known in rabbinic sources as מתנת בריא (a deed of gift of a healthy man). The transaction involved the immediate transfer of ownership of the property from the healthy donor to the donee, although the former retains usufruct for the duration of his life. This form of disposition

---

[31] Following the accentuation of BAGD, 569, and rendering the comparative rather than the antithetical sense (so also Longenecker, *Galatians*, 127).

[32] So J. B. Lightfoot, *St. Paul's Epistle to the Galatians* 5th edn. (London: Macmillan, 1876), 143.

[33] See Hans Dieter Betz, *Galatians: A Commentary on Paul's Letter to the Churches in Galatia* (Philadelphia: Fortress Press, 1979), 155–6; and Longenecker, *Galatians*, 127–30, for a survey of the literature.

[34] 'Gottes ΔΙΑΘΗΚΗ (Gal. III. 15–17) und das Jüdische Rechtsdenken', NTS 6 (1960), 313–19.

[35] *Gifts in Contemplation of Death in Jewish and Roman Law* (Oxford: Clarendon Press, 1960). See now his update in 'Acts of Last Will in Jewish Law' in *Actes à Cause de Mort*, Recueils de la Société Jean Bodin pour l'histoire comparative des institutions, 59 (Brussels: De Broeck Université, 1992), 29–45.

is irrevocable once executed and it is this gift that stands behind Paul's reference to a human διαθήκη.

Questions of a general or particular kind have been raised against the identification of *diatheke* with *mattenat bari*. Accordingly, it has been pointed out that terminologically Paul's διαθήκη does not correspond to מתנה ('gift') but דייתיקי (the Hebrew transliteration of διαθήκη), a revocable form of inheritance disposition.[36] And even if this identification were correct, for argument's sake, it is uncertain how Gentile Christians in Galatia could be expected to understand this specifically Jewish institution.[37]

Yaron's discussions of gifts in contemplation of death are careful to distinguish between the biblical and talmudic periods. Dispositions that depended upon the state of health of the donor, מתנת בריא for the hale and מתנת שכיב מרע for the sickly, do not come into full form until the Amoraic period;[38] however, their precursors can already be traced to the institutions of מתנה and דייתיקי respectively.[39] Broadly speaking the *diatheke*-type of disposition is Greek in origin, has no effect before the death of the donor, and is revocable, whereas *mattana* is native to Judaism, whose ownership of property is immediately transferred to the donee and is irrevocable. Assimilation, however, did take place and a revocable form of *mattana* is also found. Notable in Yaron's discussion are the features of irrevocability: registering with public authorities and payment of the transfer-tax and the use of such formulae as κύρια εἶναι or βέβαια εἶναι, 'to be valid and secure'.

The recent 1989 publication of the Greek papyri of the Babatha Archive may shed further light on Galatians 3: 15 and the irrevocability of διαθήκη.[40] Among the finds in the Cave of Letters by Nahal Ḥever is PYadin 19, a document which the editor, Napthali Lewis, describes as a 'deed of gift'. Like others found in the archive, PYadin 19 belongs to the relatively rare type of 'double document'.

---

[36] Longenecker, *Galatians*, 130.

[37] Betz, *Galatians*, 155.

[38] Yaron, *Gifts in Contemplation of Death*, 61–3.

[39] Characteristic of this type of disposition is the formula μετὰ τὴν τελευτήν (ibid. 46). The earliest deed of this kind is dated to 127 BCE and is a disposition of property by the Egyptian Psenthotes to his daughter and wife (*BGU* 993). This document calls itself δόσις and συγγραφὴ δόσεως. See Yaron, *Gifts in Contemplation of Death*, 26–30 and 46.

[40] N. Lewis, Y. Yadin, and J. C. Greenfield, *The Documents from the Bar Kokhba Period in the Cave of Letters: Greek Papyri. Aramaic and Nabatean Signatures and Subscriptions* (Jerusalem: Israel Exploration Society, 1989).

This means that the entire text was copied out twice, written across the fibres, on the same sheet of papyrus, the top being rolled and tied up in the presence of witnesses to become the inner text and the bottom is left as the outer text.[41] It is unusual to find documents presented in this diplomatic format by this date, the practice having fallen into disuse in Egypt, but it would seem that it did persist in the eastern Roman provinces. Suprisingly, the inner and outer texts often differed quite substantially. In Ptolemaic Egypt, the inner text became a summary of the outer text.[42]

PYadin 19 is dated by the consular year, the Roman and Macedonian calendars to the 16 April 128 CE. It is a 'deed of gift' that Judah son of Elazar Khthousion gave to his daughter Shelamzious eleven days after her marriage to Judah Cimber (cf. PYadin 18). It was found among the documents of the archive belonging to Babatha, a Jewish woman from Maoza, a village on the southern tip of the Dead Sea in the Roman province of Arabia. Babatha, a young widow with a son, married Judah son of Elazar, an En-gedian who had moved to Maoza. He already had a first, living wife (Miriam), and it is for their daughter Shelamzious (or Shelamzion in Aramaic) that he executed this deed of gift. Bigamy, it would seem, was not uncommon.

It is not known how Babatha's archive came to be found in a cave near En-gedi, but Lewis has suggested that the family may have fled to this home region of Judah during the Bar Kokhba revolt. The dates of Babatha's documents range from 93/4 CE to 132 CE, the latest of which is also the first year when fighting broke out.

The document proper is written in koine Greek by a semi-literate scribe[43] and the subscription from Judah is in Aramaic. The outer text, which is well preserved, reads in part:[44]

Judah son of Elazar Khthousion, an En-gedian domiciled in Maoza, willed ([δι]έθετο) to Shelamzious, his daughter, all his possessions in En-gedi, viz. half of the courtyard across from (?) the synagogue (?) [ ] including (?) half of the rooms and upper-storey rooms therein, but excluding the small old court near the said courtyard, and the other half of the courtyard and

---

[41] Perhaps the variant ἔξωθεν of Rev. 5: 1 derives from this scribal convention.

[42] Lewis, Yadin, and Greenfield, *Documents from the Bar Kokhba Period*, 7–8. Cf. the differences in PYadin 18 and 20.

[43] Lewis lists the emendations of the Greek in *Documents from the Bar Kokhba Period*, 85.   [44] Ibid. pls. 20, 21.

rooms Judah willed (διέθετο) to the said Shelamzious [to have] after his death (μετὰ τὸ αὐτὸ[ν] τε⟨λε⟩υτῆσαι); of which courtyard and rooms the abutters [are], on the east [property] of Jesus son of Maddaronas and empty lot, on the west the testator (ὁ διεθετῶν), on the south a market, on the north a street . . . so that the aforesaid Shelamzious shall have the half of the aforesaid courtyard and rooms from today, and the other half after the death of the said Judah (μετὰ τὲ τελ[ευ]τῆσαι του αὐτοῦ Ἰούδα), validly and securely for all time (κυρίω[s και βε]βαίως εἰς τὸν ἄπαντα χρόνον), to build, raise up, raise higher, excavate, deepen, possess, use, sell and manage in whatever manner she may choose, all valid and secure (πάντα κύρια καὶ βέβαια). And whenever Shelamzious summons the said Judah he will register (τευχίζει) it with the public authorities (διὰ δημοσίων).

(Trans. N. Lewis)

Below the main text and written in Aramaic is a confirmation by Judah (or, in Aramaic, Yehudah) that he has given the courtyard and house (דרתה וביתה)[45] to Shelamzious, and on the back of the document are the signatures of at least six witnesses (μάρτυς/שהד).

PYadin 19 may have been the kind of document that Paul had in mind when he compared the Abrahamic promise and covenant to the irrevocability of a human will. Here, the testator Judah wills to his daughter Shelamzious all his possessions in En-gedi, half to have immediately[46] and the other half after his death (μετὰ τὲ τελ[ευ]τῆσαι τοῦ αὐτοῦ Ἰούδα, l. 23). This may be paralleled in the story of Tobit when Raguel promised by oath during the wedding of his daughter that Tobias should have half his possessions at once and the other half after his and his wife's deaths (Tob. 8: 21; 10: 10).[47]

Strikingly for the comparison with Paul's διάθηκη in Galatians is the legal nature of PYadin 19. Judah, in contemplating his own death, wills over to Shelamzious all his possessions. There is no mention of him being ill, although PYadin 20–6 show that Judah died sometime in the next two years. διέθετο (ll. 11, 15–16), an aorist signifying that the action took place on that day, and participle διαθετῶν (corrected form of l. 18) probably derive from the previously unattested verb διαθετέω (a derivative from τίθημι)[48]

---

[45] Greenfield points out that the Kefar Bebayu conveyance also used these terms (ibid. 144). Many thanks to Jonas Greenfield, ל״ז, for having discussed PYadin with me on several occasions in the 1994 summer before his tragic death.

[46] The editor's reconstruction in l. 22 ἀ[πὸ τῆς σήμερον καὶ τὸ] ἄλλο ἥμ[ι]συ fits the space and context.   [47] *Documents from the Bar Kokhba Period*, 83.

[48] Ibid. 81 nn. 3 and 32–3, and 86–7 n. 18.

or less likely (διά)θέτω for which the διάθηκη (from διατίθημι) of Galatians 3: 15 is a cognate noun. Napthali Lewis does read a tantalizing διαθή[κ]ην in line 3 of the inner text, but it would be imprudent to place too much weight upon such a badly mutilated line.[49]

The irrevocability of the deed of gift is suggested above all by Judah's registering it (αὐτὴν referring to διαθήκην?[50]) with the public authorities or archives (διὰ δημοσίων). It is supported by Judah's own declaration of having given to Shelamzious 'according to what is written above . . .' (כדי על [כתב]), a statement that is confirmed by the phrase 'Yehudah wrote it' (יהודה כתב). The entire document is ratified by the signatures, written in Greek and Aramaic script, of at least six witnesses. The phrases, 'validly and securely for all time' (κυρίω[ς καὶ βε]βαίως εἰς τὸν ἄπαντα χρόνον in l. 23) and 'all valid and secure' (πάντα κύρια καὶ βέβαια in l. 25), are formulaic and attest to the inviolability of the will.

Paul may have been referring to a document like PYadin 19 in Galatians 3: 15.[51] There, the irrevocability of the will is expressed in terminology that is semantically related to the key verbs and phrases in PYadin (κεκυρωμένην), even if some of the terms are negatively conceived (οὐδεὶς ἀθετεῖ ἢ ἐπιδιατάσσεται). It is suggestive, in view of the giving of half the possessions now and half later, in PYadin 19 that he had in mind also a two-stage Abrahamic promise and subsequent coming of the seed Jesus, but this would be pressing the analogy beyond what Paul probably intended.

By comparing the Abrahamic promise to διαθήκη, Paul is able to play on the term, which has for him the *double entendre* of the Abrahamic covenant (Gal. 3: 17) and a human will. Just as a human διαθήκη is inviolable, so too the διαθήκη of Abraham ratified by God cannot be annulled by the law.[52]

[49] Perhaps διαθή[κ]ην was inserted between Ἰούδα and κυρίως καὶ βεβαίως (cf. l. 24) in the inner text.

[50] Lewis suggests that the antecedent is the courtyard, *Documents from the Bar Kokhba Period*, 87.

[51] It is still not clear what specific type of disposition it is. See R. Katzoff's preliminary comments, 'פפירוס ידין 19: שטר מתנה ממדבר יהודה והתפתחות דיני הצוואה בישראל', in *Proceedings of the Tenth World Congress of Jewish Studies, Jerusalem, August 16-24, 1989* (Jerusalem: The World Union of Jewish Studies, 1990), 1-8.

[52] A similar pun is found in Heb. 9: 15-22 although there the point is that just as the will comes into effect at the death of the testator, so the death of Christ inaugurates the new covenant.

On Seed and Seeds

It is curious that Paul should express the irrevocability of the human will in notions that resemble the addition–subtraction terminology of Deuteronomy. He could, for example, have stated that just as a human will is 'valid and secure' for all time, so too is the promise and covenant of Abraham inviolable. Perhaps with the verbs 'to nullify' (ἀθετέω) and 'to add fresh clauses' (ἐπιδια-τάσσομαι), he is purposefully evoking notions similar to those of Deuteronomy 4: 2 and 13: 1, the strict legal requirement of which he expects his opponents to obey.[53] In any case, the pithy statement about the human will does lead Paul to assert that the promise made to Abraham and his one seed is irrevocable.

The argument for the singular meaning of 'seed' (σπέρμα) is the clearest instance of literalism in Paul.[54] In Galatians 3: 16, Paul argues that the promises were made to Abraham and his one offspring. His insistence on the grammatical singular meaning of 'seed' (σπέρμα) is explicit: 'It does not say "and to seeds" (καὶ τοῖς σπέρμασιν), referring to the many, but referring to the one, "and to your seed" (καὶ τῷ σπέρματί σου), which is Christ'. Here, Paul is appealing to the text of Genesis[55] and its singular meaning. The phrase 'and to your seed' occurs in numerous places in Genesis (12: 7; 13: 15; 15: 18; 17: 8; 24: 7) and refers to the promise that God made to Abraham and his descendants to possess the land (26: 3, 4; 28: 4; 28: 13).

In Genesis, the phrase 'and to your seed', while in the singular, refers collectively to the descendants who are promised to Abraham. Paul, however, insists on the literal, singular meaning and argues against ('it does not say') his opponents' more natural interpretation of seed.[56] The formulation of the argument in Galatians 3: 16 is reminiscent of the rabbinic technique where variants are introduced to the written texts by a formula such as . . . אלא . . . אל תקרי (ʾal tiqrei; 'do not read . . . but . . .).[57] There is,

---

[53] Cf. προσετέθη (3: 19) and ἀθετῶ (2: 21). 'To break' (the covenant) is a common alternative.

[54] Cf. James Dunn, *The Epistle to the Galatians* (London: A. & C. Black, 1993), 183-4.

[55] Scripture, in its recording of God's promise, is the subject of οὐ λέγει (cf. ἡ γραφή in 3: 22).

[56] In view of Gal. 4: 21-9, it may be supposed that the 'seed' of Genesis whom Paul identifies with Christ is Isaac.

[57] See further, Ch. 8.

however, a twist and it occurs in Paul drawing attention to what is written in the scriptural text itself rather than appealing, as is common, to a variant or interpretation of it. Perhaps Paul is again turning his opponents' exegetical technique on its head: whereas his opponents say 'do not read "seed" (as written in the text of Genesis), but "seeds"', Paul counters by pointing out that the text actually says 'and to (your) seed' and not 'and to seeds'.

The insistence upon the literal meaning of seed allows Paul to argue for the one true heir of Abraham's promise, Christ. Σπέρμα in the singular does have a range of meanings, from the many descendants of Abraham noted above to a particular offspring (e.g. Seth is described as זרע אחר/σπέρμα ἕτερον ('another child') in Genesis 4: 25 and Samuel as זרע אנשים/σπέρμα ἀνδρῶν ('a son') in 1 Samuel 1: 11).[58] In Galatians 3: 16, Paul has chosen the singular meaning of σπέρμα for his own purposes, but he is not unaware of its plural sense either. Later in Galatians 3: 29 (cf. Rom. 4: 13-18), 'seed' refers to all those who are believers in Christ. The use of the singular sense of 'seed' here and the plural there may strike the modern reader as inconsistent and to be involving a sleight-of-hand, but such criticisms would be misplaced in the ancient world. The fact that σπέρμα can be both singular and plural accords with the nature of many ancient Jewish exegeses that read more than one meaning out of the same written word. The literal is but one of several senses of the biblical text. This hermeneutical principle will be discussed in greater detail below with respect to the Qumran pesharim.

In Galatians 3: 16, Paul is insisting on the singular meaning of 'seed', so that he can argue that the promise of Abraham is fulfilled in the one heir Christ and not the many descendants who observe the law. By verse 29 of that same chapter, however, he understands the term 'seed' to refer to all the heirs of Abraham's promise. It may be possible that what Paul has in mind is the 'corporate solidarity'[59] of the believers with Christ who is the true seed of Abraham: those who believe have through faith become sons of God (v. 26) and Abraham's offspring.

---

[58] Wright, *Climax of the Covenant*, 163-4, however, seeks the meaning of a singular, unified family in σπέρμα, a view that better suits Acts 3: 25 and its reference to the αἱ πατριαὶ τῆς γῆς.

[59] Longenecker, *Galatians*, 132.

CONCLUSIONS

Features of literalism are indeed found in the Qumran pesharim and Pauline letters. Attention to the biblical text, however, is often conflated with a figurative, allegorical, or non-literal interpretation where the sense is more important than the actual words used.

The issue of modification of the biblical text is not a modern notion anachronistically retrojected to the ancient world. The features of literalism identified in the previous chapter and also here do indeed belong to the world of the ancient exegete. It will be the task of Part III to see how ancient exegesis handles the wording of the biblical text.

PART III
Pesherite Exegesis and Hermeneutics

5

Did the Pesherists alter their Biblical Quotations?

Having reflected on the distinction between rewritten bibles and the explicit citation-forms of Bible interpretation and the significance of post-Qumran textual criticism for exegesis in Part I, and literalism and notions of sacredness in Part II, attention must now turn to pesherite exegesis and hermeneutics. Did the Qumran commentator simply cite his biblical texts or did he also modify the very words of holy scripture? If he did alter his scriptural texts, how can this be shown? Given the diversity of text-types in this period and the profusion of variants for individual verses, how does one know that an exegete has changed his biblical text and not simply quoted an extant variant? Moreover, what are the hermeneutical principles which allow the Qumran pesherist to modify the words of sacred writ? Is the hermeneutical centre to be found in the biblical texts themselves or is it vested in authoritative interpretation? This chapter will discuss the putative *Vorlage* of the biblical quotations; Chapter 6 will reinvestigate the issue of exegetical modifications in the pesharim; and Chapter 7 will discuss broadly the hermeneutical principles underlying Qumran exegesis.

ON EXEGETICAL VARIANTS

Underlying suggestions that the pesherist has reshaped his biblical text are notions of the original reading and variance that must be addressed. If a reading is described as a 'variant', it is because that reading varies from a particular standard. Thus, in characterizing a particular text, for example, a reading that differs from its counterpart in the MT, LXX, or SP is referred to as 'a variant' or 'a variant reading'. 'Variant' here does not necessarily imply actual derivation from the standard, unless its text can be securely fixed within a stemmatic relationship to that standard. The characterization is formal and descriptive.

When an exegetical variant is advanced, however, it almost always means that an interpreter has actually modified a reading in conformity with his exposition.[1] Here, 'variant' is not merely a descriptive term of its relationship to a textual standard, but is a change that has apparently taken place. Exegetical variants are actual changes from unmodified, original readings. The difficulty, of course, is that there are few occasions where *both* the original readings and exegetical variants are found. From which textual standard was the exegetical variant derived? What is often meant by the assertion that '*x* is an exegetical variant' is that *x* has been altered from a reading to be found in the MT, LXX, or SP.

In previous studies on the exegetical variants of the Qumran pesharim, this methodological issue has not been adequately addressed.[2] While there are those who exercise laudable caution,[3] many scholars assume that the Masoretic Text lies behind the pesherite quotations. The original text is simply asserted to be the Masoretic Text and no effort is made to examine such a presupposition.[4]

A discussion of a well-known example will help illustrate the methodological issues raised here. In 1QpHab 8. 3, the biblical quotation of Habakkuk 2: 5 reads as follows:

ואף כיא הון יבגוד גבר יהיר

moreover, wealth will deceive an arrogant man

or

---

[1] e.g. George J. Brooke, 'The Biblical Texts in the Qumran Commentaries: Scribal Errors or Exegetical Variants?', in *Early Jewish and Christian Exegesis: Studies in Memory of William Hugh Brownlee* (Atlanta: Scholars Press, 1987), 85–100.

[2] See my 'Eschatological Orientation and the Alteration of Scripture in the Habakkuk Pesher', *JNES* 49 (1990), 186–9. For a more extensive review of scholarship up to 1991, see my D.Phil. diss., 'Attitudes to Holy Scripture in the Qumran Pesharim and Pauline Letters', Oxford (1991), ch. 3.

[3] Exemplary are the remarks of Maurya Horgan, 'The Bible Explained (Prophecies)', in Robert A. Kraft and George W. E. Nickelsburg (eds.), *Early Judaism and its Modern Interpreters* (Philadelphia: Fortress Press, 1986), 253, who states that further investigation should include 'a detailed examination of the biblical texts that are preserved in the pesharim'.

[4] Among many others, see e.g. Raphael Weiss's discussion of Nahum in 4QpNah: 'I shall refer only to the Masoretic Text which is apparent behind the verses quoted in the *Pešer* . . .', 'A Comparison between the Massoretic and the Qumran Texts of Nahum III, 1–11', *RQ* 4 (1963–4), 433.

moreover, a haughty man will act treacherously (because of) wealth

The MT, by contrast, has:

ואף כיא היין בוגד גבר יהיר

moreover, wine is treacherous, an arrogant man . . .

The differences are striking: 'wine' is the subject of 'to act treacherously' in the MT whereas the pesherite quotation can be understood to render either the 'haughty man' or 'wealth' as subject.[5]

Several scholars[6] have suggested that the pesherist has changed the word from 'wine' to 'wealth', since they are graphically very similar (הון/היין) and 'wealth', or perhaps more appropriately 'possessions', is considered by the Qumran community as one of the three moral vices, disguised as righteousness, with which Belial traps Israel[7] (CD 4.12–5.11). While this is possible, the assertion presumes that (1) the pesherist also changed the verb בגד from the participial form to the imperfect; and (2) the original Habakkuk text that the pesherist had before him was more or less a proto-Masoretic Text.

The second assumption is the one that needs to be unpacked. Was the pesherite biblical text *originally* proto-Masoretic? How would one know this? Since the *only* extant biblical text of the pesher is the one embedded in the commentary, the supposed *original* text then must be hypothetical, a reconstructed text of a stage supposedly prior to the formation of the pesherite lemmata. But why should it be assumed in the first place that the supposed

---

[5] The syntax is notoriously difficult and translations can vary. Most scholars take 'wealth' rather than 'arrogant man' as subject (Johann Maier, *Die Texte vom Totem Meer* (Munich: Ernst Reinhardt Verlag, 1960), i. 153; Maurya Horgan, *Pesharim: Qumran Interpretations of Biblical Books* (Washington: Catholic Biblical Association of America, 1979) 17; Michael Knibb, *The Qumran Community* (Cambridge: Cambridge University Press, 1987), 236; and J. J. M. Roberts, *Nahum, Habakkuk and Zephaniah* (Louisville, Ky.: Westminster/John Knox Press, 1991), 112–13). Geza Vermes's translation ('the arrogant man seizes wealth without halting', *DSSE*, 344), however, has to its credit a rendering of the quotation as it is understood by the pesherist: the haughty man/wicked priest is the subject who robbed and amassed wealth (ll. 10, 12).

[6] Lim, 'Eschatological Orientation', 186–9.

[7] Jonas C. Greenfield, 'The Words of Levi Son of Jacob in Damascus Document IV, 15–19', *RQ* 13 (1988), 319–22, has called this sectarian reading of 'wealth/possession' into question. He (along with E. Puech) argues that הון or more correctly היין was an error for פחז. While not many have taken up his emendation, it does address the difficulty that 'wealth' is nowhere interpreted in CD 4.

unaltered pesherite biblical text was proto-Masoretic rather than, say, septuagintal or 'non-aligned'?

No reasons have been given for this widespread assumption. Perhaps, it arises out of the practice (common, it would seem) of reading the pesharim (or even just 1QpHab) with *BHS* open. While reading the pesharim, a casual comparison between the MT and the pesherite lemmata often takes place. There is a sense that the text-types are the same and the presence of variants in the pesherite quotations is attributed to the creative activity of the exegete, especially since the Qumran commentators do display lexical plays similar to those found in the Midrashim. Whatever the reasons may be, the end result is to assume that the *Vorlage* of the pesherite biblical quotations was a proto-Masoretic Text, a premiss that is open to question.

PROTO-MASORETIC TEXT-TYPE?

Another reason for the above assumption may be that the pesherite biblical texts *as they stand* in the commentaries may be classified as belonging to the textual group of the proto-Masoretic Text.[8] Is this, in fact, true? When the biblical quotations are reconstituted and compared to that standard, do they in fact stand in the same tradition as the MT?

An examination of the overall profile of the pesherite quotations against the MT is in order.[9] The following, therefore, is a list and discussion of the orthographical differences and substantive variants of the sixteen continuous pesharim.

The Readings Collected

The categorization of the variants below is based upon the comparison of the biblical lemmata of the pesharim with the MT. Subjective judgement no doubt plays a role in any categorization of

[8] As the remarks of Robert Haak indicate ('Habakkuk', *VTS* 44 (Leiden: E. J. Brill, 1992), 3: 'while 1QpHab does reflect individual variants from MT, it still stands within the same tradition').

[9] Comparison with the LXX is not relevant here, since this is not a textual classification as such, but an examination of the presumed proto-Masoretic Text of the pesherite *Vorlage*. For the textual characterization of the biblical text of 1QpHab, see L. Vegas Montaner, 'Computer-Assisted Study on the Relation between 1QpHab and the Ancient (Mainly Greek) Biblical Versions', *RQ* 14 (1989), 307–23. Also L. A. Sinclair, 'Hebrew Text of the Qumran Micah Pesher and Textual Traditions of the Minor Prophets', *RQ* 11 (1983), 253–63.

variants, but an effort has been made to keep this to a minimum here.

In the Tables, conjunctions, prepositions, definite articles,[10] and pronomial suffixes are consistently counted as separate units. Only partial and whole words are counted: that is, enumerating restorations but not reconstructions. Repetition of citations are not counted nor are different spellings of the same word (e.g. קצוות/קצות of Habakkuk 2: 10 in 1QpHab 9. 3-14 and 10. 2), although the latter will be noted. Finally, a semantic shift in the Hebrew that does not require a consonantal change is not counted (e.g. ו of והתבוננת and ואתבוננת in Psalm 37: 10 of the MT and 4QpPsᵃ 1-10. ii. 7).

Variants are categorized according to the number of their differences. Thus, for example, יומרו of Habakkuk 2: 6 in 1QpHab 8. 7 is classified as both an orthographical variant of אמר and a substantive variant of the MT יאמר. The following collation is based upon my own re-examination of all the texts from the photographic collection of the Israel Antiquities Authority at the Rockefeller Museum in Jerusalem in 1989-90. The publications consulted are too numerous to be listed here; these can be found in the Select Bibliography. Notable, however, are the following works: William Brownlee (*editio princeps*[11] and subsequent study[12] and commentary[13]), J. T. Milik,[14] Stanislav Segert,[15] Karl Elliger,[16] Johann Maier,[17] Jean Carmignac,[18] Jean Ouellette,[19] John Allegro,[20]

[10] The definite article is counted only when it is represented by a consonantal letter. Thus e.g. בטיש is counted as two (ב/טיש) rather than three (ב/ה/טיש) units.

[11] *The Dead Sea Scrolls of St. Mark's Monastery*, i. *The Isaiah Manuscript and the Habakkuk Commentary*, ed. Millar Burrows with the assistance of J. C. Trever and William H. Brownlee (New Haven: American Schools of Oriental Research, 1950).

[12] *The Text of Habakkuk in the Ancient Commentary from Qumran*, JBL Monograph Series, 11 (1959).

[13] *The Midrash Pesher of Habakkuk* (Missoula, Mont.: Scholars Press, 1979).

[14] In *DJD* i. 77-81.

[15] 'Zur Habakuk-Rolle aus dem Funde vom Toten Meer I-IV', *AO* 21 (1953), 218-39; 22 (1954), 99-113, 444-59; 23 (1955), 178-83, 364-73, and 575-619.

[16] *Studien zum Habakuk-Kommentar vom Toten Meer* (Tübingen: J. C. B. Mohr (Paul Siebeck), 1953), plus insert: 'Der Hebräische Text des Habakuk-Kommentars vom Toten Meer (DSH) in Umschrift'. [17] *Texte vom Totem Meer*.

[18] 'Notes sur les Peshârîm', *RQ* 3 (1961-2), 505-38.

[19] 'Variantes Qumrâniennes du livre des Psaumes', *RQ* 7 (1969), 105-23.

[20] *DJD* v. This volume should be read along with the substantial review by John Strugnell, 'Notes en marge du volume V des *Discoveries in the Judaean Desert of Jordan*', *RQ* 7 (1969-71), 163-276.

John Strugnell,[21] Dennis Pardee,[22] Maurya Horgan,[23] L. Vegas Montaner,[24] and Bilha Nitzan.[25] References to fragments, columns, and lines follow Horgan.

TABLE 1. *Isaiah*

3QpIsa

Variants

Isa. 1: 1	3QpIsa	2	ישעיה	MT	ישעיהו
1: 1		2	ויותם		יותם
1: 1		2	וי[חזקיהו]		יחזקיהו

Summary
No. of words of the biblical lemmata: 9
No. of variants: 3

4QpIsa[a]

Orthographical differences
Plene

Isa. 10: 31	4QpIsa[a]	2-6. ii. 24	[ו]שבי[י]	MT	ישבי
11: 1		7-10. iii. 15	משו[רשיו]		משרשיו
11: 2		7-10. iii. 15, 16	חוכמה		חכמה
11: 3		7-10. iii. 27	אוזניו		אזניו

לוא

11: 3 (7-10. 26) (2X)

Variants
Minus

Isa. 10: 22	4QpIsa[a]	2-6. ii. 6	—	MT	כי
10: 34		7-10. iii. 6, 10, 11	לבנון		הלבנון
11: 5		7-10. iii. 20	א[מונה]		האמונה

Other

Isa. 10: 22	4QpIsa[a]	2-6. ii. 6	הי[ה]	MT	יהיה
10: 26		2-6. ii. 13-14	ויע[ור]		ועורר
10: 28		2-6. ii. 21	אל		על
10: 28		2-6. ii. 21	עיתה		עית
10: 29		2-6. ii. 22	למו		לנו

[21] Ibid.

[22] 'A Restudy of the Commentary on Psalms 37 from Qumran Cave 4 (Discoveries in the Judean Desert of Jordan, vol. V no. 171)', *RQ* 8 (1973), 163-94.

[23] *Pesharim.*

[24] *Biblia del Mar Muerto: Profetas Menores: Edición crítica según manuscritos hebreos procedentes del Mar Muerto* (Madrid: Instituto 'Arias Montano', 1980), esp. pp. x-xxiv ('Lista de Variantes').

[25] מגילת פשר חבקוק ממגילות מדבר יהודה (1QpHab) (Jerusalem: Bialik, 1986).

10: 29	2–6. ii. 22	חל[חה]		חרדה
10: 30	2–6. ii. 23	קולכי		קולך
10: 33	7–10. 9	בת		בית
10: 34	7–10. 6	ינקפו		נקף
10: 34	7–10. 6	ינקפו		נקף
10: 34	7–10. 6	סובכי		סבכי
11: 3	7–10. 26	לוא		ולוא

Summary

No. of words of the biblical lemmata: 101
No. of orthographical differences: 6
No. of variants: 15

4QpIsa[b]

Orthographical differences
Plene

Isa. 5: 12	4QpIsa[b]	2. 3	תוף	MT	תף
5: 14		2. 5–6	חוק		חק

Defective

Isa. 5: 11	4QpIsa[b]	2. 3	ידלקם	MT	ידליקם
5: 13		2. 5	המנו		המונו
5: 14		2. 6	המנה		המונה
5: 14		2. 6	שאנה		שאונה
5: 25		2. 9	כסחה		כסוחה

Variants
Minus

Isa. 5: 12	4QpIsa[b]	2. 3	יין	MT	ויין
5: 24		2. 7	—		כי
5: 24		2. 7	—		צבאות

Other

Isa. 5: 5	4QpIsa[b]	1. 1	יהי	MT	היה
5: 12		2. 3–4	ותוף		תף
5: 12		2. 4	הביטו		יביטו
5: 12		2. 4	מעש*		מעשה
5: 12		2. 4	ידו		ידיו
5: 13		2. 4	כבדו		כבודו
5: 13		2. 4–5	צחי		צחה
5: 14		2. 6	עליז		עלז
5: 14		2. 6	בא		בה

Summary

No. of words of the biblical lemmata: 131
No. of orthographical differences: 7
No. of variants: 12

Table 1 (cont.):

4QpIsaᶜ

Orthographical differences
Plene

Isa. 9: 11	4QpIsaᶜ	4, 6–7. i. 1	בכול	MT	בכל
9: 16		4, 6–7. i. 11	[אל]מנותו		אלמנתיו
9: 20		4, 6–7. i. 20, 21	יחדיו		יחדו
10: 23		6–7. ii. 19	אדוני		אדני
10: 24		6–7. ii. 21	כוה		כה
10: 24		6–7. ii. 21	אדוני		אדני
14: 26		8–10. 5	זואת	2X	זאת
14: 30		8–10. 14	יהרוג		יהרג
19: 9		11. ii. 1	אורגים		ארגים
19: 11		11. ii. 3, 4	פרעוה		פרעה
29: 11		15–16. 3	[א]ותו		אתו
29: 15		17. 1	רואנו		ראנו
29: 18		18–19. 1	מאופל		מאפל
29: 20		18–19. 3	שוקדי		שקדי
29: 22		18–19. 5	כוה		כה
29: 22		18–19. 5	יעקוב		יעקב
30: 16		23. ii. 6	רודפיכמה		רדפיכם
30: 17		23. ii. 6, 7, 8	רואש		ראש
30: 17		23. ii. 7	תנוסון		תנסן
30: 19		23. ii. 16	זועקכה		זעקך
30: 21		23. ii. 18, 19	אוזניכה		אזניך

לוא

9: 16 (4, 6–7. i. 11, 17); 9: 18 (4, 6–7. i. 17); 9: 19 (4, 6–7. i.
19); 10: 33 (2–6. ii. 6); 30: 1 (21. 10); 30: 15 (23. ii. 4); 30: 16
(23. ii. 4); 30: 20 (23. ii. 17)

כול

9: 11 (4, 6–7. i. 1); 30: 18 (23. ii. 8, 9)

Defective

Isa. 8: 7	4QpIsaᶜ	2. 3	אפיקו	MT	אפיקיו
8: 8		2. 4	כנפו		כנפיו
9: 16		4, 6–7. i. 11–12	[אל]מנותו		אלמנתיו

כיא

10: 12 (6–7. iii. 1); 14: 29 (8–9. 12); 30: 15 (23. ii. 3); 30: 16
(23. ii. 4); 30: 18 (23. ii. 9); 30: 19 (23. ii. 15); 30: 21 (23. ii.
19); 31: 1 (25. 5, 6) (2X)

ה-

Isa. 9: 14	4QpIsaᶜ	4, 6–7. i. 9	הואה	MT	הוא
10: 20		6–7. ii. 10	ההואה		ההוא

10: 22		6–7. ii. 13	עמכה		עמך
14: 8		8–10. 2	כה[ל]		לך
19: 12		11. ii. 5	לכה		לך
29: 10		15–16. 1	מה[עליכ]		עליכם
29: 10		15–16. 2	אשיכמה[ר]		ראשיכם
29: 11		15–16. 2	לכמה		לכם
30: 15		23. ii. 4	אביתמה		אביתם
30: 16		23. ii. 6	רדפיכמה		רדפיכם
30: 18		23. ii. 8	לחנ[נכ]מה		לחננכם
30: 18		23. ii. 9	לרחמכמה		לרחמכם
30: 19		23. ii. 16	זועקכה		זועקך
30: 21		23. ii. 18	אוזניכה		אוניך

Other

Isa. 30: 17	4QpIsa^c	23. ii. 7	תנוסון	MT	תנסו
30: 21		23. ii. 18, 19	תימ[ינו]		תאמינו

Variants
Minus

Isa. 29: 11	4QpIsa^c	15–16. 3–4	ספר	MT	הספר
30: 15		23. ii. 3	—		אדני
30: 15		23. ii. 4	בטחה		בבטחה
30: 17		23. ii. 6, 7, 8	הר		ההר
30: 17		23. ii. 6, 7, 8	גבעה		הגבעה
31: 1		25. ii. 5	—		לעזרה

Other

Isa. 8: 8	4QpIsa^c	2.4	[וה]יו	MT	והיה
9: 17		4, 6–7. i. 16	תצית		ותצת
9: 18		4, 6–7. i. 17	[נה]עם		נעתם
14: 8		8–10. 3	עלימו		עלינו
19: 11		11. ii. 9	אנו		אני
19: 11		11. ii. 9	בני		בן
30: 15		23. ii. 4	בטח		בטחה
30: 18		23. ii. 8, 9	לכן		ולכן
30: 18		23. ii. 8	אדני		יהוה
30: 20		23. ii. 17	יכניף		יכנף

Summary
No. of words of the biblical lemmata: 366
No. of orthographical differences: 60
No. of variants: 19

Table 1 (cont.):

4QpIsa^d

Orthographical differences
Plene

Isa. 54: 12	4QpIsa^d	1. 6	כו]ל[	MT	כל
54: 12		1. 3-4, 6	שמשותיך		שמשתיך

Variant
Plus

Isa. 54: 12	4QpIsa^d	1. 4	כול	MT	—

Summary
No. of words of the biblical lemmata: 10
No. of orthographical differences: 2
No. of variants: 1

4QpIsa^e

Orthographical differences
Plene

Isa. 21: 11	4QpIsa^e	5. 3	שומר	MT	שמר

ה-

Isa. 21: 10	4QpIsa^e	5. 2	[לכמ]ה	MT	לכם
Isa. 32: 7	4QpIsa^e	6. 5	הואה	MT	הוא

Variants
Plus

Isa. 15: 4	4QpIsa^e	4. 1	ו[נפשו]	MT	נפשו

Minus

Isa. 11: 11	4QpIsa^e	11. 4	מכוש†	MT	ומכוש

Other

Isa. 11: 11	4QpIsa^e	11. 3	שאה†	MT	שנית
21: 15		5. 5a, 5	נדד		נדדו
32: 6		6. 4	להכ]ות§		להריק
40: 12		1-2. 4	שקל		ושקל

Summary
No. of words of the biblical lemmata: 51
No. of orthographical differences: 3
No. of variants: 6

---

* Alternatively, the yod may be construed as the Qumran spelling of the singular construct (*HDSS*, 100. 34). So perhaps also צחי.
† Reading with Strugnell, 'Notes en marge', 199.
‡ There is some doubt on the placement of the fragment.
§ Other possibilities include [להמ]ית (Allegro) and [להכ]רית (Strugnell, 'Notes en marge', 198).

TABLE 2. *Hosea*

4QpHosᵃ (4Q166, *olim* 4QpHosᵇ)

Orthographical differences

Plene

Hos.		4QpHosᵃ			MT	
2: 9	4QpHosᵃ	1. 15	[הרא]ישון	MT		הראשון
2: 10		2. 1-2	אנוכי			אנכי
2: 11		2. 9	פישתי			פשתי
2: 12		2. 10	נבלותה			נבלתה
2: 14		2. 14	השמוותי			השמתי

לוא
   2: 12 (2. 11)

כול
   2: 13 (2. 15) (2X)

כיא*
   2: 9 (1. 15)

ה-

Hos. 2: 14	4QpHosᵃ 2. 17-19	הם	MT	המה

Variants

Minus

Hos. 2: 8	4QpHosᵃ 1. 17	—	MT	ודרתי את גדרה
2: 10	2. 2	—		לה

Other

Hos. 2: 8	4QpHosᵃ 1. 7	[דרכ]ה		דרכך
2: 11	2. 9	מלכסות		לכסות
2: 13	2. 14-15	מועדיה		מועדה
2: 14	2. 17-19	אתנם		אתנה

Summary

No. of words of the biblical lemmata: 89
No. of orthographical differences: 10
No. of variants: 9

4QpHosᵇ (4Q167, *olim* 4QpHosᵃ)

Orthographical differences

Plene

Hos. 5: 14	4QpHosᵇ 2. 2	אנוכי	MT	אנכי
8: 6	11-13. 3, 5	שו[בבים]		שבבים
8: 7	11-13. 6, 7	סופות]		וסופתה

ה-

Hos. 6: 4	4QpHosᵇ 5-6. 3	לכה	MT	לך
6: 11	10a. 1	לכה		לך

Table 2 (cont.):

Variants
Other

Hos. 6: 9	4QpHos^b 10, 26. 1	ואשר†	MT	כי
8: 6	13. 3; 12. 2	היה		יהיה
8: 7	11–13. 6, 7	[סופתה]		וסופתה

Summary
No. of words of the biblical lemmata: 49
No. of orthographical differences and variants: 5
No. of variants: 3

---

* NB כי in 5: 14 (2. 2) and 8: 6 (13. 3; 12. 2).
† So Vegas Montaner, 'Lista de Variantes', p. x. This could alternatively be a re-citation formula.

TABLE 3. *Micah*

1QpMic

Orthographical differences
Plene

Mic. 6: 16	1QpMic 17–18. 4	מועצותם	MT	מעצותם

Palaeo-Hebrew script

Mic. 1: 2	1QpMic 1–5. 1	palaeo-Heb.	MT	יהוה*
כול				
Mic. 1: 5 (1–5. 4)				

Variants
Minus

Mic. 1: 6	1QpMic 10. 8	שדה	MT	השדה

Plus

Mic. 1: 3	1QpMic 1–5. 3	האר[ץ]	MT	ארץ

Other

Mic. 1: 5	1QpMic 10. 3	מה	MT	מי
1: 8	11. 2	שלל		שילל†

Summary
No. of words of the biblical lemmata: 47
No. of orthographical differences: 3
No. of variants: 4

---

* Evidently the Qumran lemma reverses the order of the MT אדני יהוה (so J. T. Milik, *DJD* i. 77).
† MT *qere*: שולל.

TABLE 4. *Nahum*

4QpNah

Scribal errors

Nah. 2: 13	4QpNah	3-4. i. 6	הורה	MT	הוריו
3: 3		3-4. ii. 3	—		חרב
3: 3		3-4. ii. 4	וגויתם		בגויתם

Orthographical differences
Plene

Nah. 2: 13	4QpNah	3-4. i. 4	טורף	MT	טרף
2: 13		3-4. i. 4, 6	מעונתו		מענתיו
3: 1		3-4. ii. 1	כולה		כלה
3: 3		3-4. ii. 4	רוב		רב
3: 4		3-4. ii. 7	מרוב		מרב
3: 6		3-4. iii. 1	שקוצים		שקצים
3: 7		3-4. iii. 2	רואיך		ראיך
3: 7		3-4. iii. 6	שודדה		שדדה
3: 10		3-4. iv. 1	גולה		גלה
3: 10		3-4. iv. 2	ירוטשו		ירטשו

כול

3: 7 (3-4. iii. 2); 3: 10 (3-4. iv. 2)

Defective

Nah. 1: 4	4QpNah	1-2. ii. 5	לבנך*	MT	לבנון
2: 13		3-4. i. 4, 6	מעונתו		מענתיו

ה-

Nah. 2: 14	4QpNah	3-4. i. 9	כפיריכה	MT	כפיריך

Other

Nah. 3: 1	4QpNah	3-4. ii. 1, 3	ימוש	MT	ימיש
3: 8		3. 4. ii: 8-10	מנו		מנא

Variants
Plus

Nah. 1: 5	4QpNah	1-2. ii. 10	ממנו		—
2: 13		3-4. i. 4-6	טרף		—
3: 1		3-4. ii. 1	הדמים		דמים
3: 2		3-4. ii. 3	וקול		קול
3: 8		3-4. iii. 10	ומים		מים
3: 9		3-4. iii. 12	ה[לובים]		לובים
3: 11		3-4. iv. 5	ותהי		תהי
3: 11		3-4. iv. 7	בעיר		—

Other

Nah. 1: 4	4QpNah	1-2. ii. 3	יוב[שהו]	MT	יבשהו
1: 5		1-2. ii. 10	מלפני[ו]		מפניו
2: 12		3-4. i. 1	ארי		אריה

Table 4 (cont.):

2: 12	3-4. i. 1	לבוא†	לביא
2: 12	3-4. i. 1	ארי	אריה
2: 13	3-4. i. 4	ארי	אריה
2: 13	3-4. i. 4	גוריו	גרותיו
2: 13	3-4. i. 4	לביוֹתיו	לבאתיו
2: 14	3-4. i. 9	[ט]רפה‡	טרפך
3: 3	3-4. ii. 3	להוב	ולהב
3: 3	3-4. ii. 3	להוב	להב
3: 3	3-4. ii. 4	וכבוד	כבד
3: 3	3-4. ii. 4	וכבוד	כבד
3: 3	3-4. ii. 4	קץ	קצה
3: 3	3-4. ii. 4	וכשלו	יכשלו
3: 3	3-4. iii. 4	וכשלו	יכשלו
3: 4	3-4. ii. 7	הממכרת	המכרת
3: 4	3-4. ii. 7	בזנותה	בזנוניה
3: 5	3-4. ii. 10	גלית	גליתי
3: 5	3-4. ii. 11	הרא[י]ת	הראיתי
3: 6	3-4. iii. 2	כאורה	כראי
3: 7	3-4. iii. 2	ידודו	ידוד
3: 7	3-4. iii. 5	אמרו	אמר
3: 7	3-4. iii. 6	אבקשה	אבקש
3: 8	3-4. iii. 8	התיטיבי	התיטבי
3: 8	3-4. iii. 8	חילה	חיל
3: 8	3-4. iii. 10	ומים	מים
3: 8	3-4. iii. 10	ח[ו]מותיה	חומתה
3: 8	3-4. iii. 10	ח[ו]מותיה	חומתה
3: 8	3-4. iv. 1	בגולה	לגלה
3: 10	3-4. iv. 2	עילוליה	עלליה
3: 10	3-4. iv. 2	יורה	ידו

Summary

No. of words of the biblical lemmata: 237

No. of scribal errors: 3

No. of orthographical differences: 20

No. of variants: 40

---

* NB, however, ל[ב]וֹן in the comment (1-2. ii. 7).

† LXX: τοῦ εἰσελθεῖν.

‡ טרפו in 3-4. i. 11.

TABLE 5. *Habakkuk*

1QpHab

Scribal errors

Hab.	1QpHab		MT	
1: 8	3. 6	וקול	MT	וקלו
1: 9	3. 9	פני הם		פניהם
1: 15–16*	5. 14–15	לחרמו על		לחרמו ויקטר
2: 7	8. 13	פת]ן [אום†		פתע
2: 9	9. 12	השצע†‡		הבצע
2: 16	11. 9	מבוד		מכבוד

Orthographical differences:

Plene

Hab.	1QpHab		MT	
1: 5	2. 1	יסופר	MT	יספר
1: 7	3. 2	איום		אים
1: 8	3. 8	יעופו		יעפו
1: 9	3. 8	כול]ו[		כלה
1: 10	4. 4	יצבור		יצבר
1: 11	4. 9	כוחו		כחו
1: 11	4. 9	אלוהו		אלהו
1: 17	6. 9	להרוג		להרג
2: 1	6. 12	אעמודה		אעמדה
2: 2	6. 15	הלוחות		הלחות
2: 3	7. 9	בוא		בא
2: 3	7. 9	יבוא		יבא
2: 4	7. 14	עופלה		עפלה
2: 6	8. 6	כולם		כלם
2: 6	8. 7	ויומרו		ויאמר
2: 7	8. 14	למשיסות		למשסת
2: 8	9. 8	יושבי		ישבי
2: 12	10. 5	בונה		בנה
2: 13	10. 8	לאומים		לאמים
2: 17	12. 1	יושבי		ישבי
2: 18	12. 10	יצריו		יצרו

לוא

1: 2 (1. 1); 1: 6 (3. 2); 1: 13 (5. 2); 1: 17 (6. 9); 2: 3 (7. 6, 9) (2X); 2: 4 (7. 14); 2: 5 (8. 3, 4) (2X); 2: 6 (8. 7)

כול

1: 10 (4. 4); 2: 5 (8. 5) (2X); 2: 8 (8. 15; 9. 3, 8) (2X); 2: 17 (12. 1); 2: 20 (13. 1)

Defective

Hab.	1QpHab		MT	
1: 8	3. 6	סוסו	MT	סוסיו
1: 8	3. 7	פרשו		פרשיו
1: 13	5. 2	הבט		הביט

Table 5 (cont.):

1: 17	6. 9	יחמל		יחמול
2: 5	8. 5	אלו	(2X)	אליו
2: 6	8. 7	עלו		עליו
2: 6	8. 7	עבטט		עבטיט
2: 7	8. 14	היתה		היית
2: 13	10. 7	ינעו		יינעו
2: 15	11. 3	הבט		הביט

Palaeo-Hebrew script

Hab. 2: 2	1QpHab 6. 14	(palaeo-	MT	יהוה
2: 14	10. 14	Heb.)		יהוה

כיא

1: 6 (2. 10); 1: 16 (6. 5); 2: 3 (7. 5, 9) (2X); 2: 5 (8. 3); 2: 11 (9. 14); 2: 14 (10. 14); 2: 18 (12. 10-11) (2X)

ה-

Hab. 2: 7	1QpHab 8. 14	מזעזעיכה	מזעזעיך
2: 7	8. 14	היתה	היית
2: 8	8. 15[§]	שלוחה	שלות
2: 8	8. 15[¶]	ישלוכה	ישלוך
2: 10	9. 13	יעצתה	יעצת
2: 10	9. 14	ביתכה	ביתך
2: 10	9. 14	[נפ]שכה	נפשך
2: 16	11. 8	שבעתה	שבעת
2: 16	11. 10	עליכה	עליך
2: 16	11. 11	כבודכה	כבודך

Other

Hab. 1: 6	1QpHab 2. 10b	הכשדאים	MT	הכשדים
1: 14	5. 12	תעש		תעשה
1: 16	6. 5	בהם		בהמה
2: 6	8. 7	יומרו		יאמר
2: 7	8. 14	מזעזעיכה		מזעזעיך
2: 9	9. 13	לנצל		להנצל
2: 10	9. 14	קצוות‖		קצות
2: 20	13. 1	הרץ		הארץ

Variants
Minus

Hab. 1: 8	1QpHab 3. 7-9	—	MT	יבאו
1: 17	6. 8	תמיד		ותמיד
2: 3	7. 6	יפיח		ויפח
2: 6	8. 6	—		אלה
2: 13	10. 7	ינעו		וייגעו
2: 15	11. 3	אף		ואף
2: 18	12. 10	פסל		פסלו

84

Plus

Hab. 1:4	1QpHab 1.14	המשפט	MT	משפט
1:10	4.3	והוא		הוא
1:12	5.1	מוכיחו		הוכיח
1:13	5.7	ברע		רע
1:15	5.13	ויגרהו		יגרהו
1:17	6.9	ולוא		לוא
2:1	6.13	מצורי		מצור
2:2	6.16	הקורא		קורא
2:3	7.9	ולוא		לא
2:6	8.7	ולוא		לא
2:13	10.8	ויעפו**		יעפו
2:14	10.15	הים		ים
2:19	12.14	ה[אומר]		אמר

Morphological

Hab. 1:11	1QpHab 4.9	זה	MT	זו

Other

Hab. 1:8	1QpHab 3.7	פשו	MT	ופשו
1:8	3.7	ופרשו		פרשיו
1:8	3.7	פרשו		ופרשיו
1:9	3.9 (14)	קדים		קדימה
1:10	4.1	יקלס		יתקלס
1:10	4.4	ילדהו		ילדה
1:11	4.9	ישם		אשם
1:12	5.1	מוכיחו		הוכיח
1:13	5.8	תביטו		תביט
1:13	5.8	ותחריש		תחריש
1:14	5.13	למשל		לא משל
1:15	5.13	יעלה		העלה
1:15	5.14	יסףהו		יאספהו
1:16	6.5	ברי		בראה
1:17	6.8	העל		על
1:17	6.8	חרבו		חרמו
2:3	7.6	יפיח		יפח
2:4	7.14	יושרה		ישרה
2:5	8.3	הון		היין
2:5	8.3	יבגוד		בוגד
2:5	8.5	יאספו		יאסף
2:5	8.5	יקבצו		יקבץ
2:6	8.6	משל עליו		עליו משל
2:6	8.7	מליצי		מליצה
2:6	8.7	יומרו		יאמר

Table 5 (cont.):

2: 6	8. 7	יכביד	ומכביד
2: 6	8. 7	יכביד	מכביד
2: 7	8. 13	פתה[]אום	פתע
2: 7	8. 13	ויקומו	יקומו
2: 7	8. 14	יקצו	יקצו
2: 8	8. 15††	וישלוכה	ישלוך
2: 10	9. 14‡‡	חוטי	חוטא
2: 12	10. 6	יכונן	כונן
2: 13	10. 7	מעם	מאת
2: 13	10. 7	יגעו	וייגעו
2: 15	11. 2	רעיהו	רעהו
2: 15	11. 3	חמתו	חמתך
2: 15	11. 3	אל	על
2: 15	11. 3	מועדיהם	מעוריהם
2: 16	11. 1	הרעל	הערל
2: 17	12. 1	יחתה	יחיתן
2: 18	12. 11	מרי	מורה
2: 18	12. 11	עליהו	עליו
2: 19	12. 15	דומם	דומה
2: 20	13. 1	מלפניו	מפניו

Summary

No. of words of the biblical lemmata: 544§§

No. of scribal errors: 6

No. of orthographical differences: 78

No. of variants: 63

---

* The re-citation of Hab 1: 15-16 as ויקטר על כן יזבח לחרמו in 1QpHab 6. 2-3, 5 indicates that a scribal error (perhaps homoioarchton) is responsible for the form of the first quotation.

† There is enough space for one letter and the original may well have been a scribal error that conflated פתע and פתאום (see the double occurrence in 1QH 17. 5; Num. 6: 9; Isa. 29: 5 (cf. Isa. 30: 13)).

‡ So also Nitzan, מגילת פשר חבקוק, 185, 'reading'.

§ Also in 9. 3.

¶ Cf. Nitzan, מגילת פשר חבקוק, 185.

‖ קצות in 10. 2.

** So also Nitzan, מגילת פשר חבקוק, 187.

†† Also in 9. 3.

‡‡ Also in 10. 2.

§§ Hab 1: 16 of 1QpHab 5. 14-15 is not counted.

Did Pesherists alter Biblical Quotations?

TABLE 6. Zephaniah

1QpZeph

Variant

Zeph. 2: 2	1QpZeph 2-4	כניץ*	MT	כמץ

Summary
No. of words of the biblical lemmata: 18
No. of variants: 1

4QpZeph

Orthographical difference
לוא
Zeph. 1: 12 (1-2. 1)

Variant

Zeph. 1: 13	4QpZeph	[מ]שוסה	MT	משסה

Summary
No. of words of the biblical lemmata: 8
No. of orthographical differences: 1
No. of variants: 1

* With Jean Carmignac, 'Notes sur les Peshârîm', 520, who maintains that the reading must be כנ'ץ since the second partly mutilated letter can ony be ו, ז or נ. Cf. the LXX's ὡς ἄνθος παραπορευόμενον ('as a flower which passes') which presupposes either כצ''ץ or כנ'ץ.

TABLE 7. Psalms

1QpPs

Orthographical difference
Plene

Ps. 68: 13	1QPs	3. 3	יד[ו]ן	MT	ידדון

Variant

Ps. 68: 31	1QPs	9. 2	נערת	MT	גער

Summary
No. of words of the biblical lemmata: 11
No. of orthographical differences: 1
No. of variants: 1

4QpPs[a]

Orthographical differences
Plene

Ps. 37: 8	4QpPs[a] 1-10. ii. 17	עזוב	MT	עזב

Table 7 (cont.):

37: 11	1-10. ii. 9	רוב	רב
37: 12	1-10. ii. 13	זומם	זמם
37: 12	1-10. ii. 13	חורק	חרק
37: 19	1-10. ii. 27	יבושו	יבשו
37: 22	1-10. iii. 9	מבורכ[ו]	מברכיו
37: 22	1-10. iii. 9	מקללו	מקלליו
37: 34	1-10. iv. 10	שמור	שמר
37: 38	1-10. iv. 17	פושעים	פשעים
45: 2	1-10. iv. 25	או[מר]	אמר

לוא

37: 21 (1-10. iii. 8); 37: 25 (1-10. iii. 17); 37: 36 (1-10. iv. 13)

Defective

Ps.	37: 11	4QpPs^a	1-10. ii. 9	יירשו	MT	יירשו
	37: 9		1-10. ii. 4	ירשו		יירשו
	37: 22		1-10. iii. 9	מקללו		מקלליו

Ps.	37: 11	4QpPsᵃ	1-10. ii. 9	יירשו	MT	יירשו
	37: 9		1-10. ii. 4	ירשו		יירשו
	37: 22		1-10. iii. 9	מקללו		מקלליו

כיא

37: 9 (1-10. ii. 2); 37: 13 (1-10. ii. 13) (2X); 37: 17 (1-10. ii. 24); 37: 20 (1-10. iii. 2); 37: 22 (1-10. iii. 9); 37: 24 (1-10. iii. 14) (2X)

ה-

Ps.	37: 34	4QpPsᵃ	1-10. iv. 10	ירוממכה	MT	ירוממך

Other

Ps.	37: 9	4QpPsᵃ	1-10. ii. 2	יכרתו	MT	יכרתון
	37: 9		1-10. ii. 4	קואי		קוי
	37: 14		1-10. ii. 16	לפיל		להפיל
	37: 20		1-10. iii. 3	יובדו		יאבדו

Variants

Plus

Ps.	37: 36	4QpPsᵃ	1-10. iv. 13	על מ[ן]קו[מו	MT	—

Other

Ps.	37: 7	4QpPsᵃ	1-10. i. 25	ואל*	MT	אל
	37: 7		1-10. i. 25	תחר		תתחר
	37: 8		1-10. ii. 1	ואל		אל
	37: 8		1-10. ii. 1-2	תחר		תתחר
	37: 10		1-10. ii. 7	אהבוננה		הבוננת
	37: 13		1-10. ii. 13	יהוהׄ		אדוני
	37: 13		1-10. ii. 14	בא		יבא
	37: 14		1-10. ii. 16	וידרוכו		דרכו
	37: 14		1-10. ii. 16	וידרוכו		דרכו
	37: 14		1-10. ii. 17	ולטבוח		לטבוח
	37: 15		1-10. ii. 17	קשתותיהם		קשתותם

37: 17	1–10. ii. 24	אזרוע]ות[	זרועות
37: 19	1–10. iii. 2	רעב	רעבון
37: 20	1–10. iii. 5a	אוהבי	איבי
37: 20	1–10. iii. 5a	כורים	כרים
37: 20	1–10. iii. 7	כולו	כלו
37: 20	1–10. iii. 7	כעשן	בעשן
37: 25	1–10. iii. 17	וגם	גם
37: 28	1–10. iv. 1	נשמדו	נשמרו
37: 33	1–10. iv. 7	ובהשפטו‡	בהשפטו
37: 36	1–10. iv. 13	אעבר	יעבר
37: 38	1–10. iv. 18	יחד	יחדו
37: 38	1–10. iv. 18	ואחר]ית[	אחרית
37: 40	1–10. iv. 20	ימלטם	יפלטם
37: 40	1–10. iv. 20	ויפלטם	יפלטם
60: 8	13. 4	אמדדה	אמדד

Summary
No. of words of the biblical lemmata: 285
No. of orthographical differences: 29
No. of variants: 27

4QpPs[b]

Variant

Ps. 129: 8	4QpPs[b] 4. 2	על]יכ[ם	MT	אליכם

Summary
No. of words of the biblical lemmata: 9
No. of variants: 1

---

* Maybe resulting from dittography (Pardee, 'Restudy', 190).
† Palaeo-Hebrew script.
‡ Following Horgan who has restored the deleted conjunction.

ANALYSIS AND DISCUSSION

Column 2 of Table 8 enumerates the total number of orthograph-ical differences and variants divided by the number of extant words in the biblical lemmata of each pesher. Column 3 lists only the variants divided by the number of extant words in the biblical lemmata of each pesher.

There is no attempt here to give a sophisticated statistical ana-lysis of the pesherite texts in comparison to the MT, since it may be doubted whether existing statistical models of the physical and social sciences are applicable to textual variants of the Bible. It is no more than a rough attempt to take a broader look at the

TABLE 8. Analysis of Tables 1–7

Pesher	Orthographical differences and variants/no. of words	Variants/no. of words
3QpIsa	3/9 (33%)	3/9 (33%)
4QpIsa^a	21/101 (21%)	15/101 (15%)
4QpIsa^b	19/131 (15%)	12/131 (9%)
4QpIsa^c	79/366 (22%)	19/366 (5%)
4QpIsa^d	2/10 (20%)	1/10 (10%)
4QpIsa^e	9/51 (18%)	6/51 (12%)
4QpHos^a	19/89 (21%)	9/89 (10%)
4QpHos^b	8/49 (16%)	3/49 (6%)
1QpMic	7/47 (15%)	4/47 (9%)
4QpNah	60/237 (25%)	40/237 (17%)
1QpHab	144/544 (26%)	66/544 (12%)
1QpZeph	1/18 (6%)	1/18 (6%)
4QpZeph	2/8 (25%)	1/8 (13%)
1QpPs	2/11 (18%)	1/11 (9%)
4QpPs^a	56/285 (20%)	27/285 (9%)
4QpPs^b	1/9 (11%)	1/9 (11%)

biblical lemmata in comparison to the MT standard. What this means, for instance, is that the entire concept of what constitutes a statistically significant sample-size cannot be determined, since such a criterion depends upon other cases, whose data are derived in a similar or identical fashion.

What is important here, and specifically as regards the assumption of the MT, is that these percentages give us some idea of the degree of variance of each pesher from the standard. Of course, the number of extant words in the biblical lemmata may skew the textual picture. For example, only nine partial or whole words of the biblical lemmata are extant in 3QpIsa and of these three words are variants. The 33 per cent derived from such a small sample is clearly misleading, since one variant would radically alter the percentage.[26]

These caveats duly noted and the limitations of enumeration notwithstanding, the following general features of the pesherite biblical texts are clear. The lemmata of 4QpNah have a larger

[26] e.g, if [יחזקיהו]‏ו (the MT is without the conj. יחזקיהו) of 3QpIsa 2 were incorrectly restored, then the percentage would change dramatically from 33% to 22% (2/9).

percentage of variants (17%), whereas those of 4QpHos[b] (6%) and 4QpIsa[c] (5%) have the lowest percentages of variants. Orthographical differences are few in some pesharim, but account for more than half of the differences in others (e.g. 1QpHab). In this regard, it is interesting to note that in 4QpIsa[c] the percentage plunges from 22 per cent to 5 per cent when the orthographical differences are removed. That is to say, that the biblical lemmata of 4QpIsa[c] vary from the MT primarily in orthography.

The following percentages may be derived from column 3 of Table 8:

1. Overall percentage of variants of all the pesharim divided by the number of pesharim: 12 per cent.

2. Percentage of variants of pesharim with the number of biblical words exceeding 20: 10 per cent.

3. Percentage of variants of pesharim with the number of biblical words exceeding 50: 11 per cent.

4. Percentage of variants of pesharim with the number of biblical words exceeding 100: 11 per cent.

5. Percentage of variants of pesharim with the number of biblical words exceeding 200: 11 per cent.

The criteria of 20+, 50+, 100+, and 200+ words are purely arbitrary. They are simply attempts to take readings based upon various groupings. While the relationship of the biblical lemmata to the MT should be determined individually—and Table 8 provides this information—there is something to be gained in describing larger groups or even the entire corpus of the pesherite biblical texts. It is clear that in nos. 2–5, the readings vary from the MT at an average of 11 per cent.

To return to the present question: are the pesherite biblical texts proto-Masoretic Texts? The answer to this question depends upon the definition of what a Masoretic Text is. If the definition allows for approximately 10 per cent variance from the Leningrad manuscript standard, then the overall percentage of 11 per cent falls just out of that range, and not too much weight should be placed upon the 1 per cent difference. Individual pesher, such as 1QpHab (12%) and 4QpNah (17%), do, however, have percentages of variants that are slightly or more substantially significant.

As mentioned above, most judgements of texts as Masoretic Texts are subjective and depend for the most part upon the individual text critic's experience and thus no cut-and-dried criteria are ever given. In this regard a few other important points should be raised which militate against such a description of the pesherite lemmata. First, comparative evidence from other Qumran scrolls may illuminate the relationship between pesherite lemmata and the MT. We have applied precisely the same analysis of the pesharim to Isaiah 10 of 1QIsaᵃ. 1QIsaᵃ was chosen because its characteristics are well known: orthographically it is fuller,[27] but it may be classified as belonging more or less to the proto-Masoretic Text type. Chapter 10 was chosen because it is a portion of Isaiah which has the longest extant corresponding text in the Isaiah pesharim. Moreover, two pesharim, 4QpIsaᵃ and 4QpIsaᶜ, preserve verses from it.[28] The data that have been derived are given in Table 9.[29]

TABLE 9. Analysis of Isaiah 10 of 1QIsaᵃ

	No.
Words of Isa. 10 in 1QIsaᵃ (pls. IX, X)	604
Orthographical differences	65
Plene	40
Defective	4
לוא	12
כיא	3
‑ה	1
Other	5
Variants	17
Plus	1
Minus	6
Other	10

From Table 9 the following percentages may be adduced: (1) number of orthographical differences and variants divided by the number of words of the biblical text (14%); and (2) number of variants divided by the number of words of the biblical text (3%).

[27] Emanuel Tov, *Textual Criticism of the Hebrew Bible* (Minneapolis: Fortress Press, 1992), 108–9 and 114–15, classifies it as a text written in 'Qumran practice'.

[28] It is in a sense a random choice, since the decision was based upon what was preserved.

[29] This enumeration is based upon the textual work of E. Y. Kutscher, *The Language and Linguistic Background of the Isaiah Scroll (1QIsa A)*, Eng. trans. (Leiden: E. J. Brill, 1974); and Elisha Qimron, *Indices and Corrections* (Leiden: E. J. Brill, 1979).

Compared to Isaiah 10 of 1QIsa[a] the overall percentage of variants of the pesharim from the MT is the same at 11 per cent. Individual percentages, of course, vary in degree from pesher to pesher.

Second, an important, though little-known and seldom discussed, feature of the pesherite lemmata must be taken into account: verses and entire sections of the MT are sometimes absent in the lemmata. 1QpHab simply ends at Habakkuk 2: 20; the first part of Hosea 2: 9a in 4QpHos[a] (4Q166) is absent; 4QpHos[b] (4Q167) omits Hosea 5: 14b; 4QpIsa[b] (4Q162) does not have Isaiah 5: 15-24; and 4QpIsa[c] (4Q163) lacks Isaiah 9: 12 and 14: 9-25.[30] These are not caused by mutilations in the scrolls or doubtful joins of the fragments by the editors, but are simply not there in the texts.[31] These minuses were not counted in Table 9,[32] but it is clear that had they been the percentages of variants would have been much higher.

Third, and in anticipation of objections, certain questions should be answered. Is this argument of absent verses and sections an argument from silence? Yes, it is. But it should be pointed out that every 'minus', no matter how slight, is in fact an argument from what is not there. Second, is it not sometimes argued that the pesherist of 1QpHab lost interest or simply found nothing worthy of comment in Chapter 3?[33] This argument may well account for the method of the Habakkuk pesherist, though it is not entirely clear how the 'missing' verses of the other Qumran commentaries can be thus explained, but it is important to realize that it is an *exegetical* explanation. At the level of textual comparison, the lemmata of 1QpHab simply do not include chapter 3 of Habakkuk.

If one presses the case that the biblical lemmata cannot be classified precisely because textual and exegetical variants are inextricably intertwined in 1QpHab, then it may be asked how it is

---

[30] It is also possible that Isa. 10: 1-11 and 10: 13-19 may have been absent from 4QpIsa[c] (so Horgan, *Pesharim*, 95 and 111-12).

[31] Cf. a clear example of this phenomenon which can be seen in pl. VI of *DJD* v: col. 2 l. 6 of 4QpIsa[b] ends its quotation at Isa. 5: 14 whereas col. 2 l. 7 of the same document begins with Isa. 5: 24.

[32] Only words and short phrases.

[33] As an aside, it is notable that material unsuitable to the pesherist's programme as such is not necessarily an argument for the deliberate omission of ch. 3. Uninteresting material may simply be cited without comment (see e.g. 4QpIsa[c] where the lemmata are much longer and the comments are short and insubstantial).

that one knows that exegetical variants exist in the commentary in the first place.

CONCLUSIONS

In sum, the above discussion has questioned the entire procedure by which previous scholarship frequently asserts that the Qumran commentators modified this or that word of holy scripture simply by comparing the pesherite lemmata to the Masoretic Text. Such a procedure is highly questionable. Even if, for argument's sake, it is granted that the pesherite lemmata are proto-Masoretic Texts, the sheer number of different readings enumerated above should at the very least give one pause to reflect as to what these supposedly unmodified readings were and how we know that they were so.[34]

[34] Vegas Montaner, 'Computer-Assisted Study', 318: 'If the text allegedly altered in *1QpHab* is the Masoretic one, it must be considered that pre-Masoretic texts were not so unified as the MT itself is.'

6

Modifying the Biblical Text

The ancient exegete modified his biblical text. This is the premiss on which this study is based, since reinterpreting biblical texts and recasting their words are ways of renewing the sacred message, fixed in written words, for subsequent generations. Scripture is believed to be holy not because it is unchangeable and static, but because it is divinely inspired. Yet the occasional emphasis upon the preservation of the literal word of the written text suggests that ancient exegetes worked with a more complex set of procedures. It was not simply a matter of moulding holy scripture, whether by paraphrase of whole passages or modification of verbatim quotations, to say something quite different from its written form, but there existed a tension between a multiplicity of interpretative forces which will be explored in the following chapters.

Despite the intuitive conviction about the malleability of holy scripture, however, a closer examination of previous scholarship on the pesharim has uncovered precious little evidence to support one of its central assumptions that holy scripture was freely altered by the Qumran commentators. Exegetical variants advanced by past research have often turned on the unreflected belief that the original unmodified pesherite reading is found in the MT, an assumption that has been called into question by the previous chapter.

ON IDENTIFYING EXEGETICAL ALTERATIONS

A more defensible approach to the entire question of exegetical modifications, given the diversity of text-types in the Second Temple period, is to steer clear of the assumption that the pesherite biblical texts are proto-Masoretic texts. Instead, attention is turned inwards to evidence that points to possible exegetical alterations of the biblical texts, whether these be found in the re-citation or internal coherence of the biblical lemmata.

This chapter will examine the pesharim collectively. This means, of course, that the distinctive characteristics of individual pesher will not stand out. For example, the relatively more frequent occurrence of atomization and identification in 4QpNah (e.g. ומלאכיו הם ציר frs. 3–4. ii. 1) would not be mentioned in a discussion of pesherite techniques generally. Moreover, combining the analyses of these documents implies an identity of attitude to the sacredness of scripture, an assumption that needs to be shown in the first place not only for each group of commentaries, such as the Isaiah pesharim, but also for individual documents—that is, for example, 4QpIsaᵃ (4Q161), 4QpIsaᵇ (4Q162), and the rest. Unfortunately, the fragmentary nature of the majority of pesherite texts has determined the presentation of the evidence. There is simply not enough material for devoting a section to each pesher.

Apart from the relatively better-preserved documents, such as 1QpHab, 4QpNah, and 4QpPsᵃ (Ps. 37), the other pesharim are fragments rather than sizeable scrolls. Of course, the sheer number of smallish fragments of 4QpIsaᶜ (4Q163), taken together, would probably be as long as 4QpNah or 4QpPsᵃ; however, the higher ratio of its lines of quotations to commentary, a feature which seems to be characteristic of all the Isaiah pesharim, as well as the wellnigh complete mutilation of the interpretation render the desired description impossible. It is in the interplay between lemmata and comments that features of pesherite exegesis emerge. As for the pesharim to Micah (1QpMic) and Zephaniah (4QpZeph and 1QpZeph) what little is left of the original texts is rather difficult to decipher. So, while it would be exemplary to deal with each pesher individually, it should be underscored that the datum is less than ideal.

There is no intention to suggest that the pesharim have an identical attitude towards holy scripture, even if the following synthesis may inadvertently be so understood. The assumption here is that *prima facie* the pesharim will share a range of attitudes towards scripture similar enough to allow for results drawn from one document to be applied to another. Thus, if it is found that a pesherist has changed scripture in one passage, then it will be assumed that the biblical text may also have been reworked elsewhere in the scroll, since the author has already crossed the threshold between the realm of immutability and change. Moreover, similar alterations will also be looked for in other pesharim.

1. *Habakkuk 2: 17 in 1QpHab 12*

The citation, interpretation, and re-citation of Habakkuk 2: 17 in column 12. 1-10 of 1QpHab constitute a striking instance of scriptural alteration. Lines 1-7 read:

[*For the violence of Lebanon shall cover you and the destruction of beasts shall*]
(l. 1) *destroy you. Because of (the) blood of man and violence of land, town and all who dwell in it* (Hab. 2. 17). (l. 2) The interpretation of the matter concerns the wicked priest—to repay him (l. 3) his recompense which he has done to the poor. For the *Lebanon* is (l. 4) the council of the community and the *beasts* are the simple ones of Judah who observe (l. 5) the torah—whom God will judge for destruction, (l. 6) just as he devised to destroy the poor. And as it said: *because of (the) blood of* (l. 7) *(the) town and violence of land*. Its interpretation: the *town* is Jerusalem in which the wicked priest committed deeds of abomination and defiled the sanctuary of God. And *violence of land* are the cities of Judah where he stole the possession of the poor.

Part of Habakkuk 2: 17 appears as lemma in line 1: (lit.) 'Because of (the) blood of man and violence of land, town and all who dwell in it' ([1] מדמי אדם וחמס ארץ קריה וכול יושבי בה) and is re-cited with the formula 'and as it said' ([2] ואשר אמר) as 'because of blood of town and violence of land' (מדמי קריה וחמס ארץ) at the end of line 6 and the

---

[1] This verse occurs twice in the prophecy of Habakkuk, here and in Hab. 2: 8 (1QpHab 9. 8-12).

[2] The phrase is used in four other places in 1QpHab, six times in 4QpIsa[a-c], once in 4QFlor, and twice in CD. In the Damascus Document, ואשר אמר occurs in 9. 2 and 16. 6, but not as a re-citation formula. Note that the variation of משפט[ה] (with אשר אמר) of Deut. 9: 5 and 7: 8 in CD 8. 14 and 19. 26 is due to manuscriptal difference. The lemma of 2 Sam. 7: 11 in 4QFlor 1. 7 is most likely a re-citation; however, only traces of a few letters of one word are left of the first citation. It is impossible to be sure whether this phrase functions as a re-citation formula in 4QpIsa[a-c], since the initial citations are all mutilated (4QpIsa[a] 2-6. ii. 6-8; 4QpIsa[b] 1. 3; 4-5; 4QpIsa[c] 6-7 . ii. 7; 22. 4; 24. 2). In 1QpHab, there is no doubt that this is a re-citation formula. Apart from the above instance in 12. 6, the lemmata cited in 7. 3 and 9. 3 are identical to the initial citations and 10. 2 differs only in the spelling of קצוה/קצוח. The re-cited lemma of 6. 2 differs from the possible initial citation of 5. 13-14. Cf. Millar Burrows, 'The Meaning of ''šr 'mr in DSH', *VT* 2 (1952), 255-60; Karl Elliger, *Studien zum Habakuk-Kommentar vom Toten Meer* (Tübingen: J. C. B. Mohr), 123-5, for what he calls the *Wiederaufnahme-formel*; Joseph A. Fitzmyer, 'The Use of Explicit Old Testament Quotations in the Qumran Literature and in the New Testament', in *ESBNT*, 3-58; Maurya Horgan, *Pesharim: Qumran Interpretations of Biblical Books* (Washington: Catholic Biblical Association of America, 1979), 239-44; and most recently Moshe Bernstein, 'Introductory Formulas for Citation and Re-citation of Biblical Verses in the Qumran Pesharim', *DSD* i. 30-70, for a comprehensive discussion of all the citation and re-citation formulae.

beginning of line 7. Some have argued that the text of Habakkuk 2: 17 in lines 6 and 7 is an elliptical quotation, the intervening phrase having been omitted, and is a phenomenon that would be represented by three dots in modern style-sheets ('because of blood . . . and violence of town').[3]

This solution does not adequately explain the modification of the construct state from 'because of blood of man' to 'because of blood of town', nor does it account for the displacement of 'and violence of land' (וחמס ארץ) to the position after 'town'. Moreover, what has happened to 'man' (אדם)?[4]

The modern analogy of representing the omitted phrase by three dots is inadequate in accounting for this phenomenon, since the two forms of Habakkuk 2: 17 do not have the same meaning: the first version refers to human bloodshed and urban violence, while the second to the defilement of blood sacrifice at the sanctuary in Jerusalem and the robbing of the poor in the cities of Judah. Instead, this is a clear instance of exegetical alteration of the biblical text for interpretation. The pesherist needed a reading that could be interpreted to be the Wicked Priest's deeds of abomination in the city of Jerusalem. 'Because of (the) blood of man and violence of land, town and all who dwell in it' as it stands in line 1 will not allow him, unless of course he departs substantially from the text (which he is not doing), to comment upon the cultic pollution which the Wicked Priest performed in Jerusalem, but 'because of blood of town' can. The pesherist is operating with a more literalistic interpretation at this point. Why he does so will be the subject of the following chapter on pesherite hermeneutics. Here, it will suffice to remark that exegetical modification was identified without recourse to readings from the MT.

2. *Habakkuk 1: 13 in 1QpHab 5*

Another instance of exegetical modification can be detected in 1QpHab 5. 8–12 where Habakkuk 1: 13b is quoted.

---

[3] William Hugh Brownlee, *The Text of Habakkuk in the Ancient Commentary from Qumran*, JBL Monograph Series 11 (1959), 119–20.

[4] *Pace* Herb Basser, 'Pesher Hadavar: The Truth of the Matter', *RQ* 49–52 (1988), 405, who simply maintains that מדמי קריה is the result of the reordering of the words. Our own view is that the pesherist may have felt that אדם (מדמי) had already been interpreted previously in 9. 8–12, a passage in which the Wicked Priest was reported to have been handed over by God to his enemies on account of his iniquity against the Teacher of Righteousness and the men of his council.

(l. 8) *Why do you regard, O treacherous ones, and keep silent when* (l. 9) *a wicked swallows up one more righteous than he?* (Hab. 1: 13b) Its interpretation concerns the house of Absalom (l. 10) and the men of their council who remained silent when the Teacher of Righteousness (l. 11) was reproved and did not help him against the man of the lie who rejected (l. 12) the torah in the midst of all their council.

A key passage for theories about the origin and history of the Qumran community,[5] 1QpHab 5. 8–12 interprets Habakkuk's question of theodicy that Yahweh used the Chaldeans to punish the wicked in Israel as a prophecy about the betrayal of the Teacher of Righteousness by those who should have helped him against the Liar. Those who remained silent during this confrontation between the opposing leaders are given the negative sobriquet, 'house of Absalom', an allusion that evokes the treachery of Absalom (2 Sam. 15) and may also refer to his namesake in 1 and 2 Maccabees.[6]

Though not transparent in the English translation, the Hebrew text of Habakkuk 1. 13b betrays, so to speak, an exegetical adjustment:

למה תביטו בוגדים ותחריש בבלע רשע צדיק ממנו

(lit.) *why do you regard* (pl.), *O treacherous ones, and you keep silent* (sing.) *when a wicked one swallows up one more righteous than he?*

The incongruous verbal numbers, 'you regard' in the plural and 'you keep silent' in the singular, compel translators to choose as the subject between the treacherous ones and Yahweh (so also in the MT and LXX). Maurya Horgan, for example, translates the sentence with Yahweh as subject and the treacherous ones as object: 'Why do you (i.e. Yahweh) heed traitors, but are silent when a wicked swallows up one more righteous than he?'[7] A serious objection to this translation, however, arises in the comment, where the subject (which according to this rendering would be the Lord God) is identified with the house of Absalom who were silent in the time of the chastisement of the Teacher of

---

[5] The identification of the 'wicked' in the lemma with 'the man of the lie' supports the view that the Wicked Priest, if there be only one, and the Liar are one and the same man (see my 'The Wicked Priests of the Groningen Hypothesis', *JBL* 112 (1993), 422–3).

[6] D. N. Freedman, 'The "House of Absalom" in the Habakkuk Scroll', *BASOR* 114 (1949), 11–12.

[7] *Pesharim*, 15 and 33.

Righteousness (5. 10), a rendering of the text that is difficult to reconcile with the author's manifest reverence for the Almighty.

An alternative solution is to adopt 'the treacherous ones' as subject and to read 'you keep silent' as an implied plural. Geza Vermes, for example, renders the verse 'O traitors, why do you stare and stay silent when the wicked swallows up one more righteous than he?'[8] This translation has the advantage of avoiding the overt irreverence and complements the pesherite explanation that the house of Absalom and the men of their council remained silent (נדמו) at the reproof of the Teacher of Righteousness. In view of the pesherite understanding of the verse, this latter solution is preferable to the former one, but it too requires a translational gloss to smooth over the incongruity of the verbal numbers.

How should this numeral discrepancy be explained? Given the precedent of the exegetical modification of Habakkuk 2: 17 in 1QpHab 12 discussed above, it may be that this too is an exegetical adjustment of the biblical text for the sake of interpretation.

A discussion of this complex passage must begin with the context. In the MT, 1: 13b belongs to Habakkuk's second complaint to Yahweh, a section that runs from 1: 12 to 1: 17. The MT of 1: 12 to 1: 14a reads as follows:

1: 12a. Are You not from of old, O Yahweh, my God, my holy one? We shall not die.

1: 12b. O Yahweh, for judgement have You placed him and O Rock, for reproof have You established him.

1: 13a. Too pure of eyes to see evil, and You are unable to regard trouble.

1: 13b. Why do You regard treacherous ones, keep silent when a wicked swallows up one more righteous than he?

1: 14a. And You have made man as the fish of the sea, like a creeping thing for whom there is no ruler.[9]

From Habakkuk 1: 12a to 1: 14a, then, the subject in the MT is consistently the Lord God. Conscious of this, the scribal tradition reflected in the 'changes of the scribes' (*tiqqune ha-sopherim*) has altered the verse from 'You shall not die' to 'we shall not die' in order to avoid any hint that God could die. To safeguard against

---

[8] *DSSE*, 343. So also, Michael Knibb, *The Qumran Community* (Cambridge: Cambridge University Press, 1987), 227.

[9] 1QpHab 5. 13 reads 'to rule over him'.

the unintended implication of the negative 'You shall not die'—
that is, God will not die, but he could do so—the scribes shifted the
subject to a first person plural, presumably referring to the Prophet
and the righteous ones whom he represents.

In the Habakkuk Pesher, however, there are different subjects to
be found in the biblical quotations and commentary.

	MT	Lemma	Commentary
1: 12b	God	God (5. 1)	God (5. 4)
			('God will appoint him for judgement . . .')
1: 13a	God	God (5. 1–2)	community (5. 7–8)
			('they did not whore after their eyes . . .')
1: 14a	God	God (5. 12–13)	God?

In 1QpHab, God is the subject of both Habakkuk 1: 12b and its
exegesis: God has appointed him for judgement (למשפט שמתו). The
object suffix 'him' of the biblical text is identified with 'His chosen
ones' (בחירו, defectively spelt) in the commentary, those who are to
execute divine judgement upon the nations (וביד בחירו יתן אל את משפט
כול הגוים). These elected ones, moreover, are those who continued
to observe the divine commandments in their distress.

In Habakkuk 1: 13a, God remains the subject of the biblical
quotation as is suggested by 'You are not able' in the second
singular (תוכל; 5. 2). Only part of that verse ('too pure of eyes to
see evil'), however, is interpreted in the commentary and it refers
to the faithful community who did not whore after what their eyes
could see during the time of wickedness (5. 6–8). In 1: 14, God is
again the subject of the biblical quotation as shown in the second
person singular, 'and You have made man as the fish of the sea'.
The only extant interpretation, however, reveals that the Kittim
(Romans[10]) are the ones who are gathering their wealth and their
spoils as 'the fish of the sea' (1QpHab 6. 1–2), a comment that
makes use of the fishing imagery in 1: 14 and 1: 15 ('and he
gathers him up . . .', 1QpHab 5. 14).

Although the end of column 5 is mutilated, it is likely that the
first clause of Habakkuk 1: 14 ('You (i.e. God) have made man') is
not interpreted. The second clause is reworded slightly[11] and incor-

---

[10] This identification is suggested above all by the mention of Kittim/Romans
sacrificing to the standards. See p. 105.

[11] 'Fish' is written as a masculine plural in the lemma (דגי; 1QpHab 5. 12) a
feminine singular in the intepretation (דגת; 1QpHab 6. 2).

porated into the interpretation of the Kittim at the beginning of column 6, but the reference to 'the fish of the sea' most probably arises out of the notion of gathering with the fishing-net in Habakkuk 1: 15. Phrased differently, the Habakkuk pesherist has dissected the two clauses of 1: 14a and combined the latter clause with his interpretation that the Kittim have gathered booty like the fish of the sea. God, however, remains the subject of 'You have made man' in 1: 14a.

The procedure of dividing up verses or clauses of verses is often described in the scholarly literature as atomization. Such a technique, characteristic of pesherite exegesis, helps explain the numeral incongruity in Habakkuk 1: 13b. The passage immediately preceding the interpretation of Habakkuk 1: 13b reads as follows:

(l. 1) *for judgement You have set him and O Rock, for reproof have You established him. Too pure of eyes* (l. 2) *to see evil and You cannot look upon trouble* (1. 12b–13a). (l. 3) The interpretation of the verse is that God will not destroy His people by the hand of the nations, (l. 4) but by the hand of His chosen ones God will give the judgement of all the nations and in their reproof (l. 5) all the wicked ones of His people will be guilty. (His chosen are those) who kept His commandments (l. 6) in their distress, for this is what it said, *too pure of eyes to regard* (l. 7) *evil* (1. 13a). Its interpretation is that they did not whore after their eyes in the time (l. 8) of wickedness.

The syntax of 1QpHab 5. 3–8 is not straightforward, the difficulty being with the position of the relative clause 'who kept His commandments in their distress' (ll. 5–6)[12] immediately following the mention of the wicked ones. This relative clause is better understood to be qualifying 'his chosen ones', through whom God will judge the nations and by whose reproof the people will be found guilty, rather than the wicked ones.[13] Thus, the sense is that the chosen ones are not only the instruments of divine judgement and reproof, but they also continued to observe the commandments in their distress in that they did not commit acts of fornication.

The acts of fornication are expressed in visual terms, 'they did not whore after their eyes in the time of wickedness', that corres-

---

[12] אשר שמרו את מצוותו בצר למו.

[13] So also Knibb, *Qumran Community*, 227, who translates: '(the reproof of those) who have kept their commandments in their distress'.

pond in the biblical text to the mention of God's eyes being so pure
as to be unable to look upon evil. In the first citation of the lemma
in lines 1–2, God is the one who is unable to look upon trouble
because his eyes are too pure to see evil. When the phrase is re-
cited in lines 6–7, however, it is the chosen ones who are
identified as those whose eyes are too pure to see evil.

Noteworthy is the dissection of Habakkuk 1: 13a into two
halves, separating 'too pure of eyes to regard evil' from the
immediately following 'you are not able to regard upon trouble'.
This atomization of Habakkuk 1: 13a allows the pesherist to read
out of the latter clause the fidelity and chastity of the chosen ones.

At this point, the pesherist turns to the next half of 1: 13b.
Here, he encounters the treacherous ones (בוגדים) in the biblical
text, about whom he has previously written in column 2, lines
1–10. Unfortunately, the lemma cannot be atomized as in
Habakkuk 1: 13a. Habakkuk's question is clearly directed to the
Lord God: 'Why do you regard treacherous ones and keep silent
when a wicked swallows up one more righteous than he?' The
verb to regard (תביט) also gives rise to a contrast between the
faithful chosen ones whose eyes are to pure to see (מראות) evil, in
the immediately preceding lines. The linkage between the two
verbs for seeing (נבט and ראה) is strengthened by the parallel use of
תביט in the lemma of 1: 13a (5. 2).

Faced with this difficulty, the pesherist was forced to modify the
singular verb תביט to the corresponding plural תביטו, thus shifting
its subject from 'God' to the 'treacherous ones' (בוגדים). Habakkuk's
question of divine theodicy is now understood to be an implicit
charge of inaction against those who remained silent at the rebuke
of the Teacher of Righteousness: 'Why do you, O treacherous
ones, look on and stay silent when a wicked swallows up one more
righteous than he?' The bystanders are reprimanded for standing
silent at the public rebuke of the Teacher of Righteousness.

This modification is exegetically motivated, due in part to the
pesherist's concern for commenting on the 'treacherous ones' in
the biblical text and contrasting their betrayal to the fidelity of the
chosen ones. The alteration also has the theological advantage of
avoiding any imputation of irreverence against the Almighty. Why
the pesherist changed only one of the two verbs (the verb of 'You
stay silent' remains in the singular) is a puzzling question. Part of
the explanation is surely the atomizing mind-set with which the

pesherist exegeted scripture:[14] the pesherist worked with sense-units as he himself defined them. Modifying 'why do you regard' to the plural is sufficient for interpreting the entire verse as a reference to the betrayal of the treacherous ones. Another contributing element may well be his conservative attitude to the sacredness of the biblical text.

3. *Habakkuk 1: 14-15 in 1QpHab 5. 12-15*

There may be another modification of the biblical text in 1QpHab 5-6. In 1QpHab 5. 12-15 there is a partially mutilated text of Habakkuk 1: 14-15. The lemma and commentary in column 5 read as follows:

(l. 12) *You have made man as the fish of the sea* (l. 13) as roamers to rule over it. He will bring all of it up with a fish hook and drag it into his net (l. 14) and gather it in [his se]ine. [Therefore he will sacrif]ice to his net. Therefore he will rejoice (l. 15) [and be gla]d [and make sacrifices smoke to his fish net, for by them] his portion is fat [(l. 16) and his food is rich].

Although the last few lines of column 5 are mutilated, there is general agreement on the restoration of the text, reconstructed as it is on the basis of the extant phrases 'therefore he will rejoice' (l. 14) and 'his portion is fat' (l. 15). Compared to the MT, this biblical lemma differs in a number of places,[15] the most significant of which is in the order of the three phrases about sacrificing to and rejoicing in his net: (1) [Therefore he will sacrif]ice to his net. (2) Therefore he will rejoice [and be glad and] (3) [make sacrifices smoke to his fish net]. The MT orders them as (2), (1), and (3). When the biblical lemma is re-cited in 1QpHab 6. 2-3, however, the second and third phrases now correspond to the MT, i.e. (1) and (3).

It is possible to explain away the order in the first citation as an inadvertent inversion of the first two phrases resulting from the identical beginnings, 'therefore' (כן על).[16] However, such an explanation is predicated on the questionable assumption that the original order was that of the MT.

Alternatively, the biblical lemma at the end of column 5 need

---

[14] Or due to the erratic nature of scribal emendation.

[15] למשל, 'to rule over' as opposed to לא משל, 'there is not one ruling over', and יעלה, 'he will lift up' for העלה, 'he has lifted up'.

[16] So Horgan, *Pesharim*, 35; and Knibb, *Qumran Community*, 230.

not be interpreted as a scribal error requiring an adjustment from the reader. As it stands, the text has a chiastic structure:

a   therefore he will sacrifice to his net,
b   therefore he will rejoice and be glad,
a' and he will make sacrifices smoke to his fish net,
b' for by them his portion is fat and his food is rich.

Here, the sacrifice to his net is echoed in causing sacrifices to smoke to his fishing-net, and the rejoicing and gladness in the declaration that his food is rich. Whether the MT understands the verses this way is not the issue, for it is clear that it does not. The point is that the biblical lemma, *as it stands* in column 5, does have its own coherence of thought. The neo-Babylonians of Habakkuk's complaint, interpreted by the pesherist as the Kittim/ Romans, sacrificed burnt offerings and rejoiced because they had become wealthy by means of their net ('by them' refers to מכמרת/ חרם).

This reading of the biblical lemma underscores the importance of the role that the fishing-net plays in the pesher and provides a possible explanation for the order of the biblical phrases in column 6. 2–3, 'therefore he will sacrifice to his net and burn incense to his fish net'. Not unlike 1QpHab 12, the pesherist reorders his biblical text in the re-citation, and thus produces a text that is more succinct and corresponds more closely to his interpretation. It is the Chaldean sacrifice to the fishing-net which interests the pesherist, for one of the practices of the Kittim/Romans of his day was to pay homage to their standards and weapons of war (see Josephus, *AJ* 6. 6. 1 (316)). Thus, it states in column 6. 3–5: 'its intepretation is that they sacrifice to their standards and the weapons of their war are objects of reverence'. The Habakkuk pesherist found little of comment in the rejoicing of Habakkuk 1: 15, but more to say on the nets which he interprets to be the standards and weapons of the Kittim/Romans, as column 6. 5–12 also indicates.

4. *Nahum 3. 5 in 4QpNah frs. 3–4. ii*

In fragments 3–4. ii. 10–11 to 3–4. iii. 1 of 4QpNah, the pesherist may have changed the two verbs 'to lift up' and 'to expose' of Nahum 3: 5 from first to second person. The pesherite lemma and commentary read: '(l. 10) *Behold I am against you, says the Yahweh of h[osts]. Now you will lift up* (l. 11) *[your]skirts over your face and expos[e to] nations your nakedness and to kingdoms your shame.'* In the biblical prophecy of Nahum, verse 5 of chapter 3 belongs to the oracle of woe (3: 1–17) against Nineveh. Yahweh charges the Assyrian capital with oppression and deceit and warns that her might will not save her from punishment. After opening with an imagery of charging chariots, depicting a devastating attack on Nineveh, the oracle turns in verse 4 to the description of the city as a harlot. Like the harlot, Nineveh seduces the nations and betrays the peoples with her charms, and because of this her punishment will involve exposure of her nakedness (v. 5) and public humiliation (vv. 6–7). Pesher Nahum interprets the harlotry of Nineveh as the impurities,[17] filth, and abominations related to the cities of the east and nations. Whether it is the wickedness practised by the nations is not clear, given the mutilation of the top of column 3.

What is evident is that in the pesherite lemma there are awkward changes of persons: first, the Lord of hosts proclaims 'Behold I am against you' (הנני אליך נאם יהוה צ[באו]ת), which is immediately followed by a shift to the second person 'you will lift up . . . and you will show' (והרא[י]ת and וגליה); after the interpretation, the lemma reverts to the first person, 'and I shall cast . . . and I shall treat you with contempt and I shall make you . . .' (השלכתי, ושמתיך and ו[נ]בלתיך). The shift from first to second and back to first person is possible, though rather awkward in syntax, particularly in view of the immediately following the Lord's proclamation, 'I am against you'. Something seems to be amiss with the two second person singular verbs standing out within a section where the subject is in the first person and refers to the Lord.

The MT supported by the LXX reads as follows: 'Behold I am against you, says the Lord of hosts. Now *I will lift up* your skirts over your face and *I will expose* to nations your nakedness and to kingdoms your shame' (my italics). It is possible that the pesherite *Vorlage* of Nahum 3: 5 also originally had the first person singulars גליתי and הראיתי, but the pesherist modified this to the second person in order to avoid any irreverence that may be

---

[17] Reading בנדתם with Horgan, *Pesharim*, 185, rather than ביןתם 'between them' (John Allegro, *DJD* v. 38, 40), or 'their daughters' (John Strugnell, 'Notes en marge du volume V des *Discoveries in the Judaean Desert of Jordan*' *RQ* 7 (1969–71), 207–8).

implied in the act of lifting up the skirts and exposing the nakedness of the harlot.[18]

5. *Nahum 2: 14 in 4QpNah 3-4. i*

In 4QpNah, the words 'your lion' and 'its prey' of Nahum 2. 14
(frs. 3-4. i. 9-10) are atomized and identified with 'his great ones',
whoever they may be, and the wealth amassed by the Jerusalemite
priests.

Distinctive in these instances is the modification of the nouns
and their pronominal suffixes from 'your lion' (כפיריכה) and 'its prey'
(טרפ[ה]) to 'his young lion' (כפריו) and 'his prey' (טרפו). This change
may be explained by the demands of Hebrew grammar: the use of
pronominal suffixes is a common way of expressing possession and
it may well be that only the nouns (without their suffixes) are
atomized: thus, his 'young lion' and his 'prey'. There are, of
course, other ways of atomizing the biblical text[19] and expressing
possession.

However the words are construed, it is clear that the pesherist
did not regard the word and letter of the biblical text to be
immutable. There is no strict adherence to the lexical morpheme of
כפיריכה and טרפה.[20] Why he felt it necessary to divide the biblical
words in this manner cannot now be known for certain, although
it is tempting to see this as an adaptation of the biblical text to the
furious young lion, Alexander Jannaeus. It was Alexander
Jannaeus' 'young lions' who were identified with the great ones
and it was his prey that was understood to be the wealth of the
Jerusalemite priests.[21]

6. *Psalm 37: 20 in 4QpPs^a 1-10. iii*

There may also be an exegetical modification in the biblical text of
Psalm 37: 20 in 4QpPs^a 1-10. iii. 5-8. It has been suggested that
the pesherite phrase 'the lovers of the Lord' (אוהבי יהוה) was altered
from 'the enemies of the Lord' (איבי יהוה as in the MT) and that the

---

[18] The sectarian concern for sexual matters and impurities is well known.

[19] e.g. טרפה הוא ההון and כפיריכה הם גדוליו.

[20] מלאכיו in frs. 3-4. ii. 1 may also be another instance of the alteration of the
suffix.

[21] Similarly Knibb, *Qumran Community*, 213, although he assumes that the
original suffixes were feminine as in the MT and that the lemma has already been
modified.

artificiality of this change may be seen from its broken context.[22] Arguments for this deliberate manipulation of the verse may be granted if one assumes that the original had 'the enemies of the Lord', as in the MT.[23] The introduction of 'the lovers of the Lord', then, breaks the context of the burning of the evil ones (Ps. 37: 19b–20).

Fortifying this suggested exegetical alteration is the absence of support from the versions. What is more, 'as the *splendour* of pastures' (כיקר כרים) seems a rather inappropriate phrase in the context of the utter destruction of the enemies of the Lord (cf. כלו כלו בעשן כלו), a difficulty which may have prompted the pesherist to recast the verse.

Against identifying an exegetical change are questions about the putative original Psalm 37: 20 of the pesherist. Did his text contain the reading 'enemies' rather than 'lovers'? If the lemmata of the pesher were understood without reference to the MT, they would form a parallel pattern of a b/a' b'—the perfect will be satisfied (v. 19b); the evil perish (v. 20a); the lovers of the Lord will be as precious as rams (כיקר כור[ם]); they (= the evil) shall vanish as smoke completely[24]—and no break in context need be seen:

> In the days of famine they will be [sati]sfied,
>   but the wicked will perish.
> The lovers of the Lord will be like the splendour of the pastures,
> All of them (i.e. wicked) will vanish like smoke.

There are reasons for and against identifying an exegetical alteration in the pesherite lemma of Psalm 37: 20. It is attractive to see the change from 'enemies' to 'lovers' as a solution for the awkwardness of comparing Yahweh's enemies to the glory of the field. The commentary identifies the lovers with the princes and

---

[22] Geza Vermes proposed this in the 2nd edn. of his *DSSE*, 243 (so also Knibb, *Qumran Community*, 254). George J. Brooke, 'The Biblical Texts in the Qumran Commentaries: Scribal Errors or Exegetical Variants?', in Craig A. Evans and William F. Stinespring (eds.), *Early Jewish and Christian Exegesis: Studies in Memory of William Hugh Brownlee* (Atlanta: Scholars Press, 1987), 95, describes this as an instance of *'al tiqre*.

[23] Joseph D. Amousine, 'Observatiunculae qumraneae', *RQ* 7 (1969–70), 533–5, proposed the spelling of 'the enemies' as אואבי, which was misunderstood by the commentator to mean 'the lovers' and was rewritten as אוהבי.

[24] So Dennis Pardee, 'A Restudy of the Commentary on Psalms 37 from Qumran Cave 4 (Discoveries in the Judean Desert of Jordan, vol. V no. 171)' *RQ* 8 (1973), 192.

chiefs, but does not provide decisive clues in favour of one interpretation or the other.

7. *Psalm 37: 10 in 4QpPsª 1–10. ii*

Psalm 37: 10 in 4QpPsª 1–10. ii. 5, 7 reads 'I shall consider diligently' (אתבוגנה), whereas the MT has the second person singular.
Some have argued that this is a restylization into divine speech of
the biblical text[25] (cf. Temple Scroll) while others maintain that this
is the pesherist's self-reference.[26] The interpretation, however,
which includes the much discussed 'end of the forty-year period'
(cf. CD 20. 14–15), does not exploit this first person variant.[27] In
fact, the comment is not at all concerned with the one who has
'considered diligently', but rather with the peril and disappearance
from the land of the wicked (ll. 7–9). It is possible that the biblical
text was adapted by the pesherist, but it is difficult to identify his
reasons for doing so.

CONCLUSIONS

The approach adopted here, that is to confine the search for
exegetical variants to internal evidence found in the pesharim
(e.g. re-citations, grammatical congruity), has been careful to
impute to the pesherists exegetical modifications simply because
their biblical texts differed from the MT. Each possible case of
exegetical modification has been assessed on its own merits, without any undue influence of MT readings. As a result there are
fewer examples that can pass the stricter criteria in view here and
some of these are different from the ones often mentioned in the
scholarly literature.

These results are modest, but more defensible within the context
of a greater awareness of the pluriformity of the biblical texts. They
are also significant enough to show that the Qumranians were not
mere commentators, but also in some sense authors of the biblical
texts, a theme that will be developed in subsequent chapters.

[25] Hartmut Stegemann, 'Der Pešer Psalm 37 aus Höhle 4 von Qumran
(4QpPs37)', *RQ* 4 (1963–4), 248 n. 45.
[26] Brooke, 'Biblical Texts', 88.
[27] Pardee, 'Restudy', 192, has wondered whether this reading was not simply a
reflexion of the first singular in v. 36 without theological implications.

7

Nature of Pesherite Interpretation

Now it has been shown that in their exegeses the pesherists did not always adhere strictly to the wording of their biblical texts, whichever version they happen to have had before them, it would seem useful to turn to the nature of sectarian biblical interpretation. Why did they modify the very words of scripture when there existed a range of exegetical techniques by which a desired meaning might be drawn out of or read into the biblical texts? What is it in the constitution of the Qumran community that allowed its biblical interpreters to cross the threshold from commentary to composition? And is this, as was claimed in the conclusion of the previous chapter, evidence that the Qumran exegetes were also acting in some sense as biblical authors?

It is not the intention here to go over ground already covered, since the hermeneutical principles and exegetical techniques have been discussed previously in scholarship, some studies of which are useful,[1] while others tendentious or not wholly illuminating.[2] To point out that this or that pesherite verbal twist resembles, say, some rabbinic exegetical technique stops well short of penetrating

---

[1] The best of these include, Karl Elliger, *Studien zum Habakuk-Kommentar vom Toten Meer* (Tübingen: J. C. B. Mohr (Paul Siebeck) 1953); Geza Vermes, 'Interpretation, History of. B. At Qumran and in the Targums', in *IDBS*, 438–43; Bilha Nitzan, (1QpHab) מגילת פשר חבקוק ממגילות מדבר יהודה (Jerusalem: Bialik, 1986); Maurya Horgan, *Pesharim: Qumran Interpretations of Biblical Books* (Washington: Catholic Biblical Association of America, 1979); Lou H. Silberman, 'Unriddling the Riddle: A Study in the Structure and Language of the Habakkuk Pesher', *RQ* 3 (1961), 323–64; F. F. Bruce, 'Biblical Exposition at Qumran', in R. T. France and D. Wenham (eds.), *Gospel Perspectives. Studies in Midrash and Historiography* (Sheffield: JSOT Press, 1983), iii. 77–98; P. S. Alexander, 'Midrash and Pesher', in Speaker's Lecture Series, 'Midrash and the New Testament: The Interpretation of Scripture in the Synagogue and in the Early Church', University of Oxford, 10 Nov. 1987.

[2] William H. Brownlee's thirteen hermeneutical principles being a case in point ('Bible Interpretation among the Sectaries of the Dead Sea Scrolls', *BA* 19 (1951), 54–76), which have been correctly criticized by George Brooke, *Exegesis at Qumran: 4QFlorilegium in its Jewish Context* (Sheffield: JSOT Press, 1985), 282–8, for confusing exegetical techniques with hermeneutical principles.

the underlying motivations and reasoning. Nor are attempts to identify the genre of the pesher able to answer the questions posed here. To be sure the pesher genre is related to ancient Near-Eastern (Akkadian) and biblical (Joseph and Daniel) dream interpretations, the New Testament's variegated exegeses of the Old Testament, and the rabbinic Midrashim, but such similarities of form, whether real or imagined, only scratch the proverbial surface. The issue of pesherite genre will be discussed in a subsequent chapter, but for the present it will suffice to state that the pesher is best regarded as *sui generis*. Titles, such as 'Midrash pesher', are vagaries best avoided as they conceal the lack of analytical precision.

HOUSE OF STUDY

Not surprisingly, the Qumran-Essene community did not address the issue of scriptural modification in its writings, since questions of biblical authority and sanctity are formulations of modern discussions, although it was earlier argued that biblical consciousness—the awareness that certain writings stood apart—was already evident in the Second Temple period. For the covenanters of Qumran, taking liberties with the biblical texts did not conflict with a punctilious observance of the Mosaic law or a view of itself as the true Israel. In fact, it is precisely because the Qumran community sought to live according to the Sinaitic precepts and saw itself as the embodiment of biblical prophecy that it engaged in the renewal and development of the biblical message.

Column 8, lines 12–16 of the Rule of the Community from Cave 1 offer a clear statement of sectarian ideology:

(l. 12) When these (i.e. members) become a community in Israel according to these norms, (l. 13) they shall separate from the session of the men of deceit by walking into the wilderness in order to prepare His way.[3] (l. 14) As it is written: *in the wilderness, prepare the way of the Lord, make level in the desert a highway for our God* (Isa. 40: 3). (l. 15) This (i.e. way) is the study of the torah which He commanded through Moses to do

[3] 4QSᵉ (4Q259) דרך האמת 'way of the truth' for הואהא and James H. Charlesworth, *Rule of the Community and Related Documents* (Tübingen: J. C. B. Mohr (Paul Siebeck), 1994), 37 n. 210, suggests that the latter reading be read as another substitute for YHWH corresponding to the four dots of the Isaianic quotation. If correct, this would be yet another substitute for the divine name (cf. האו in CD 9. 5 (Nah. 1: 2) and הו אות in 4Q266); see J. Baumgarten, 'A New Qumran Substitute for the Divine Name and Mishnah Sukkah 45', *JQR* 88 (1992), 1–6.

according to everything which has been revealed time and again, (l. 16) and according to what the prophets revealed by His holy spirit.

As is often pointed out, this statement is programmatic for the very existence of the Qumran community: they separated themselves from deceitful men in order to establish a house of study in the wilderness, the act of scripture reading and meditation being equated with the fulfilment of Isaiah's prophecy to prepare the way of the Lord (cf. 1QS 9. 19-20).

Whether this version represents an earlier or later view of the emerging Qumran community remains unclear at this point. Of the copies from Cave 4, the Isaianic biblical proof-text is extant in 4QS^e, but missing from 4QS^d. Geza Vermes, one of the two official editors of the Cave 4 material for the *DJD* series, has recently argued that 1QS represents a developed version of the Community Rule after the Zadokites took over the leadership of the community.[4] If true, this would require that eight of the ten 4QS manuscripts (apart from 4QS$^{a, c}$) be considered later copies of texts more primitive than 1QS, since palaeographical estimates date the latter to 100-75 BCE and the former ones to between 50 BCE and 50 CE.[5] The first quarter of the second century BCE is the *terminus ante quem* of the Cave 1 scroll, making 1QS an early copy of the presumed developed version of the Community Rule. Whereas 4QS$^{b, d, e, f, g, h}$ are late copies of more primitive versions of the composition. An alternative explanation would view 1QS as reflecting an earlier stage of redaction and the copies from Cave 4 as later abridgements.

Notwithstanding present uncertainties of its literary development, column 8 of 1QS has conventionally been understood to be representing the idealized community whose existence was forged out of a displeasure with the *status quo* at the Jerusalem cultus. Isaiah 40: 3 is interpreted both figuratively, the 'preparation of the way of the Lord' becoming the study of the torah (מדרש התורה), and literally, setting up a community in the wilderness (במדבר). In a later section, there is an explicit reference back to this passage in

---

[4] See 'Preliminary Remarks on Unpublished Fragments of the Community Rule from Qumran Cave 4', *JJS* 42 (1991), 250-5 and '4QS Manuscripts' (forthcoming in *Festschrift* for M. Hengel). Many thanks to Geza Vermes for sending me his pre-publication copy.

[5] Frank Moore Cross, 'Palaeographical Dates of the Manuscripts', in Charlesworth (ed.), *Rule of the Community*, 57.

column 8 when it states that the wise leader (משכיל) shall himself
walk according to 'the ordinances, discern the mysteries of the
end-time and the qualities of the individual members, and guide
and teach them in the way that they should go, for this is the time
to prepare the way to the wilderness[6] (1QS 9. 12-20).

Pride of place in the sectarian exposition of the biblical texts
eventually went to the unidentified figure known only as the
Teacher of Righteousness, although it should be remembered that
it was the entire community and its continuous study and observance of the precepts that qualified and defined its form of ongoing
revelation.[7] From the initiation procedures of new volunteers to the
mundane maintenance of an organized community, the law was
interpreted and applied by chosen leaders and ordinary members
alike.[8] For example, in meetings of the community presided by the
overseer (המבקר), judgement or counsel is taken after an ordered
and considered discussion by the priests, elders, and all the rest of
the people (1QS 6. 8-13). To this 'assembly of the many', each
man is to bring his knowledge (מדעו) to the council of the community.

Furthermore, if the identification of the Qumran community
with the Essenes be admitted,[9] then it may be noted that continual
study also figured prominently in Philo and Josephus' descriptions
of the sect.[10] In *Quod omnis probus liber sit*, 81-6, Philo depicts the
Essenes as continually engaged in study (ἀναδιδάσκονται μὲν καὶ
παρὰ ἄλλον χρόνον), but especially on the Sabbath when they
abstained from work and congregated in synagogues (συναγωγαί)
to hear scripture being read (τὰς βίβλους ἀναγινώσκει) and its
difficulties explained (ὅσα μὴ γνώριμα παρελθὼν ἀναδιδάσκει). Given

---

[6] 'To the wilderness' suggests that the withdrawal of the community is in the
future (Michael Knibb, *The Qumran Community* (Cambridge: Cambridge University
Press, 1987), 143; and Preben Wernberg-Møller, *The Manual of Discipline* (Leiden:
E. J. Brill, 1957), 138 n. 48).

[7] So Michael Fishbane, 'Use, Authority and Interpretation of Mikra at Qumran',
in *Mikra*, 339-78.

[8] See recently, Steven D. Fraade, 'Interpretive Authority in the Studying
Community at Qumran', *JJS* 44 (1993), 46-69.

[9] For parallels between the scrolls and classical sources, see Geza Vermes and
Martin Goodman (eds.), *The Essenes According to the Classical Sources* (Sheffield: JSOT
Press, 1989), 1-17; and Todd S. Beall, *Josephus' Description of the Essenes Illustrated
by the Dead Sea Scrolls* (Cambridge: Cambridge University Press, 1988), 123-30.

[10] Philo was influenced by Stoicism in his characterization of the Essenes as
'athletes of virtue' (ἀθλητὰς ἀρετῆς), whereas Josephus likened them to the
Pythagoreans. *AJ* 18. 18-22 (5) appears to be dependent upon Philo.

his well-known fondness for allegorical interpretation, it is not surprising that Philo characterizes this exposition as given through symbols (διὰ συμβόλων), the idealized aim of which is to foster the love of God (φιλοθέου), love of virtue (φιλοαρέτου), and love of man (φιλοανθρώπου). Josephus corroborates this bibliocentric approach of the Essenes when he states that as regards ethical matters and prophecy there are some among them who, trained in the study of holy books (Βίβλοις ἱεραῖς), purifications (ἀγνείαις), and prophetic sayings (προφητῶν ἀποφθέγμασιν), become foretellers of the future (*BJ* 2. 159 (12)).

If the Therapeutae and Therapeutridae of Egypt are also related to the Qumran-Essene community, then they too gave the study of scripture a central place.[11] According to Philo's spiritually perfect portrayal in *de Vita Contemplativa*, 24–8, individual members entered a sanctuary and small room (σεμνεῖον καὶ μοναστήριον), bringing with them nothing but the laws (νόμους), inspired prophetic oracles (λόγια θεσπισθέντα διὰ προφητῶν), hymns (ὕμνους), and other worthy books (τὰ ἄλλα οἷς ἐπιστήμη καὶ εὐσέβεια συναύξονται καὶ τελειοῦνται). They prayed, and read the holy books (τοῖς ἱεροῖς γράμμασι), and drew out their philosophy by allegory, since they considered literal meanings (τὰ τῆς ῥητῆς ἑρμηνείας, 'the interpretation according to the word') to be outward symbols of an inner and hidden nature. Corporate study also took place on sabbaths (30–1) and on the great banquet of the Festival of Weeks (64–90). In the course of the latter, the president (ὁ πρόεδρος) examines some scriptural text (ζητεῖ τι τῶν ἐν τοῖς ἱεροῖς γράμμασιν) or explicates another passage (ὑπ' ἄλλον προταθὲν ἐπιλύεται) by exegeses of holy scripture (αἱ δὲ ἐξηγήσεις τῶν ἱερῶν γραμμάτων) in order to reveal the hidden meanings. The ordinary members, for their part, must meekly listen and by a little exercise of memory (ἐκ μικρᾶς ὑπομνήσεως) understand obscurities by what has been made clear.

---

[11] Even if unpublished evidence from 4QTLev ar^b, 'the name of his holy one' (שם קדשה; Frank Moore Cross, *The Ancient Library of Qumran*, 3rd edn. (Sheffield: Sheffield Academic Press, 1995), 183, calls into question the etymological argument of אסא for θεραπευταί, the similarities between the Qumran Community, Essenes, and Therapeutae are none the less undeniable.

PROPHETIC INSPIRATION

Column 8 of the Community Rule defines 'the study of torah' as doing (לעשות) everything according to all that is revealed (ככול הנגלה) and according to what the prophets revealed by His holy spirit (גלו הנביאים ברוח קודשו כאשר). Evidently, Torah study was not restricted to the meditation of the first five books of Moses, but correctly observing all the laws that have been revealed continuously (עת בעת).[12] As a community that sought to live according to the precepts of God, the Qumranians had to supplement the Pentateuch with laws shared commonly with Jewish tradition (e.g. calendrical calculations with Jubilees[13]) and their own sectarian halakhot. The latter is reflected, for instance, in the extension of the law on incest (Lev. 18: 13) where the Mosaic law (משפט העריות) is said to apply 'also to women' (כהם הנשים; CD 5. 10). Such adaptations of existing laws have precedents in inner biblical exegeses (e.g. the extension of sabbatical laws for sown fields to vineyards (Exod. 23: 10-11) in such a way as to obscure the innovative element (Lev. 25. 3-7)).[14]

For some who consider the Temple Scroll sectarian, there is a further non-biblical holiness code which is identified with the 'second law' (משנה התורה or התורה השנית) that the Teacher of Righteousness revealed to the Qumran community and sent to the Wicked Priest (4QpPsᵃ 1-10. iv. 8-9 and 4Q177 1-4. 14).[15] This 'second law' may also have been called the 'book of meditation' (ספר הגו/הגי) (derived from the והגית of Josh. 1: 8)) with which the sacerdotal leadership must be thoroughly familiar (CD 10. 4-6; 13. 2-3; 14. 6-8; and 1QSa 1. 6-8). Others would alternatively see in the 'law' mentioned in the Psalms Pesher a reference to another halakhic work known as 'Some Precepts of the Torah' (4QMMT).[16]

There is no need to enter into this issue here, since the sectarian or non-Qumranic character of both the Temple Scroll and 4QMMT

[12] Formally, this may be described as Torah and *mishpat* (so Fraade, 'Interpretive Authority', 66).
[13] See Annie Jaubert, *La Date de la cène* (Paris: J. Gabalda, 1957).
[14] On this whole phenomenon, see Michael Fishbane, *Biblical Interpretation in Ancient Israel* (Oxford: Clarendon Press, 1985).
[15] Yigael Yadin, *The Temple Scroll* (Jerusalem: Israel Exploration Society, 1983), i. 390-2. Yadin's edition is based only on 11Q19. See now Ben Zion Wacholder with Martin Abegg, 'The Fragmentary Remains of 11Q Torah (Temple Scroll)', *HUCA* 62 (1991), 1-116; and Emanuel Tov and Sidnie White in *DJD* xiii. 319-34, for 4Q365a (4QTemple?).   [16] Elisha Qimron and John Strugnell, *DJD* x. 119-20.

remains debatable. Suffice it to say that the Qumran community had in its 'library' texts that were non-biblical and that may or may not be related to other extra-canonical texts mentioned in the sectarian documents. Being learned in the law, for the Qumran community, is not equated with a study of only the five books of Moses, in whatever version they happen to have had before them, but also other authoritative works besides.

Another feature of the 'study of torah' is the inspiration of the 'holy spirit'. This spiritual dimension is seldom given its due emphasis in scholarly discussions and as will be seen is one feature which the pesharim share with the Pauline letters. The Qumran community is admonished to observe all that the prophets have revealed by God's holy spirit.[17] It is highly unlikely that the conception of 'His holy spirit' (רוח קודשו) here falls in line with later Christian formulations of the Trinitarian Godhead.[18] Rather, this sacred spirit is akin to that which inspired the biblical prophets and psalmist (cf. Isa. 63: 10 and Ps. 51: 13).[19]

The corollary of this obedience is to be found in CD 2. 12, where God instructs the members of the community 'through the anointed ones of his holy spirit' (ביד משיחי רוח קודשו). A further link between the prophets ('anointed ones'; cf. 1 Kgs. 19: 16) and the spirit is also plausibly restored in CD 6. 1: the removers of the boundary erred in preaching rebellion against the divine commandments given through Moses and 'and also by those who were anointed with the holy spirit'.[20] This same holy spirit unifies men who enter God's covenant: it is 'by his holy spirit[21] of the community in his [God's] truth that he [man] can be cleansed from all his guilt' (1QS 3. 7).

It can only be speculated as to what the observance of prophetic revelations entailed, but the role attributed to the Teacher of Righteousness does cast some light into the inner workings of the Qumran community and the mind of its biblical interpreters.

---

[17] The syntax in ll. 15-16 makes this explicit, as the verb 'to do' (לעשות) also governs the clause וכאשר גלו הנביאים ברוח קודשו.

[18] *Contra* J. C. O'Neill, *Who Did Jesus Think He Was?* (Leiden: E. J. Brill, 1995), who attempts to argue that the trinitarian formulation is already evident in nascent Judaism and in the Early Church.

[19] Wernberg-Møller, *The Manual of Discipline*, 130 n. 49, points out that the targums understand these passages to be referring to the prophetic spirit.

[20] Ibid. Reading במשיחי רוח הקודש.

[21] Reading with Elisha Qimron in *Rule of the Community*, 12 n. 57, from 4QS[a] (ברוח קודשו).

TEACHER OF RIGHTEOUSNESS

The teacher *par excellence* of the Qumran community was someone known only by the sobriquet 'the Teacher of Righteousness' (מורה הצדק). The fact that he is not named can be explained by the intra-mural orientation of the sectarian writings. Just as everyone at New College is expected to know who 'the Dean' is, so too the Qumranians did not need any other reference beyond his title within their walls. For historical purposes, however, such coded language hinders a secure identification.

Evidence from the scrolls indicates that he was the founder of the Qumran community (CD 1. 11[22] and 4QpPs^a 1–10. iii. 16), who held a dual role, also being supreme interpreter of the law and prophecies (cf. 1QS 8. 12–13). In his capacity as an expert of the law he came into confrontation with a rival leader called 'the Liar' (איש הכזב), who is usually distinguished from his sacerdotal opponent, 'the Wicked Priest' (הכוהן הרשע).[23] The latter apparently pursued him on Yom Kippur (thus indicating a calendrical difference) to his house of exile at Khirbet Qumran (1QpHab 11. 6–8)[24] and later attempted to murder him (4QpPs^a 1–10. iv. 8). Whereas the former rejected his teachings in the midst of all the congregation (1QpHab 5. 8–12). Faith in the teachings of the Teacher of Righteousness[25] not only guaranteed compliance with the perceived will of God, but also a member's place in the salvific plan.[26] He is often identified with the eschatological figure of the 'one teaching righteousness' (יורה הצדק; CD 6. 11)[27] of the 'well midrash', or less probably with the 'messiah of righteousness' (הצדק משיח, 4QcommGen A 5. 3 (*olim* 4QpGen^a).

The Teacher of Righteousness was possibly regarded as 'the

---

[22] The lack of a definite article (מורה צדק) can be explained by its poetical context.

[23] On the debate over the identification of one or two figures, as well as the number of wicked priests, see my 'The Wicked Priests of the Groningen Hypothesis', *JBL* 112 (1993), 415–25.

[24] O'Neill, *Who Did Jesus Think He Was?*, 55–66, renders 'to swallow' (בלע) as 'to destroy', 'to put to death', and even 'to crucify', a sense that is otherwise expressed by the verbs המית (4Q285, fr. 5. l. 4; 4QpPs^a 1–10. iv. 8) and תלה (4QpNah 3–4. i. 7; 11QTS 64. 6–13). בלע as understood by the Habakkuk pesherist himself means 'rebuke' (תוכחה) in 1QpHab 5. 10.

[25] ואמנתם במורה הצדק, 'and in their faith in the Teacher of Righteousness' (1QpHab 8. 2).

[26] בישועתו, CD 20. 34.

[27] Although challenged recently by Fraade, 'Interpretive Community', 62.

unique teacher' (מורה היחיד; CD 20. 1), the uncertainty occurring in
the reading of the second word. As it appears in MS B of the
medieval recension, the second word should mean 'unique'. The
spelling of *vav* and *yod* being problemmatic in the Cairo Geniza
document, this is often emended to 'the community' (היחד).
Reading the phrase as 'the teacher of the community' will add to
his didactic role among the Qumranians, whereas 'unique' will
single him out as the consummate teacher. Both readings are
equally suitable and the question should remain open.

The Teacher of Righteousness is not referred to explicitly as a
prophet, as he is a priest (הכוהן, 1QpHab 2. 8; 4QpPs[a] 1–10. iii.
15). However, his prophetic status may be inferred from what is
attributed to him. In column 7 of the Habakkuk Pesher, it states
that God had made known all the mysteries of his servants, the
prophets, to the Teacher of Righteousness (ll. 4–5). Now, the attribution here stops short of indicating prophetic status. He is an
interpreter of biblical oracles, divinely inspired to be sure, rather
than himself being a prophet. If the biblical lemma is taken into
consideration, however, then it may well tip the whole question in
favour of the view that the pesherist regarded the Teacher of
Righteousness as a prophet, or at least following in the tradition of
the biblical prophets. 1QpHab 7. 4–5 interprets Habakkuk 2: 3,
'in order that he will run who reads it'. Within the biblical book
this refers to the command for the prophet to write down the
vision. Here, the Teacher of Righteousness is being identified with
the prophet Habakkuk.

The identification, however, has a further dimension. In the
earlier lines of that passage, Habakkuk is said to have known a
partial revelation about the final generation. It is only in a subsequent revelation that God made known to the Teacher of
Righteousness all the mysteries uttered by the biblical prophet (מורה
הצדק אשר הודיעו אל את כול רזי דברי עבדיו הנבאים). The Teacher of
Righteousness, then, is not only the divinely chosen successor, but
the revelation granted to him was also more complete.

The same view is stated negatively in the manifold interpretation of Habakkuk 1: 5 in column 2: the presumed objects of the
mutilated biblical lemma, 'the nations' or 'traitors',[28] are identified

---

[28] It is uncertain whether the pesherist had בוגים as in the MT or בוגדים as in the
LXX (οἱ καταφρονηταί) and Syr. Although the גוים who will be judged in col. 13 are

with the traitors of the pesherist's own day who did not obey the subsequent revelation of the priest, the Teacher of Righteousness, in whose heart God had set the understanding to interpret (לפשור) all the words of his servants the prophets. Just as the prophetic foretelling was divinely inspired ('the word of his servants, the prophets, through whom God foretold all which is to come upon His people and his land'), so also knowledge of the fulfilment of those prophecies in the final days comes from God.[29] The divinely inspired utterance is formulated succinctly in lines 2–3: '[the words] of the Teacher of Righteousness from the mouth of God (מפיא אל)'.[30]

If what has been suggested thus far is at all correct, then it can be seen that the succession of divinely inspired prophetic interpretation was carried forward by the Qumran commentators. The link between the Teacher of Righteousness and his followers is terminologically explicit in the use of 'pesher' (פשר).[31] Just as the Teacher interpreted (לפשור) prophetic oracles eschatologically, so also his followers used the introductory formula 'the pesher of the verse' or a variation of it to comment on the biblical texts. When the final age was prolonged (1QpHab 7. 10–14)[32] and in accordance with the belief that the whole community participates in the ongoing revelation ('time and again' of 1QS 8. 12–16), his followers developed a form of interpretation that was inspired by the Teacher of Righteousness and in whose commentaries he also plays a part.[33]

It is an assumption to hold that the two techniques are identical. Even if some of the Qumran compositions were thought to

the idolatrous Gentile nations, not enemies from within, it is nevertheless possible that the pesherist read two entirely different meanings out of the same word.

[29] In 1Q22 God commands Moses to interpret ([ור]פש) the Sinaitic ordinances for the Levites and priests.

[30] Cf. 'in the book of Zechariah from the mouth [of God]', 4QpIsa[c] 8–10. 8.

[31] As is commonly noted, the term 'pesher' is used only once in the Hebrew Bible at Qoh. 8: 1, and is related to פתר, the Aramaic פשר, and the Akkadian *pishru*.

[32] Annette Steudel, *Der Midrasch zur Eschatologie aus der Qumrangemeinde (4QMidrEschat[a.b]): Materielle Rekonstruktion, Textbestand, Gattung und traditionsgeschichtliche Einordnung des durch 4Q174 ('Florilegium') und 4Q177 ('Catena A') repräsentierten Werkes aus den Qumranfunden* (Leiden: E. J. Brill, 1994), 161–211, discusses the issue of 'delayed parousia' on the basis of her reconstruction of 4Q174 and 4Q177.

[33] In a narrative dependent upon Genesis, Josephus relates how a certain Simon the Essene foretold the downfall of Archelaus by the interpretation of the ethnarch's dream (*BJ* 2. 113 (3) and *AJ* 17. 347 (3)).

have been written by him (e.g. 1QH 2. 1-9, 5. 20-6. 36), it is an unsubstantiated claim to suppose that the form of biblical commentary known in the pesharim was already practised by him. The emphasis upon his speech and repeated mention of the 'hearing' of those around him would rather suggest that he taught orally, a pattern that better accords with pedagogical models in the ancient Jewish and Graeco-Roman world.

CONCLUSIONS

In both ideological orientation and exegetical tradition, the pesherists did not consider the words of their biblical texts to be fixed and immutable. As members of a community that lived by the precepts of the law, they saw themselves as participants in the unfolding revelation of God, even when the end-time had been delayed. They adapted biblical laws and supplemented them where there were perceived gaps, and found correspondences between contemporary events and figures of biblical prophecies.

The pesherists behaved primarily as expositors of the biblical texts, but sometimes one cannot but feel that they were also acting as biblical authors. There is a formal distinction in their commentaries between what they quote as lemma and interpretation, and yet at certain points they also blur this dividing line by changing the very words of scripture. Like the 'biblical authors' who reused the legal and prophetic texts they had before them, so too the pesherists moulded scripture for their own purposes. The justification for doing so is grounded in the belief that God, by his holy spirit,[34] continues to reveal His will to his servants, both prophets and covenanters alike.

---

[34] The rabbinic definitions of 'defiling the hands' include the belief that the words found in a scroll were 'spoken by the holy spirit' (*t. Yad.* 2. 14; *b. Meg.* 7a). See Roger Beckwith, *The Old Testament Canon of the New Testament Church and its Background in Early Judaism* (London: SPCK, 1985), 278-83, for a discussion of the whole issue.

PART IV
Pauline Interpretation
of the Bible

8

Paul and Midrash Pesher

Whether Paul, too, modified his biblical text is a long-standing issue in the history of the interpretation of the New Testament. From earliest times—and particularly during the Reformation and the nineteenth century—to the present, scholars, the clergy, and laymen alike have taken sides to defend or attack the New Testament authors' handling of scriptural quotations: did they practise a form of proof-texting that completely disregards the original context? Did they alter and modify the very words of the Bible to suit their own interpretations, or is there an integrity and coherence underlying their method? If Paul intentionally changed texts from what subsequent believers regard as the first half of 'the Holy Bible', then it may be asked what implications for 'verbal inspiration', 'inerrancy', and the authority of 'the Old Testament' are to be drawn?[1]

Clearly, comprehensive answers to each one of these many questions would require extended treatments well beyond the limits of the present study. Issues relating to biblical authority are complex, touching as they do not only areas that may be addressed by argumentation, but also the personal convictions and beliefs of the individual. The question pursued in this study is much more modest and has been formulated within the context of the Second Temple Bible interpretation: did Paul view himself as a scriptural expositor or is he also in some sense a 'biblical author'? Was he a participant in the phenomenon now frequently described as 'inner biblical exegesis' or was he one of its notable commentators? Is his exegetical method to be described as 'Midrash pesher' or is such a classification artificial and misleading?

---

[1] Cf. James A. Sanders, *Torah and Canon* (Philadelphia: Fortress Press, 1972); Brevard Childs, *Introduction to the Old Testament as Scripture* (London: SCM Press, 1979); James Barr, *Holy Scripture. Canon, Authority, Criticism* (Oxford: Clarendon Press, 1983); and John Barton, *People of the Book? The Authority of the Bible in Christianity* (London: SPCK, 1988).

WHAT IS MIDRASH PESHER?

The most explicit use of the Qumran pesharim in the study of his verbatim biblical quotations is to be found in the view that Paul practised a form of exegesis that can be described as 'Midrash pesher'. E. Earle Ellis, in a number of publications dating from 1957 to the present,[2] has argued that the explanation of a textual variant cannot account for several phenomena found in the explicit citations of the letters, since the rationale underlying Paul's usage, both in its textual manifestations and theological applications, is found in the exegetical moulding of the biblical text. The problem is essentially one of interpretation and this interpretation is none other than the Midrash pesher which is also to be found in the Gospels of Matthew and John.

The Midrash pesher exegesis, Ellis contends, (1) merges pertinent verses into one strongly expressive proof-text, (2) adapts their grammar to the New Testament context and application, (3) chooses appropriate renderings from known texts or targumim, and (4) creates *ad hoc* interpretations. Thus, for example, in what he calls the most notable instance of pesherite exegesis, Ellis argues that Paul has created or selected and inserted the phrase 'in victory' ($\epsilon i s\ \nu \hat{\iota} \kappa o s$), also attested by Aquila and Theodotion but not in the LXX ($i \sigma \chi \acute{\upsilon} \sigma a s$), into the 'merged quotation' of 1 Cor. 15: 54-5 ('Death is swallowed up in victory. Where, O death, is your victory? Where, O death, is your sting?'), since the idea of death swallowed up in victory is so intimately connected with the victory of Christ's resurrection.[3] In other words, Ellis sees the variants 'in victory' as the result of Paul's conscious exegetical adaptation, whether by an *ad hoc* rendering[4] or by choosing from a reading already extant, of the biblical text for his interpretation of 'the victory of our Lord Jesus Christ' in verse 57. Moreover, Ellis maintains (with F. H. Woods) that 'in victory' is one of the meanings

---

[2] *Paul's Use of the Old Testament* (London: Oliver & Boyd, 1957); 'Midrash Pesher', republished in *Prophecy and Hermeneutics in Early Christianity: New Testament Essays* (Tübingen: J. C. B. Mohr, 1978), 173-81; 'Midrash, Targum and New Testament', in E. Earle Ellis and Max Wilcox (eds.), *Neotestamentica et Semitica: Studies in Honour of Matthew Black* (Edinburgh: T. & T. Clark, 1969), 61-9; and 'Biblical Interpretation in the New Testament Church', in *Mikra*, 691-726.

[3] *Paul's Use*, 15, 145, 148.

[4] In which case, Aquila and Theodotion presumably must be seen in the unlikely position of having been influenced by Paul.

derived from the Hebrew root נצח which also means 'to succeed' (cf. the MT לנצח 'forever').

Ellis has frequently come under fire for his uncritical handling of the Septuagint,[5] but it would be fair to say that his view of Paul's exegesis as Midrash pesher has been influential. Many New Testament scholars believe that Paul's exegetical technique may be described, with various qualifications, as Midrash pesher. C. K. Barrett, for instance,[6] in an important contribution to the New Testament's use of the Old, cites Romans 10: 6–7 as an instance of pesher exegesis.[7] The text reads as follows:

μὴ εἴπῃς ἐν τῇ καρδίᾳ σου· τίς ἀναβήσεται εἰς τὸν οὐρανόν; τοῦτ᾽ ἔστιν Χριστὸν καταγαγεῖν· (7) ἤ· τίς καταβήσεται εἰς τὴν ἄβυσσον; τοῦτ᾽ ἔστιν Χριστὸν ἐκ νεκρῶν ἀναγαγεῖν;

He, accordingly, transposes it to the pesherite pattern:

Do not say in your heart, Who shall ascend into heaven? The *pēšer* of this is, Who shall bring Christ down? (7) Do not say in your heart, Who shall descend into the deep? The *pēšer* of this is, Who shall bring Christ up from the dead?[8]

In his translation of Romans 10: 6–7, Barrett inserts the additional *pēšer* before τοῦτ᾽ ἔστιν, presumably because he believes that latent in the formula τοῦτ᾽ ἔστιν is the meaning of *pēšer*. Ellis, commenting recently on the use of Genesis 21: 12 and 18: 10 in Romans 9: 7–9, similarly makes this assertion when he states that οὗτος (ἔστιν), which is a variation of τοῦτ᾽ ἔστιν (cf. Rom. 9: 7–9), 'is an equivalent of the Qumran *Pesher*'.[9] Is the technical term 'pesher' nothing more than 'it is' or 'this is'? And can this so-called exegesis of 'Midrash pesher' be described simply as 'this is that'?[10]

---

[5] Most recently by James Barr, 'Paul and the LXX: A Note on Some Recent Work', *JTS* 45/2 (1994), 593–7.

[6] So also Martin McNamara, *Palestinian Judaism and the New Testament* (Wilmington, Del.: Michael Glazier, 1983), 232–3; Morna D. Hooker's description of 2 Cor. 3 as 'midrash pesher' (*From Adam to Christ: Essays on Paul* (Cambridge: Cambridge University Press, 1990) 141, 150–1); and James A. Sanders, 'Habakkuk in Qumran, Paul and the Old Testament', rev., in Craig A. Evans and James A. Sanders (eds.), *Paul and the Scriptures of Israel* (Sheffield: Sheffield Academic Press, 1993), 107.

[7] 'The Interpretation of the Old Testament in the New', in *CHB* i. 377–411.

[8] Ibid. 392. McNamara has also identified this passage as a pesher and has transposed Rom. 10: 5–13 accordingly, but he does this in order to draw out the targumic elements (*Palestinian Judaism*, 232).

[9] 'Biblical Interpretation in the New Testament Church', 696–7.

[10] So F. F. Bruce, *The New Testament Development of Old Testament Themes* (Exeter:

Before considering its exegetical characteristics, however, it should be asked what a Midrash pesher is, whence this genre is derived, and if it is a useful description of Pauline exegesis.[11] The genre of Midrash has traditionally referred to the classical exegetical *œuvres* of the rabbinic period (e.g. *Gen. Rab.*, *Sifre*, and *Sifra*). With the introduction of the term 'midrash' into literary and biblical criticism,[12] so many different meanings have become attached to it, that it has become abstruse and ill-defined.[13] One even suspects that the term sometimes means nothing more than a sexy synonym for exegesis.[14]

Among the Qumran scrolls, it is difficult to distinguish the term 'pesher' from 'midrash', since both can have a general meaning. 4Q174 (also known as '4QFlorilegium') provides clear evidence that the two overlapped semantically: '(this is) the midrash of (מ[ד]רש) of *Blessed is the man who does not walk in the counsel of the wicked* (Ps. 1: 1). The interpretation of the verse concerns פשר הדבר](ר ([המה]) those who turn from the way . . .' (col. 3, l. 14).[15] Here, the pesher formula is redundant, signalling again that verse 1 of Psalm 1 was to be interpreted. Significantly, the comment is immediately followed by two other supporting proof-texts from Isaiah 8: 11 and Ezekiel 44: 10, a practice not commonly found in the *pesharim continus* (exceptionally 4QpIsa[c] cites Hos. 6: 9a and Zech. 11: 11), but followed in the thematic pesharim (e.g. 11QMelch). Certainly, it would be tendentious and anachronistic to argue that this tech-

---

Paternoster Press, 1968); and Richard Longenecker, *Biblical Exegesis in the Apostolic Period* (Grand Rapids, Mich.: Eerdmans, 1975), 129-32. Cf. Acts 2: 16 and Peter's declaration: 'This is that which is spoken . . .'.

[11] Decades ago, Matthew Black suggested that Midrash pesher was a modern invention best forgotten ('The Christological Use of the Old Testament in the New Testament', *NTS* 18 (1971), 1).

[12] See above all the pioneering work of Renée Bloch, 'Midrash', in *SDB* v. 1263-81.

[13] A devastating critique of current usage is offered by Philip S. Alexander, 'Midrash and the Gospels', in C. M. Tuckett (ed.), *Synoptic Studies: The Ampleforth Conferences of 1982 and 1983* (Sheffield: JSOT Press, 1984), 1-18.

[14] Jacob Neusner, *What is Midrash?* (Philadelphia: Fortress Press, 1987), p. xi, observes: 'the reason for prevailing confusion about Midrash is that a common English word "exegesis", meaning "interpretation and explanation" is replaced by an uncommon Hebrew word'.

[15] Following A. Steudel's transcription and reconstruction in *Der Midrasch zur Eschatologie aus der Qumrangemeinde (4QMidrEschat[a.b]): Materielle Rekonstruktion, Textbestand, Gattung und traditionsgeschichtliche Einordnung des durch 4Q174 ('Florilegium') und 4Q177 ('Catena A') repräsentierten Werkes aus den Qumranfunden* (Leiden: E. J. Brill, 1994), 25.

nique alone identifies 4Q174 as a rabbinic Midrash; however, the formal similarities are also undeniable.

Based primarily on this passage in 4Q174, W. H. Brownlee has suggested that Midrash was indeed the title of the Qumran commentaries and proposed that a new category of exegesis, the Midrash pesher, be created.[16] This suggestion was taken up by Krister Stendahl in his study of Matthean formula quotations and in turn by Ellis for Pauline exegesis.[17] The claim for its titular use in the continuous Qumran commentaries falters on syntactical and literary grounds. The word 'midrash' (מ[ד]רש), as commonly restored, is understood by Brownlee to be grammatically linked to the biblical lemma: thus he translates, 'A midrash of "Blessed is the man . . ."'.[18] It is, he asserts, 'a heading of the unitary Psalm (= our Pss. 1-2)'.[19]

This explanation, however, is unlikely if only for the simple reason that 4Q174 does not cite the first two psalms of the traditional Psalter. To be sure Psalm 2: 1 is interpreted subsequently, but the intervening verses are left out and replaced by passages from Isaiah and Ezekiel. Moreover, it is to be doubted that 'Midrash' in 4Q174 was the title of an embedded Qumran commentary on the first two psalms. To apply this supposed titular sense of 'Midrash' to the continuous pesharim, which do not use this term, is to fudge the literary distinctions between 4Q174 and 1QpHab and compound the problems.

Even if 'Midrash pesher' is not to be considered a literary genre, as has been argued, a case could nevertheless be made for the 'Midrashic' features of pesherite exegesis.[20] As discussed previously, the Qumran community defines its own preparation of the way in the wilderness as 'a midrash of the torah' (1QS 8. 12-16). It regarded itself as a 'house of torah' (בית התורה; CD 20. 10, 13)

[16] First suggested in his article, 'Bible Interpretation among the Sectaries of the Dead Sea Scrolls', *BA* 19 (1951), 54-76, it finds full expression in his commentary, *The Midrash Pesher of Habakkuk* (Missoula, Mont.: Scholars Press, 1979), 23-8.

[17] *The School of Matthew and its Use of the Old Testament* (Lund: C. W. K. Gleerup, 1954), 182-94, and *Paul's Use*, 139-47, respectively.

[18] *Midrash Pesher of Habakkuk*, 25.

[19] Ibid.

[20] e.g. George J. Brooke, *Exegesis at Qumran: 4QFlorilegium in its Jewish Context* (Sheffield: JSOT Press, 1985), 283-92; 'The Biblical Texts in the Qumran Commentaries: Scribal Errors or Exegetical Variants?', in Craig A. Evans and William F. Stinespring (eds.), *Early Jewish and Christian Exegesis: Studies in Memory of William Hugh Brownlee* (Atlanta: Scholars Press, 1987), 85-100; and Ellis, 'Biblical Interpretation', 692-701.

where a quorum of ten men study the law continuously (1QS 6. 6–8) and in which the young are instructed in the Book of Hagu as well as the laws of the covenant (1QSa 1. 6–8). It may also be argued that pesherite exegeses parallel such rabbinic techniques as *'al tiqre, hilluf, paronomasia,* and *gezera shawa.*[21]

Whether one is convinced of pesherite interpretation as midrashic exegesis depends in part upon the persuasiveness of the individual techniques identified. For example, it is often stated that the pesharim used the rabbinic technique of *'al tiqrei,* 'do not read', to change the 'wine' (היין) of Habakkuk 2: 5 to 'wealth' (הון; 1QpHab 8. 3). Now, this technique occurs in several places in the rabbinic literature to introduce a different reading of a particular text, whether it involves alternative vocalizations or also alterations of the consonants: thus, 'do not read (אל תקרי) X, but (אלא) Y'.[22] For instance, in the *Mek. de-rabbi Ishmael* at Exodus 12: 17, the commandment to observe Passover regulations is interpreted twice, the second of which required a revocalization of the consonants from 'unleavened bread' to 'commandments': '"And you shall observe the (feast of) unleavened bread (הַמַצוֹת)". R. Josiah says: Do not read it so (אל תקרא כן), but (אלא): "you shall observe the commandments (הַמִצוֹת)".' This repointing of the key word changes the whole meaning of Exodus 12: 17 and allows the Darshan to make the point that the observant should also be quick to perform his religious duty, just as he should not be slow in making the unleavened bread. Unfortunately, nowhere is this formula to be found in the pesharim and its presence as a technique is to be doubted.[23]

Another difficulty in characterizing pesherite exegesis as such is that many of the so-called Midrashic techniques are not altogether distinctive to the genre. As David Daube has shown long ago, the seven *middot* that Hillel prescribed were derived from Alexandrian

---

[21] Brooke, *Exegesis at Qumran.*

[22] Variants involving consonantal changes are found in e.g. *Ber.* 15b; *ARN* 3; *Yalkut Ps.* 765. See A. Rosenzweig, 'Die Al-Tikri-Deutungen: Ein Beitrag zur talmudischen Schriftdeutung', in M. Brann and J. Elbogen (eds.), *Festschrift zu Israel Lewy* (Breslau: M. & H. Marcus Verlag, 1911), 204–53; N. H. Torczyner, 'אל תקרי' in ישראלית אשכול אנציקלופדיה (Berlin: 1932), ii. 376–86; and Carmel McCarthy, *The Tiqqune Sopherim and other Theological Corrections in the Masoretic Text of the Old Testament* (Göttingen: Vandenhoeck & Ruprecht, 1981), ch. 4.

[23] The view that there are 'implicit' *'al tiqrei* techniques (i.e. without the introductory phrase) is to be rejected (*contra* M. Gertner, 'Midrashim in the New Testament'), since the technique *by definition* requires some form of the formula.

rhetoric and jurisprudence of the Hellenistic period (e.g. *a minori ad maius*).[24] How useful then would the invocation of 'Midrash' be?

Given these added complexities, it would seem best to leave this genre out of consideration of pesherite exegesis. At most, it may be said that the pesharim are midrashic, in the general and non-specific meaning of the word.[25] In other words, while it is undeniable that some of the techniques found in the Midrashim also appear in the pesharim, these exegetical features are not exclusively found in them nor is recognition of their similarities sufficient to allow a simple equation of the one genre with the other.

COMMON FEATURES OF PESHERITE EXEGESIS

The analytical advantage in avoiding the use of Midrash is that the pesher may be examined on its own terms without the further entanglement of another genre, since describing the exegetical characteristics of a pesher is more difficult than is realized. What often comes to mind with the word 'pesher' is the more or less intact scroll of the commentary on Habakkuk, supplemented by other notable passages from the pesharim to Isaiah, Nahum, Hosea, and Psalms. By virtue of its early publication date and preservation, 1QpHab's exegetical techniques have sometimes been taken to be typical, when in fact the exegesis is much more varied than is commonly supposed, even within one pesher.

Moshe Bernstein has recently argued against the primacy of 1QpHab in the classification of the Qumran pesharim. While the general thrust of the argument is sound, Bernstein overstates the case with his emphasis upon the order of publication.[26] He argues that scholarly discussions on the pesharim have been influenced by the study of the Habakkuk pesher and this is due to the 'significance of firstness'.[27] By 'significance of firstness', Bernstein

---

[24] 'Rabbinic Methods of Interpretation and Hellenistic Rhetoric', *HUCA* 22 (1949), 239–64. Recently, Alexander, 'Midrash and the Gospels', has argued that these lists of hermeneutical rules, whether there be 7, 13, or 32, do not correspond all that closely to the exegesis as practised in the Midrashim.

[25] Maurya Horgan, *Pesharim: Qumran Interpretations of Biblical Books* (Washington: Catholic Biblical Association of America, 1979), 252, states that 'the term "midrash" is neither a useful nor an informative term by which to characterize the pesharim'.

[26] 'Introductory Formulas for Citation and Re-citation of Biblical Verses in the Qumran Pesharim', *DSD* i. 31, 65–70.

[27] Ibid.

means that publication of the Habakkuk pesher occurred before that of all other pesharim. While this may be true to a degree, it is the discovery of an exegetically illuminating prophecy of Habakkuk that has shaped the classification of the genre more than the order in which it appeared.

Even if 4QFlor and 4QCatena[a] were published before 1QpHab, as in Bernstein's hypothetical reconstruction, it would not *necessarily* have led to his more nuanced classification. Given its much better state of preservation in comparison to the fragmentary state of others, it is not surprising that the commentary on the first two chapters of Habakkuk's prophecy looms large in scholarly discussions. That is to say, both the chance preservation of so much of the text and its inherent exegetical qualities, more than the order of publication, determine Habakkuk Pesher's central place in scholarly discussions. The classification of the Qumran commentaries by Jean Carmignac into the continuous and thematic pesharim is based upon typological issues rather than such concerns as the dates of publication: the former more or less follows sequentially continuous biblical passages while the other draws its proof-texts from a variety of biblical books around a particular theme.[28] Moreover, it is in any case to be doubted that Habakkuk Pesher *alone* exercised the kind of overwhelming influence that Bernstein attributes to it.

Bernstein is, however, correct in drawing attention to the varied nature of pesherite exegesis. As regards their use of quotation formulas, he argues that these texts do not constitute one monolithic genre of the continuous pesharim, but that they instead stand as points along a continuum, the closest to the thematic pesharim being 4QpIsa[c], followed by 4QpIsa[e], 4QpIsa[b], 1QpHab, and 4QpIsa[a].[29] This nuanced classification of the continuous and thematic pesharim is a welcome advance in the discussion,[30] but it may be asked whether Bernstein has gone far enough to consider issues of genre and hermeneutical method.

Among the Qumran scrolls, the term 'pesher' is found in three broad exegetical contexts. First, it appears as the key term of inter-

[28] 'Le Document de Qumrân sur Melkisédeq', *RQ* 7 (1969–71), 342–78.

[29] 'Introductory Formulas', 69–70.

[30] A very similar conclusion was already reached in my D.Phil. dissertation, 'Attitudes to Holy Scripture in the Qumran Pesharim and Pauline Letters': 'between the thematic and continuous categories is 4QpIsa[c]' (p. 105).

pretative formulas (e.g. 'the *pesher* of the matter', 'its *pesher*', etc.) in scrolls and fragments that systematically comment on more or less continuous sections of selected biblical books.[31] As already noted, there is variety within this group of continuous pesharim, some citing biblical texts from other books, others discontinuous when compared to the MT. It is conventional to assume that these fifteen or sixteen scrolls represent the 'pesher', a literary genre that presumably originated from or developed as a result of the teachings of the Teacher of Righteousness. 'Pesher' as a literary genre has also been extended to describe other fragmentary texts that either do not contain any commentary (4QpMic? [4Q168])[32] or interpret texts that have not been identified (4QpUnid [4Q172]).[33]

Second, 'pesher' is found in the introductory formulas of scrolls that do not systematically follow a biblical book. Here, the biblical lemma and its pesherite interpretation are used to bolster a theme and subject (11QMelch, 4QFlor [4Q174], 4QCatena[a] [4Q177][34]). To be included in this group are the interpretations of Isaiah 24: 17 in CD 4. 13-17 and Genesis 49: 3-4 in 4Q252, fragment 4, lines 5-7.

Third, the technical term is used to interpret a concept or biblical law, rather than a verbatim quotation of a scriptural text: 4Q180 interprets the ages of creation according to the predetermined design of God;[35] 4Q464, column 2 possibly preserves an interpretation of Abraham's promise;[36] and 4Q159, fragment 5, appears to be an interpretation of Levitical law.[37]

This brief survey shows that the technical term 'pesher' has a wider range of meanings than is often supposed.[38] Even within its

---

[31] Biblical verses are absent from 4QpHos[a] (Hos. 1: 15), 4QpIsa[b] (Isa. 5: 15-24), and 4QpIsa[c] (Isa. 9: 12 and 14: 9-25). Whether this is due to the intentional omission of the pesherists is not self-evident.

[32] So John Allegro, *DJD* v. 36. This may well be a copy of Micah rather than being originally part of a pesher on the Minor Prophets as Allegro thought.

[33] It is dangerous to draw far-reaching conclusions from such meagre fragments, but one possibility is that this is an interpretation of non-canonical texts. Alternatively, Horgan, *Pesharim*, 263, places fr. 1 of 4Q172 with 4QpPs[a].

[34] Steudel, *Midrasch zur Eschatologie*, has recently argued that the latter two are copies of a midrash on eschatology.

[35] פשר על הקצים. See Devorah Dimant, 'The Pesher on the Periods (4Q180) and 4Q181', *IOS* 9 (1979), 77-102.

[36] Esther Eshel and Michael E. Stone, 'קטע מקומראן לשון הקודש באחרית הימים לאור', *Tarbiz*, 62 (1993), 172.

[37] Allegro, *DJD* v. 9, suggests Lev. 16: 1 as a possible source text.

[38] So also Dimant, 'Pesher on the Periods', 96.

more restricted application to lemmatic commentary alone there is variety. At one end, it characterizes the well-known revelatory and fulfilment exposition of biblical prophecy of the Teacher of Righteousness, in which divine mysteries are explained by an inspired reading of scripture. This use of 'pesher' is akin to the dream interpretations of the Joseph and Daniel stories[39] and of the ancient Near East.[40] At the other end, 'pesher' means little more than 'interpretation' without any special nuance attached to the word, as in its synonomous use with the epexegetical independent pronoun in 4QIsa^b.[41] To be sure, all instances of exegesis require some process of uncovering the meaning of the biblical text, no matter how slight it may be, but it would be misleading to read the sense derived from key passages of the Habakkuk pesher into each and every occurrence.

There is another point to be made about 'pesher' as a literary genre. This sense of the word is an abstraction of Qumran scholarship. There is no evidence in the scrolls to indicate that it was the name of the genre given by the Qumran community itself for the continuous type of biblical exegesis that it practises. As mentioned, 'Midrash' is one suggested title of this interpretation, but there are good reasons to reject it. Now, it is possible that the Qumranians themselves called their commentary 'pesher', and it would be an apt title, but nowhere is there a heading or *incipit* with this technical term to be found.[42] In the absence of a title, it would be venturous to assume that there is a clearly defined literature called 'pesher' standing beside other biblical exegeses of different genres. As already noted, even within the sixteen texts designated as 'pesher' there is variety and difference. In fact, what is commonly described as 'pesher' could alternatively be understood as a collec-

---

[39] See above all, Karl Elliger, *Studien zum Habakuk-Kommentar vom Toten Meer* (Tübingen: J. C. B. Mohr (Paul Siebeck) 1953), 155: 'Seine Auslegung gründet sich also nicht auf den Text allein, sondern in noch stärkerem Maße und im entscheidenden Punkte auf eine besondere Offenbarung.'

[40] John J. Collins points to similarities with the Demotic Chronicle of the Ptolemaic period ('Jewish Apocalyptic against its Hellenistic Near Eastern Environment', *BASOR* 220 (1975), 32); and A. Leo Oppenheim, 'The Interpretation of Dreams', *TAPA* 46 (1956), 179–355.

[41] 'These are' (אלה הם) and 'it is' (היא) in col. 2 introduce the interpretation of Isa. 5: 11–14 and 5: 24–5 respectively in the same way that the earlier pesher-formula of line 1 does. Cf. Horgan's cogent arguments against the bridging function of these pronouns (*Pesharim*, 92).

[42] Cf. the numerous headings of 'rules' (סרך).

tion of multiple pesherite interpretations that comment on larger or smaller portions of the biblical texts.

This perspective allows a better appreciation of sectarian biblical commentary, for within the so-called pesher genre is a range of interpretations, some of which exhibit the oft-repeated features of revelatory fulfilment and actualization while others are no more than glosses on the words of the biblical texts. The varied characteristics of texts conventionally regarded as the pesharim may be illustrated by 4QpIsa[a-e] (4Q161-5). Of these five, the fragmentary fourth pesher (4Q164) probably conforms most nearly to the typical view of pesherite exegesis. Fragment 1, lines 1-5. read:

I shall establish you[43] *in sapphi [res]* (Isa. 54: 11) [The interpretation of the verse is (l. 2) tha]t they established the council of the community [among] the priests and peop[le]. (mutilated end of line) (l. 3) the congregation of his chosen ones as a stone of sapphire among the stones. [*And I shall set*] (l. 4) *all your battlements of agate* (Isa. 54: 12).[44] Its interpretation concerns (פשרו על) the twelve [men in the council of the community] (l. 5) who enlighten by the decision of the Urim and Thumim [   ].

Here, the restoration of Jerusalem after the Exile is interpreted to have been fulfilled in the establishment of the council of the community (עצת היחד), known in 1QS 8. 1 to have been composed of twelve men and three priests. The Qumran community as the living Temple of men is seen to be the fulfilment of Second Isaiah's admonition that Jerusalem recognizes the rebuilding programme of Darius in her midst. This concept has close affinities to the notion of the New Jerusalem and a return to Paradise in Ezekiel (cf. 28: 15-30; 48: 30-4) and Revelation, the latter's vision of which also includes precious foundation stones (21: 18-21). It is an exegesis that is commonly described as 'actualization' or perhaps more meaningfully in English 'contemporization'.

Not all of the commentaries on Isaiah, however, interpret their biblical texts in the way of 4QpIsa[d]. Compared to other pesharim, the ones to Isaiah (4Q164 excepted) quote on the whole longer passages of the biblical text. Moreover, the commentary of 4Q162-3 and 4Q165 is slight and little more than a gloss on the texts. Thus, for example, in 4QpIsa[b], column 2, those who seek

---

[43] Lit. 'I have established you' (as MT), but understood as a future. The corrected reading of 1QIsa[a], ויסדותיך, 'your foundations', is supported by the LXX (τὰ θεμέλιά σου).

[44] 'All' is not found elsewhere.

strong drink and pleasure of Isaiah 5: 11–14 are simply identified with 'the scoffers who are in Jerusalem'. The exegetical technique seems to be no more than 'this is that'.

Pesherite exegesis not only varies from one pesher to the next, but there are also differences to be found within a single commentary. For example, 4QpPs^a (4Q171) is one of the key texts for deciphering coded historical allusions to the Pharisees, Sadducees, Wicked Priest, and Teacher of Righteousness. Selections from its commentary are often quoted in order to illustrate the 'pesher' method. Yet its exegesis, say in column 4, varies from the identification of the 'wicked' and 'righteous' of Psalm 37: 32–3 with the 'Wicked Priest' who attempts to murder the 'Teacher of Righteousness' to the mere paraphrase of Psalm 37: 39. Even in the Habakkuk Pesher, whose *loci classici* are regularly displayed when the subject of Qumran exegesis is raised, the last half of columns 12 and 13 are no more than glosses on the woes against idolatry of Habakkuk 2: 18–20.

It is uncertain why the variety of pesherite exegesis is not more apparent in scholarly discussions. Presumably it is because standard treatments in handbooks and dictionary articles often emphasize what is distinctive about pesherite exegesis. A more comprehensive view, however, would require that both its highlights and more mundane aspects be recognized.

PESHERESQUE

Whether in its more florid or plain form, pesherite exegesis shares features with other bible exegesis of the Second Temple period, not least of which is Paul's interpretation of what he describes as 'the old testament' (παλαιὰ διαθήκη, 2 Cor. 3: 14; cf. Rom. 7: 6). As is frequently pointed out, Daniel's interpretations of Nebuchadnezzar and Belshazzar's dreams have close affinities to pesherite exegesis, particularly in their use of the Aramaic terms פשר and רז. In verses 24–8 of chapter 5, the dream even involves an inscription with the enigmatic 'mene, mene, teqel and parsin', which Daniel interprets to mean that God has numbered (מנה) the days of Belshazzar's kingdom, has weighed him (תקילתה) in balances, and has divided (פריסת) the kingdom and handed it over to the Persians (פרס). The lexical play, although etymologically debatable, is similar to the well-known exegetical turns of scriptural texts in the pesharim.

Moreover, in Daniel 2: 29-30, it is said that both the dream of the statue of metals and clay and its interpretation have been divinely revealed. God has made known to Nebuchadnezzar 'what is to be', which further requires a revelatory interpretation (פשרא) by the seer. In the vision of the Ancient of Days in chapter 7, however, it was Daniel who saw the vision and one of the multitude who interpreted for him these matters.

Daniel stands in the tradition of the oneirocritical interpreters of the ancient Near East, the striking biblical parallel of which is to be found in Joseph and his interpretation of dreams in prison and in Pharaoh's household (Gen. 40-1). In a manner similar to Daniel's interpretation of the Babylonian kings' dreams, Joseph reveals the hidden meanings of the visions to the chief butler, chief baker, and Egyptian ruler, the confirmation of whose interpretation (פתרון) is to be found in the fulfilment of the events: the butler is restored to his position; the baker is hanged; and seven years of famine followed seven years of plenty in the land. Furthermore, the ability to interpret dreams is attributed to the revelatory work of God, formulated here as a man 'in whom the spirit of God (רוח אלהים) is to be found (Gen. 41: 38)'.

The relationship on the one hand between Daniel and Joseph's dream interpretations and on the other the pesharim may be further strengthened if the Qumran-Essene identification be admitted. Josephus relates how a certain Simon the Essene correctly interpreted the ears of corn (nine in *BJ* 2. 113 (3), but ten in *AJ* 17. 345 (3)) to be the number of years of Archelaus' reign and the feeding oxen to represent pain and political turmoil for the ethnarch. This episode in his narrative is clearly dependent upon Genesis, but it is nevertheless significant that Josephus knew of Essenes who interpreted dreams.

The manifest similarities between dream interpretations and pesherite exegesis cannot be denied: both are dependent upon revelation and fulfilment of the events while similar techniques of lexical play and atomization are applied.[45] Nevertheless, it should be noted that apart from the inscription in Daniel 5, these interpret visions and images rather than texts and words. In so far as they

---

[45] See Lou H. Silberman, 'Unriddling the Riddle: A Study in the Structure and Language of the Habakkuk Pesher', *RQ* 3 (1961), 323-64, and recently Maren Ruth Niehoff, 'A Dream Which is not Interpreted is Like a Letter Which is not Read', *JJS* 43 (1992), 58-84, on the affinities with the Petirah Midrashim.

do so, they are related to other visionary explications such as those found in the Book of Revelation. For example, the mystery of the seven stars and lampstands are explained as the seven angels and churches (1: 20). Or again, the seven heads of the beasts are identified with the seven hills traditionally thought to have surrounded Rome as well as the seven kings of the past, present, and future (17: 9-10). This latter passage shows that John understood the same vision to have contained several meanings, just as the pesherists considered their scriptural texts to be multivalent (e.g. the triple interpretation of Hab. 1: 5 in 1QpHab 2).

Pesherite exegesis *strictu sensu* requires the technical term 'pesher' in its interpretative formula. The characteristics of its exegesis, however, are not unique. Both its revelatory and fulfilment orientation and exegetical techniques (e.g. atomization) can be found elsewhere, especially but not exclusively in dream interpretations and apocalypses.[46] Within the Qumran scrolls themselves, there are exegetical passages, while not containing the technical term 'pesher', are indistinguishable from those that are so marked. A good illustration of this can now be found in 4Q252, one of the most fascinating texts to have emerged from the recent release of unpublished scrolls.

4Q252 is a fragmentary, though substantial, text of six columns that selects and comments on passages from Genesis 6-9, 11, 15, 18, 22, 28, 36, and 49.[47] It begins with a chronology of the Flood story that dates key events according to the 364-day solar calendar: 'In the four hundred and eightieth year of Noah's life their end was made known (lit. "came") to Noah, and God said, "My spirit will not dwell in man for ever". And their days were determined to be one hundred and twenty years until the end of the waters of the Flood.' The rest of column 1 and beginning of column 2 enumerate the precise dating of the opening of the

---

[46] e.g. 'et quoniam vidisti . . . haec est interpretatio'. See Michael Knibb, 'Apocalyptic and Wisdom in 4 Ezra', *JSJ* 13 (1982), 71; and Florentino García Martínez, 'Traditions communes dans le *IVᵉ Esdras* et dans les Mss de Qumrân', *RQ* 15 (1991), 290-1.

[47] See among many others, John Allegro, 'Further Messianic References in Qumran Literature' *JBL* 75 (1956), 174-5; Hartmut Stegemann, 'Weitere Stücke von 4Qp Psalm 37, von 4 Q Patriarchal Blessings und Hinweis auf eine unedierte Handschrift aus Höhle 4Q mit Exzerpten aus dem Deuteronomium', *RQ* 6 (1967-9), 193-227; my 'Chronology of the Flood Story in a Qumran Text (4Q252)', *JJS* 43 (1992), 289-90; and George J. Brooke, 'The Thematic Content of 4Q252', *JQR* 85 (1994), 33-59.

windows of heaven, the forty days and nights of rain, the 150 days of mighty waters, the resting of the ark on Mt. Ararat, the abating of the waters, the three flights of the dove, and the disembarking of the animals.[48] The revelation of the proper times and days of the Flood is expressed in terms reminiscent of biblical prophecy: 'their end (קצם) came to Noah'. The Qumran commentator believed that God had revealed to Noah the appointed end (קץ) of all flesh when he declared that His spirit would not dwell in man for ever. Apparently, not only were the exact years, days of the months and weekdays made known to Noah at that time, but the Qumran commentator too, writing in his own day, knew these precise calculations of the events of the Flood.[49]

4Q252 does not itself explain why it was important to date precisely the events of the Flood, but in CD 2–3 it is stated that God had revealed to the remnant His holy sabbaths and glorious feast, so that they will not go astray in the way of all Israel. The proper observation of sabbaths and feasts presupposes correct calendrical calculations, including the events of the Flood story.[50] The genre of 4Q252 will be further discussed in the subsequent section on Paul's use of biblical excerpts. It will suffice to note here how the seemingly neutral chronology of the Flood story may be used in a polemical context about the calendar.

What is more germane for the present examination of the relationship between pesherite exegesis and other biblical commentaries are two passages from 4Q252, one containing the technical term while the other does not, but both may be described as 'pesherite' in the way that they interpret scripture. In column 4, lines 3–6, Jacob's blessing of Reuben found in Genesis 49. 3–4 is cited, followed by an interpretative pesher formula, and commentary.

(l.3) The blessings of Jacob: *Reuben, you are my first-born* (l. 4) *and the first fruit of my strength, exceeding in destruction and exceeding in power. Unstable as water, you shall no longer exceed,* (because) *you went up to* (l. 5) *your father's bed. Then you defiled it. On his couch you went up.* [vacat] Its interpretation is that (פשרו אשר) he reproved him for (l. 6) having lain with Bilhah his concubine. And he said, *you are my first-born* [ ] Reuben, he was (l. 7) the first fruit [ ]

---

[48] 'Chronology of the Flood Story'.

[49] The sectarian character of the text is revealed in its terminology (namely היחד, 'Chronology of the Flood Story', 295).

[50] Joseph Baumgarten, *Studies in Qumran Law* (Leiden: E. J. Brill, 1977), 108–9.

The structure of lemma plus commentary, followed by re-citation of a portion ('you are my first-born') of the scriptural text is reminiscent of the pesharim. The interpretative formula, incorporating the technical term 'pesher', introduces a commentary that explains why Reuben will no longer be pre-eminent, since he defiled his father's bed by having sexual intercourse with Jacob's concubine, Bilhah. The reference to Genesis 35: 22 here shows how the Qumran exegete explained one scriptural passage with another, a harmonizing practice found elsewhere, especially in the so-called 'rewritten bibles' genre.

In column 5, the commentary on Genesis 49: 10 does not include an introductory formula with the technical term, but the style of its interpretation, both in its structure and content, is similar to what is often regarded as typical pesher exegesis.

(l. 1) *A ruler shall [not] depart from the tribe of Judah* (Gen. 49: 10). When Israel will have the dominion, one sitting in it (i.e. the throne) for David (l. 2) wil[l not] be cut off. For *the staff* is (היא) the covenant of the kingdom, (l. 3) the [cl]ans of Israel are (המה) *the feet*, until the coming of the messiah of righteousness, the scion of (l. 4) David. For to him and his seed has been given the covenant of the kingdom of his people for eternal generations (l. 5) which he kept [ ] the torah with the men of the community for (l. 6) [ ] it is the assembly of the men (l. 7) [ ] he gave [ ]

Previously known as 4QPatriarchal Blessing, the text begins with the quotation of the first half of Genesis 49: 10, the interpretation of which is a paraphrase that also corresponds to Jeremiah 33: 17 ('David shall never lack a man to sit on the throne of the house of Israel'). A messianic interpretation then follows, though the rest of verse 10 is nowhere preserved.

In the MT, it reads: 'nor the staff from between his feet, until Shiloh comes and to him will be the obedience of the people'. The interpretation equates the two key words, 'the staff' (מחקק) and 'the feet' (הרגלים),[51] with the 'covenant of the kingdom' and 'clans of Israel' respectively. Moreover, it sees in the words 'he who will come' (עד כי יבא) a pregnant messianic prophecy. 'Shiloh' (שילה), commonly translated as 'to whom it belongs', is understood to be the coming of the messiah of righteousness, the scion of David. In

---

[51] Geza Vermes, *DSSE*, 302, reports that George Brooke reads דגליו 'his divisions' with the Samaritan Pentateuch.

rabbinic literature 'Shiloh' is understood as a name for the messiah and this is the tradition that is being drawn here.[52]

Structurally, the lemma followed by the comment is not dissimilar to the pesherite pattern. If Genesis 49: 10b-d were indeed absent from the commentary rather than mutilated, then its interpretation without prior citation is distinctive. In any case, the subsumed lemma is quartered and the key words of 'the staff' and 'the feet' are atomized in the way of pesherite interpretation. In terms of content, column 5 is also related to sectarian interpretation in explicitly mentioning 'men of the community' (אנשי היחד). Further, the figure of the messiah of righteousness may plausibly be identified with the interpreter of the law who arises with the branch of David, known from sectarian documents.[53]

When 'the pesher' is analysed and compared to other biblical interpretations of the Second Temple period, it is undeniable that many of its features, if not all, may also be found elsewhere.[54] Whether they be other Qumran scrolls, Daniel, Genesis, or Revelation, there are parallels to be drawn that do not necessarily include the technical term 'pesher' or its semantic equivalent. The literary genre of 'pesher' is distinctive in the way that it follows larger or smaller sections of the biblical text and uses the technical term in its interpretative formulae. Its exegetical features, however, are not unique. Many interpretative techniques and strategies that do not include the technical term may be described as pesheresque, if one so chooses.

CONCLUSIONS

Pauline exegesis may be compared to the pesherite interpretation of the Qumran scrolls. While formal distinctions between the two should not be ignored, and the pesher as a genre is *sui generis*, they nevertheless manifest commonalities that cannot be denied. The existence of 'Midrash pesher', however, is based upon a dubious reading of 4Q174 and this alleged hybrid genre should, in our opinion, be left out of a discussion of pesherite or Pauline exegeses.

[52] In *Tg. Onk.*, *Gen. Rab.*, and *b. Sanh.* 98B (John J. Collins, *The Scepter and the Star: The Messiahs of the Dead Sea Scrolls and Other Ancient Literature* (New York: Doubleday, 1995), 62-3).

[53] Ibid.

[54] See e.g. *Barn.* 6. 18-19 on Gen. 1: 28 and 9: 8 on Gen. 14: 14 and 17: 23.

9
Paul and his Old Testament Quotations

The overlap with pesherite techniques, suggested above, leads to the question of whether Paul too altered his biblical texts in the manner of the Qumran commentaries. Before answering this, however, it must be asked from the outset whether, or perhaps more suitably in view of the history of scholarship, where such exegetical alterations in the Pauline letters may be found. Study of Pauline modification of the Old Testment quotations has been a long-standing issue in New Testament research; more than once have the biblical passages been collated and analyzed.[1] The need to re-examine them now stems from the greater awareness of textual variety and the blurring of Hebrew and Greek linguistic boundaries that traditionally separate the text-types of the MT, SP, and LXX.

ON 'SEPTUAGINTAL'

As mentioned in Chapter 2, greater caution must be exercised in describing biblical quotations in the Pauline letters as a whole to be septuagintal, since such a textual characterization assumes that

---

[1] Still the most comprehensive of which is Dietrich Alex Koch, *Die Schrift als Zeuge des Evangeliums: Untersuchungen zur Verwendung und zum Verständnis der Schrift bei Paulus* (Tübingen: J. C. B. Mohr (Paul Siebeck), 1986). Other post-Qumran studies include, E. Earle Ellis, *Paul's Use of the Old Testament* (London: Oliver & Boyd, 1957); Richard N. Longenecker, *Biblical Exegesis in the Apostolic Period* (Grand Rapids, Mich.: Eerdmans, 1975); D. Moody Smith, 'The Use of the Old Testament in the New', in James M. Efird (ed.), *The Use of the Old Testament in the New and Other Essays: Studies in Honor of William Franklin Stinespring* (Durham, NC: Duke University Press, 1972), 3–65; Christopher D. Stanley, *Paul and the Language of Scripture: Citation Technique in the Pauline Epistles and Contemporary Literature* (Cambridge: Cambridge University Press, 1992); and Moisés Silva, 'Old Testament in Paul', in G. F. Hawthorne and R. P. Martin (eds.), *Dictionary of Paul and his Letters* (Leicester: InterVarsity Press, 1993), 630–42. Also notable is Richard Hays's study of intertextuality and biblical allusions in *Echoes of Scripture in the Letters of Paul* (New Haven, Conn.: Yale University Press, 1989).

the citations agree with the Septuagint over and against the MT, Samaritan, and all other text-types and recensions. To be distinctively septuagintal, as is often claimed, the cited verse or individual reading should agree with the LXX in those passages where the Septuagint differs from all other text-types. The reasoning should not simply be that a Pauline reading agrees word for word with a printed edition of the Septuagint that is being used for comparison.

For example, in his classic and still influential treatment[2] of the Septuagint, *An Introduction to the Old Testament in Greek*, H. B. Swete states that '(m)ore than half of the direct quotations from the O.T. in the Epistles of St. Paul are taken from the LXX, without material change'.[3] A spot check of the list that he provides shows that Swete bases his textual characterization primarily upon the verbal agreement between the Pauline quotations and LXX. The MT is not considered for the most part. Thus, for instance, the passage from Psalm 43: 23 in Romans 8: 36 is cited by Swete as having been drawn from the Septuagint. But in what sense is it septuagintal? The quotation reads: ἕνεκεν σοῦ θανατούμεθα ὅλην τὴν ἡμέραν ἐλογίσθημεν ὡς πρόβατα σφαγῆς 'on account of you we are being put to death all day long, we are considered as sheep of slaughter'. Compared to the Göttingen edition edited by Rahlfs, published in 1931, which was not available to Swete, the Pauline quotation differs only slightly in the use of the atticistic form of ἕνεκα. The textual characterization of 'septuagintal', however, is questionable if the MT is also compared: כי עליך הרגנו כל היום נחשבנו כצאן טבחה. Even if the כי ('for') of the MT be considered a plus, a view that is by no means necessary given ὅτι in Romans 8: 36,[4] the Hebrew text along with the Septuagint and Pauline citation exhibits a uniform textual tradition. The pu'al perfect הרגנו signifying physical state is aptly translated into Greek by the present passive θανατούμεθα, rendered in English by the continuous present 'we are being put to death'.

Swete lists the quotation of Romans 8: 36 as one which has been drawn from the Septuagint without material change, and

---

[2] Ellis, in his widely read study *Paul's Use of the Old Testament*, 12, cites Swete's description with favour.

[3] (Cambridge: Cambridge University Press, 1900), 400.

[4] This particle is either understood to be part of the introductory formula (καθὼς γέγραπται ὅτι) or biblical quotation agreeing with the MT (so Joseph A. Fitzmyer, *Romans* (Garden City, NY: Doubleday, 1992), 534).

strictly speaking that is not incorrect, but the comparison with the MT shows that such a statement is only partially true. Verse 23 of Psalm 43 does indeed agree closely with the LXX or Old Greek, so far as it is reconstructed, but it does not do so exclusively. The MT, too, textually agrees with the Pauline quotation. It is septuagintal only in the more limited sense that it is also attested by the LXX. It is likely, given their verbal similarity, that Paul quoted from a manuscript of 'the Septuagint', but the lemma is not 'septuagintal' in the sense that it is textually distinctive from the MT.

Textual comparison of the Pauline lemma should be carried out not only with extant witnesses written in Greek, but also with Hebrew sources. This point needs to be underscored since it is seldom paid its due attention in scholarship. If textual characterization of this type is carried out on the one hundred or so explicit quotations in the Pauline corpus, it can scarcely be said that Paul used primarily septuagintal biblical texts over and against the MT.[5] To be sure many of the Pauline lemmata agree almost verbatim with the Göttingen, Cambridge, and Rahlfs editions, but such agreements are characteristically septuagintal only when the textual traditions diverge at those relevant passages.

PERCENTAGE OF EXEGETICAL MODIFICATIONS?

Recognition of textual diversity among the biblical texts of this period and the presence of variants for each biblical verse means that it is now difficult to know whether Paul himself has changed the words of his scriptural quotations or whether he has simply cited an extant variant. If the latter, then no unwarranted reshaping of the words of holy scripture can be imputed to him and the theological question would rather turn on the authoritative issue of competing versions of the same biblical text. Paul, however, is a man of his time and it is unlikely that he considered every jot and tittle of his biblical texts to be immutable. Showing such modifications is the real task at hand.

Given these considerations, it is not without some surprise to

---

[5] A rough classification, based upon previous work, of the 102 passages (including those found in 1 and 2 Timothy and Ephesians) is provided by Silva, 'Old Testament in Paul', 631. Of these only seventeen are distinctively Septuagintal. Forty-two passages show that Paul, LXX, and MT share the common text. Stanley, *Paul and the Language of Scripture*, 67, however, claims that some 44/83 or 53% of the Pauline quotations in the *Hauptbriefe* agree with the Septuagint against the MT.

encounter statistically precise figures being offered by recent studies. Dietrich-Alex Koch's *magnum opus*, a work that has otherwise much to commend it, concludes that fifty-two out of ninety-three or 56 per cent of the Pauline citations show multiple modifications, and twelve out of ninety-three, or 13 per cent, have been modified three or more times.[6] Such precisions are at the very least incompatible with the nature of the evidence and the pluriform textual picture that has emerged with the discovery and study of the Qumran biblical texts.[7]

Is textual diversity of the biblical texts not also evident in the New Testament generally and Pauline letters specifically? Students of the New Testament are often struck by the divergence of the biblical lemmata in the writings of the Early Church, but explanations for such variance do not, apart from the odd reference to the MT, venture beyond the Septuagint or its inner development.[8] A discussion of selected passages will illustrate the difference in perspectives and highlight the contribution of Qumran biblical texts to the study of New Testament and Pauline biblical quotations.

Isaiah 40 in 1 Peter 1: 24–5 and 1QIsa^a

An example of both the blurring of the linguistic divide that separates the text-types and the textual diversity of New Testament biblical quotations is to be found in the quotation of Isaiah 40: 6–8 in 1 Peter 1: 24–5:

> πᾶσα σὰρξ ὡς χόρτος,
>   καὶ πᾶσα δόξα αὐτῆς ὡς ἄνθος χόρτου
> ἐξηράνθη ὁ χόρτος καὶ τὸ ἄνθος ἐξέπεσεν
> τὸ δὲ ῥῆμα κυρίου μένει εἰς τὸν αἰῶνα

> All flesh is as grass
>   and all its glory as the flower of the field (lit. grass)
> the grass withers and the flower falls off,
>   but the word of the Lord remains for ever.

---

[6] *Schrift als Zeuge*, 186–90. To a lesser degree Stanley, *Paul and the Language of Scripture*, 348–50.

[7] A critique of Koch's textual study is found on pp. 109–28 of my D.Phil. diss., 'Attitudes to Holy Scripture in the Qumran Pesharim and Pauline Letters', Oxford, 1991.

[8] The most sophisticated study of which is Koch, *Schrift als Zeuge*, 1–230, 247–56, who suggests a pre-Pauline recension similar to the proto-Theodotion textual tradition found at Nahal Hever. The issues, however, are more complex than he allows.

Here, the abiding word of Yahweh in Second Isaiah is identified with the good news that was preached to the Christians in the dispersion, a contemporizing exegetical move that is not dissimilar to the pesherite application of biblical prophecy to the Qumran community. Notwithstanding minor differences, the biblical quotation is regarded on account of its shorter reading to be Septuagintal.[9] Compared to the MT, neither the LXX nor 1 Peter attests to v. 7: 'the grass withers, the flower fades for the breath of the Lord blows upon it'. In the Great Isaiah Scroll, there is now confirmation of the shorter Isaiah 40: 6–8 of the LXX and 1 Peter. On plate XXXIII, lines 6 and 7, of 1QIsaᵃ the first scribe wrote:[10]

כול הבשר חציר (l. 6)
וכול חסדיו כציץ (l. 7) השדה
יבש חציר נבל ציץ
ודבר אלוהינו יקום לעולם

(1.6) All flesh is grass
    and all of its loveliness as the flower of (l. 7) the field
grass withers, a flower fades[11]
    but the word of our God will remain for ever.

The main differences[12] between the Petrine quotation and Qumran text are: (1) for 'all its loveliness' (חסדיו[13]) the lemma reads 'all its glory', and (2) the word of 'our God' becomes that of 'the Lord'.

They are, however, shorter in comparison to the MT and the corrector of 1QIsaᵃ who adds 'for the spirit of the Lord breathes upon it' (נשבה בוא . . . כי רוח) between lines 6 and 7, and 'grass withers, a flower fades, but the word of our God' (יבש חציר נבל ציץ ודבר אלוהינו) down the side of the left-hand margin.[14]

[9] So e.g. E. G. Selwyn, *First Epistle of St. Peter*, 2nd edn. (London: Macmillan and Co., 1947), 152: 'the deviations from the LXX are unimportant . . .'.

[10] Millar Burrows, John C. Trever, and William H. Brownlee, *The Dead Sea Scrolls of St. Mark's Monastery*, i. *The Isaiah Manuscript and the Habakkuk Pesher* (New Haven: American Schools of Oriental Research, 1950).

[11] Or 'falls off'.

[12] Both the Petrine quotation and the LXX use χόρτος for translating the closely related Hebrew terms of 'grass' (חציר) and 'field' (השדה).

[13] The MT has the singular suffix, חסדו, and the usual meaning of the noun is 'goodness', 'kindness', or 'piety'. The translation of 'loveliness' suggested by *BDB* is based upon context. The LXX translates it as δόξα ἀνθρωπέπον. The critical apparatus of *BHS* accordingly suggests emending it to הדרו 'its glory' or חמדו 'its delight'.

[14] The differences in script, orthography, and representation of the tetragram clearly indicate that the second was also a different hand by the scribe who, it is believed, also copied 1QS, 1QSa, 1QSb, and 4QTest.

The MT reads in verses 6–8:

(v. 6) כול הבשר חציר
וכול חסדו כציץ השדה
(v. 7) יבש חציר נבל ציץ
כי רוח יהוה נשבה בו אכן חציר העם
(v. 8) יבש חציר נבל ציץ
ודבר אלוהינו יקום לעולם

(v. 6) All flesh is grass
    and all of its loveliness as the flower of the field.
(v. 7) Grass withers, a flower fades,
    because the spirit of the Lord breathes upon it.
    Surely 'grass' is 'the people'.
(v. 8) Grass withers, a flower fades,
    but the word of our God will remain forever.

Clearly, the original scribe who was copying 1QIsa[a] wrote what are equivalent to verses 6 and 8. Verse 7 has at its head a phrase about the temporal character of nature that is identical to the beginning of verse 8. It is likely that a scribal error of *parablepsis*, the eye skipping from the beginning of verse 7 to the subsequent verse 8, is responsible for the shorter text. Whether the original scribe of 1QIsa[a] himself made this mistake or was simply copying out a *Vorlage* which already contained this error is not clear. If the former, then he was ultimately responsible for the shorter text which also appears in the LXX and 1 Peter. The latter case would assume that that scribal error occurred earlier in the textual transmission.

A second, different scribe corrected the error by inserting the missing phrases between the lines and along the margin. This second scribe evidently read 'a grass withers, a flower fades' (יבש חציר נבל ציץ) of line 7, not as part of verse 8, but the beginning of verse 7. He then inserted interlinearly 'for the spirit of the Lord breathes upon it' above 'but the word' (ודבר), precisely at that point where verses 7 and 8 differ. Realizing that he needed another phrase about the withering grass and fading flower, he wrote 'grass withers, a flower fades, but the word of our God' (יבש חציר נבל ציץ ודבר אלוהינו) down the left-hand margin, repeating 'but the word of our God' which he cancelled by the indication of four sublinear dots. At this point the reader of 1QIsa[a] will have to return to the line to read the complementary verbal clause 'will remain forever' (יקום לעולם). This is finally followed by a further scribal addition of the gloss 'surely "grass" is "the people"'.

The biblical quotation of 1 Peter agrees with the uncorrected text of 1QIsa[a]. They, together with the LXX, are shorter than the MT and the corrected version. Moreover, they do not attest to the gloss. It is not surprising that revisions of the LXX also included these pluses from the MT. In any case, what was once regarded as a septuagintal quotation in 1 Peter 1: 24–5 has now turned up in a Hebrew manuscript of Isaiah,[15] which has been characterized by some to be proto-Masoretic and others as one of its late descendants.[16]

Some Pauline Variants

Turning to the Pauline letters, a discussion of selected passages will illustrate the complexities of the issues in identifying exegetical variants.

Romans 10: 20 belongs to the catena of biblical quotations that condemn Israel's failure to respond to God's call. Here, a biblical proof-text from Isaiah 65: 1 is adduced to prove that even Gentiles understood the Gospel message. The verse reads:

εὑρέθην ἐν τοῖς ἐμὲ μὴ ζητοῦσιν,
ἐμφανὴς ἐγενόμην τοῖς ἐμὲ μὴ ἐπερωτῶσιν

I was found by those who did not seek me.
I have shown myself to those who did not ask for me.

Compared to the LXX, it would appear that the phrase 'I was found' and 'I have shown myself' are reversed, since they otherwise agree verbally. The LXX reads:

ἐμφανὴς ἐγενόμην τοῖς ἐμὲ μὴ ζητοῦσιν
εὑρέθην τοῖς ἐμὲ μὴ ἐπερωτῶσιν

The MT confirms this explanation:

נדרשתי ללוא שאלו נמצאתי ללא בקשני

I have allowed myself to be sought by those who have not asked.
I have been found by those who did not seek me.

---

[15] Noted already by E. Y. Kutscher, *The Language and Linguistic Background of the Isaiah Scroll (1QIsa A)*, Eng. trans. (Leiden: E. J. Brill), 556, but without reference to the New Testament.
[16] Kutscher, *Language and Linguistic Background*, 2–3. Emanuel Tov, *Textual Criticism of the Hebrew Bible* (Minneapolis: Fortress Press, 1992), 115, characterizes it as a text written in the Qumran practice.

Whether Paul himself modified his biblical text here[17] or simply used a different text is debatable. If the former, then it may be asked why no emphasis is placed upon the notion of 'finding' in the latter half of Romans 10.[18]

In the MT, the phrase 'who have not asked' requires an object when compared to the parallel 'who did not seek me'. The LXX makes explicit the implied first person object and it could be argued that the Pauline quotation is septuagintal in attesting to 'me'. 1QIsa[a] again shows that such a characterization is simplistic when it supplies the object: ללוא שאלוני, 'by those who have not asked for me'.

The contribution of 1QIsa[a] to the quotation of Isaiah 65: 1 in Romans 10: 20 raises fundamental questions about the textual characteristics of the Pauline biblical quotations and the way that they are analysed. It is no longer primarily an inner-Greek or septuagintal matter. The far-reaching implication is that biblical texts written in the Hebrew language must be given full consideration in the evaluation of Pauline citations.[19]

Another example from Romans will illustrate this broadening of the exegetical and textual horizons. In Romans 12: 19, Paul quotes Deuteronomy 32: 35: $\dot{\epsilon}\mu o\grave{\iota}$ $\dot{\epsilon}\kappa\delta\acute{\iota}\kappa\eta\sigma\iota\varsigma$, $\dot{\epsilon}\gamma\grave{\omega}$ $\dot{\alpha}\nu\tau\alpha\pi o\delta\acute{\omega}\sigma\omega$ ('vengeance is mine, I will repay'). As has been previously noted, this citation differs from the LXX in its initial phrase ($\dot{\epsilon}\nu$ $\dot{\eta}\mu\acute{\epsilon}\rho\alpha$ $\dot{\epsilon}\kappa\delta\iota\kappa\acute{\eta}\sigma\epsilon\omega\varsigma$ $\dot{\alpha}\nu\tau\alpha\pi o\delta\acute{\omega}\sigma\omega$, 'in the day of vengeance, I shall repay'), but agrees with it in the latter. The LXX presumes a reading such as ליום נקם, as attested in the SP. Conversely, the Pauline lemma agrees with the MT in its first phrase and disagrees with it in the latter: לי נקם ושׁלם, 'vengeance is mine, and he has repaid'.[20] Hebrews 10: 30 agrees entirely with the Pauline quotation and it may well be that the two together attest to a different translation of the Hebrew original.[21]

If the quotation is considered within its historical context, however, an alternative explanation of the Pauline reading emerges.

[17] Fitzmyer, *Romans*, 600.
[18] So Stanley, *Paul and the Language of Scripture*, 145.
[19] See e.g. אתם ('with them') of 1QIsa[a] against the MT אותם ('them') as attesting to the $\alpha\dot{\upsilon}\tau o\hat{\iota}\varsigma$ of Isa. 59: 20 in the LXX and Rom. 11: 26–7.
[20] *GKC* 520, however, renders it contextually as a substantive, 'recompense'.
[21] So also, Harold Attridge, *Hebrews* (Philadelphia: Fortress Press, 1989), 295 n. 62, who further argues for a corruption in the original Hebrew from ליום נקם to לי נקם.

Exemplars of biblical texts from Qumran are uniformly unpointed. This means that an ancient exegete or translator who encounters a consonantal cluster such as שלם need not read it as the pi'el third person masculine perfect. He could vocalize it as a pi'el infinitive שַׁלֵּם that complements the first person of 'vengeance is mine'. Thus, *Targum Onkelos* (אֲנָא אִישַׁלֵּם) and *Fragmentary Targum* (דהשלם אֲנָא הִיא) translate the word to the first person singular in the Aramaic. Paul or a Greek translator before him could have interpreted שלם likewise and translated it as ἀνταποδώσω, 'I will repay'.[22]

Of course, it is theoretically possible that the LXX, Paul, Hebrews, and the targumim all had a Hebrew *Vorlage* of the first person imperfect of pi'el, אשלם,[23] but there is no need to suppose this unattested Hebrew variant when the unpointed combination of consonants could read as an infinitive with an implied subject: 'vengeance is mine and (it is mine) to repay'. It is easy to see how such a reading could develop into 'vengeance is mine, I will repay'.

Reference to the MT or Qumran biblical manuscripts written in Hebrew is essential if the Pauline variants are to be properly evaluated, for once it is recalled that Paul was a polylingual Jew of the Graeco-Roman world, fluent or at least competent in Hebrew, Aramaic, and Greek, there opens up a range of possibilities beyond the intra-Greek developments of the Septuagint and its revisions.

One final example from Romans will illustrate how the post-Qumran perspective increases the complexities of studying Pauline exegetical modifications. In the well-known passages in Romans 9: 33, where Yahweh's laying of the precious stone on Zion (Isa. 28: 16) is combined with the Christologically interpreted notion of stumbling block (Isa. 8: 14–15), consideration of the readings of two Qumran biblical manuscripts helps explain the supposed exegetical variant of τίθημι, 'I am laying'.[24] The whole conflated biblical quotation of Romans 9: 33 reads:

ἰδοὺ τίθημι ἐν Σιὼν λίθον προσκόμματος
καὶ πέτραν σκανδάλου, καὶ ὁ πιστεύων ἐπ᾿ αὐτῷ[25] οὐ
καταισχυνθήσεται

---

[22] Koch, *Schrift*, 77–8, argues that the Pauline quotation is a Hebraizing revision.

[23] So Stanley, *Paul and the Language of Scripture*, 172.

[24] See e.g. Selwyn, *First Epistle of St. Peter*, 163, 272–3.

[25] Cf. James Barr, 'Paul and the LXX: A Note on Some Recent Work', *JTS* 45/2

Behold I am laying in Zion a stone of stumbling
  and a rock that causes one to trip,
but the one who believes in him
  shall not be put to shame.

For the initial verb, the LXX attests to the synonym ἐμβαλῶ. The MT is problematic in the sudden change in person: הִנְנִי יִסַּד, lit. 'behold me, he laid'. While it may be possible to construe a cryptic relative clause here ('behold, I am he (who) laid'[26]), the readings of 1QIsaᵃ (מיסד) and 1QIsaᵇ (יוסד) attest to the first person of the verbs in the LXX and Pauline quotation. The incongruity of the subjects is resolved by the participle, whether in the piʿel or qal: 'behold, I am laying'. The Septuagint's ἐμβαλῶ is one translation of the Hebrew. The Pauline τίθημι, which is also the verb of Isaiah 28: 16 in 1 Peter 2. 6, would appear to be another translation.

These examples will suffice to give an indication of the complexities in identifying Pauline modifications of biblical quotations. Statistical precisions of the kind suggested recently are apt to give a misleading impression that there is no more work to be done.[27] Quite the opposite is true: a comprehensive study of all the Pauline quotations from the perspective of textual plurality is a desideratum. A thorough study will have to be done once all the Qumran biblical scrolls have been properly edited and published.

EMBEDDED BIBLICAL *EXCERPTA*

Paul was not an inerrantist, this much is certain. Like the pesherists, he tolerated different forms of the same biblical verse and on occasion is seen to reshape the words of his lemma. Some of these exegetical variants are insubstantial (e.g. position of Ἀβραάμ (Gen. 15: 6) in Romans 4: 3 and Galatians 3: 6; the presence of ἄνθρωπος (Lev. 18: 5) in Romans 10: 5 but not in

---

(1994), 599–600, who criticizes Stanley for his neglect of the MT when evaluating the Septuagintal and recensional evidence.

[26] Cf. a discussion of this possibility in J. D. W. Watts, *Isaiah 1–33* (Waco, Tex.: Word Books, 1985), 367 n. 16a.

[27] e.g. Hays, *Echoes of Scripture*, 9, states: 'The questions that scholars have traditionally asked about Paul's use of the Old Testament have been either answered in full or played out to a dead end.'

Galatians 3: 12) while others seem to support a theological point. Again, the same biblical quotation of Isaiah 28: 16 in Romans 9: 33 is illustrative. It reads:

καὶ ὁ πιστεύων ἐπ' αὐτῷ οὐ καταισχυνθήσεται

and the one who believes in him will not be put to shame.

When he requotes the text ten verses later, he qualifies 'the one who believes' with πᾶς ('all'), it would seem in order to underscore the universal inclusion of 'Jews and Greek' in the salvific plan of the Lord (Rom. 10: 12–13).

Testimony Book Hypothesis

The Pauline toleration for variants of the same biblical verse can partly be explained by the postulate of 'testimonies' or scriptural anthologies. It has long been supposed that chains of biblical texts existed before they were included in Paul's letters. With the discovery of such biblical anthologies at Qumran it is timely to raise again the 'testimony book' theory and to show how it can help in explaining Paul's manifest tolerance for biblical variants.

It is sometimes claimed[28] that the modern conception of the testimony book hypothesis originated over a hundred years ago with Edwin Hatch's Grinfield lecture entitled 'On the Composite Quotations from the Septuagint', a paper which was published together with the other lectures of the series as *Essays in Biblical Greek.*[29] This view is misleading, since J. Rendel Harris and not Edwin Hatch was the architect of the theory that posits one lost Testimony Book against the Jews which was first compiled by Matthew, used by Paul and other New Testament writers, attested to in Papias, cited by the Church Fathers (especially Cyprian), and extant in a secondarily redacted, sixteenth-century manuscript found in the monastery of Iveron on Mount Athos.[30] The testimony book hypothesis has had few supporters and most share C. H. Dodd's reservations that Harris's theory 'outruns the evidence'.[31]

[28] e.g. Adolf Harnack, *A History of Dogma,* Eng. trans. (New York: Russell & Russell, 1958), 175 n. 1; Ellis, *Paul's Use,* 98–107; *ESBNT* 67–8.
[29] (Oxford: Clarendon Press, 1989).
[30] *Testimonies I–II* (Cambridge: Cambridge University Press, 1916, 1920).
[31] *According to the Scriptures: The Sub-Structure of New Testament Theology* (London: Nisbet, 1952), 26.

Unfortunately Hatch's own suggestion of the existence of biblical excerpts has been overshadowed by Harris's testimony book
hypothesis, even though there is much of value in his conception
of biblical *excerpta*. Hatch summarizes these ideas:

It would be improbable, even if there were no positive evidence on the
point, that the Greek-speaking Jews, who were themselves cultured, and
who lived in great centres of culture should not have had a literature of
their own. . . . It may naturally be supposed that a race which laid stress
on moral progress, whose religious services had variable elements of both
prayer and praise, and which was carrying on an active propaganda,
would have, among other books, manuals of morals, of devotion and of
controversy. It may also be supposed, if we take into consideration the
contemporary habit of making collections of *excerpta*, and the special
authority which the Jews attached to their sacred books, that some of
these manuals would consist of extracts from the Old Testament.[32]

Several points are notable here. First, Greek-speaking *Jews*, and not
Christians, were thought to have had in their possession extracts
from scripture (which Hatch inappropriately calls 'Old Testament').
This is, of course, quite different from Harris's subsequent testimony book hypothesis, where Christians were seen to possess a
book of testimonies in their controversy against the Jews. Harris
was conscious of this shift when he wrote, 'if such collections of
Testimonies on behalf of the Jews existed in early times, before the
diffusion of Christianity, then there must have been, *a fortiori*,
similar collections produced in later times, when the Christian
religion was being actively pushed by the Church in the Synagogue'.[33] What is important to underscore here is that Hatch pre-
supposed Jewish, rather than Christian, collections of biblical
verses in the string of scriptural passages that he finds in the
writings of the Early Church. For him, Christian writers had taken
over the practice of extracting verses from the Bible if not also the
very collections made by Jews in earlier times. In this connection,
it is notable that he chose 'excerpta' rather than some other theologically questionable term such as 'testimony' to describe the
phenomenon which he also finds in *1 Clement*, the *Epistle of
Barnabas*, and the *Dialogues* of Justin Martyr.

Second, Hatch proposed not only manuals of controversy used
in Jewish propaganda—whatever the truth of such activity might

[32] *Essays in Biblical Greek*, 203.
[33] *Testimonies I–II*, 2.

have been[34]—but also manuals of morals and devotion. In the catenae of biblical quotations to which he draws attention in *1 Clement* and *Barnabas*, Hatch lists biblical passages that were used for moral exhortation (on peace based on piety: *1 Clem.* 15; on good works: *1 Clem.* 34. 6; on love: *1 Clem.* 50; humility: *1 Clem.* 56; Christological teachings (on Christ's fulfilment of scripture: *1 Clem.* 22, and His passion, *Barn.* 5. 13); baptismal liturgy: *Barn.* 11; and Temple theology: Barn. 16. 2). Only selections from Justin's *Dialogue with Trypho* and his *First Apology* can be properly regarded as evidence of manuals of controversy. Justin apparently took over Jewish extracts of scriptural passages in his own argument against Trypho, the circumcised Hebrew.

Third, Hatch speaks of collections of biblical extracts and does not go so far as to propose that these were produced in book form, let alone that they were published in one book, as Harris later suggested. Finally, the textual and formal characteristics of the biblical verses varied. Some followed the LXX closely while others diverged from it (e.g. Ps. 118 (119), 21 (22) in *Barn.* 5). There were composite quotations (e.g. Dan. 7: 10 and Isa. 6: 3 in *1 Clem.* 34) and scriptural chains that lacked an overall cohesion (e.g. Ps. 117 (118), Prov. 3, and Ps. 140 (141) in *1 Clem.* 61).

Qumran Biblical Anthologies

Hatch's theory of biblical *excerpta* is preferable to the testimony book hypothesis in the way that it posits collections of biblical texts with varying textual characteristics among Jewish communities in the Second Temple period.[35] It does not suffer from the improbability of supposing that one book of these collected scriptural texts was behind the catenae of scriptural texts throughout the centuries.

Several texts discovered at Qumran support the view that Jews did indeed excerpt biblical passages. Of these, the best-known of which is 4Q175 or 4QTestimonia, a single sheet of excerpts which cite together chapters 5 and 18 of Deuteronomy (5: 28-9 and 18: 18-19), a tradition attested in the SP (at Exod. 20: 21b), Numbers

---

[34] See now, Martin D. Goodman, *Mission and Conversion: Proselytizing in the Religious History of the Roman Empire* (Oxford: Clarendon Press, 1994).

[35] Dodd's own theory of large blocks of biblical passages underlying the NT has recently been challenged by Koch who argues that as far as Paul is concerned 'The Bible of the Early Church' is 'eine Fiktion' (*Schrift als Zeuge*, 254).

24: 15–17, Deuteronomy 33: 8–11, and 4QPsJosh. The final passage does not belong to the canonical scriptures, but comprises the septuagintal lemma and an interpretation of Joshua 6: 26. It is found in fragment 22, column 2 of 4Q379, a text described by its editor as a rewritten form of Joshua.[36] Its appearance here alongside canonical texts is eloquent testimony to the way that the Qumranians considered certain extra-Biblical writings on equal footing with the canonical texts.[37]

Apart from 4Q175, there are several other texts, some of which have a manifest liturgical context (e.g. tephilin (Exod. 13: 1–10 + Deut. 5: 1–6, 9 + 10: 12–11: 21) and mezuzot (Deut. 5: 1–6, 9 + 10: 12–11: 21)),[38] while others may be characterized under broad subject headings: 4Q158 consists of pentateuchal excerpts with brief exegetical supplements; in 2QEx[b] (2Q13 fr. 8), Exodus 19: 9 immediately follows Exodus 34: 10;[39] 4QDeut[n] has been compared to the Nash Papyrus[40] and contains Deuteronomy 8: 5–10 in column 1 and Deuteronomy 5: 1–6: 1 in columns 2–6;[41] other excerpted texts of Deuteronomy are 4QDeut[j, k, l];[42] 4Q177 is a catena of Psalms, now plausibly reconstructed with 4Q175 as part of a midrash on the last days;[43] 4Q176 (4QTanh) is a text that draws together biblical passages around the theme of consolation.[44]

These excerpts lie along a continuum between the Qumran scrolls that are recognizable as biblical texts, close and freer paraphrases, and those that are clearly exegetical. Not surprisingly, it is

[36] Carol Newsom, 'The "Psalms of Joshua" from Cave 4', *JJS* 39 (1988), 58–9.
[37] See my 'The "Psalms of Joshua" (4Q379 fr. 22 col. 2): A Reconsideration of its Text', *JJS* 44 (1993), 309–12, for arguments in favour of the authoritative status of 4Q379. [38] J. T. Milik, *DJD* vi. pt. 2.
[39] So Hartmut Stegemann, 'Weitere Stücke von 4Qp Psalm 37, von 4 Q Patriarchal Blessings und Hinweis auf eine unedierte Handschrift aus Höhle 4Q mit Exzerpten aus dem Deuteronomium', *RQ* 6 (1967–9), 193–227.
[40] Ibid.
[41] Sidnie A. White, '4QDt[n]: Biblical Manuscript or Excerpted Text?', in H. W. Attridge, J. J. Collins, and T. H. Tobins (eds.), *Of Scribes and Scrolls* (New York: University Press of America, 1990), 13–20, and 'The All Souls Deuteronomy and the Decalogue', *JBL* 109 (1990), 193–206, argue for its liturgical or devotional character.
[42] Julie Duncan, 'Considerations of 4QDt[j] in Light of "All Souls Deuteronomy" and Cave 4 Phylactery Texts', in *Madrid*, i. 199–216.
[43] Annette Steudel, *Der Midrasch zur Eschatologie aus der Qumrangemeinde (4QMidrEschat[a.b]): Materielle Rekonstruktion, Textbestand, Gattung und traditionsgeschichtliche Einordnung des durch 4Q174 ('Florilegium') und 4Q177 ('Catena A') repräsentierten Werkes aus den Qumranfunden* (Leiden: E. J. Brill, 1994).
[44] John A. Allegro, *DJD* v. 60–7.

now being suggested that a number of these excerpts either underlie certain sectarian Qumran texts[45] or that they reflect a particular
textual tradition.[46]

Biblical Extracts in the Pauline Letters

It is probable that Paul too used collections of biblical texts, given
the detachable quality of many of his biblical chains embedded
within his letters (Rom. 3: 10–18; 9: 25–9; 11: 33–6; 15: 9–12;
and 2 Cor. 6: 16–18; cf. also Rom. 9: 12–13, 33; 10: 6–8,
11–13, 15–21, 18–21; 11: 8–10; 12: 19–20; Gal. 4: 27–30;
1 Cor. 3: 19–20; and 2 Cor. 9: 9–10). He or his amanuensis
either used extant anthologies or excerpted favourite biblical passages and inserted these biblical chains into the appropriate places
in the letters. The practical necessity of having handy collections of
biblical passages for reference, given the difficulties of searching for
verses through rolls or even codices, is self-evident.[47] In creating
his own anthologies he is following a practice also common in the
Graeco-Roman world.

What was problematic in previous discussions was that the
postulate of extant biblical extracts had been seen simply as the
precursor to Rendel Harris's testimony book hypothesis. As noted,
Hatch differs from Harris in a number of important respects and
his views have the further advantage of avoiding the anachronistic
designation of 'testimony book'—a title which is borrowed from
Cyprian's *ad Quirinum: Testimoniorum libri tres*[48]—and of supporting the unlikely thesis that one book of biblical proof-texts had
such influence throughout the centuries.

---

[45] Joseph M. Baumgarten, 'A "Scriptural" Citation in 4QFragments of the
Damascus Document', *JJS* 43 (1992), 95–8, argues that the quotations of Deut. 30:
4 and Lev. 26: 31 in 4Q266 and 4Q270 were created by the exegete.

[46] Emanuel Tov, 'Groups of Biblical Texts found at Qumran' in D. Dimant and
L. H. Schiffman (eds.), *Time to Prepare the Way in the Wilderness: Papers on the
Qumran Scrolls* (Leiden: E. J. Brill, 1995), 85, suggests that Deut. 33 of 4Q175 is
quoted from 4QDeut^h.

[47] T. C. Skeat's observation that a codex-format would be no easier than a roll for
locating a passage is true only for surveying texts within four or five columns
('Early Christian Book-Production: Papyri and Manuscripts', in *CHB* ii. 70). It does
not account for distant passages in a long biblical book (e.g. Isaiah) nor for cross-
referencing between books.

[48] It would seem that F. C. Burkitt, *The Gospel History and its Transmission*
(Edinburgh: T. & T. Clark, 1907), 128, was the first to use this term: 'the First
Evangelist draws his proof-texts direct from the Hebrew (or rather from a collection
of Testimonia derived from the Hebrew)'.

According to Luke–Acts, it was Paul's custom to argue (διελέξατο) with his Jewish opponents in the synagogue 'from the scriptures (ἀπὸ τῶν γραφῶν), explaining (διανοίγων) and proving (παρατιθέμενος) that it was necessary for Christ to suffer and to rise from the dead' (Acts 17: 2–3). In Thessalonica, he did so for three weeks, winning some converts while also inciting jealousy among his Jewish brothers. If the Lukan account on the Pauline mission can be believed, the controversy in the Thessalonican synagogue was over the Christological interpretation of the scriptural texts. Paul wished to proclaim the Gospel and to argue that the suffering and resurrection of Jesus were already prophesied in the biblical texts. This exegetical debate was not exceptional: it was, according to Luke, customary (κατὰ τὸ εἰωθὸς) for Paul to engage his mission-field opponents in this way.

Within the context of such a ministry, it would be improbable (to paraphrase Hatch) that Paul would not have had, in addition to biblical texts, manuals of controversy. There is evidence in the deutero-Pauline corpus for the existence of such manuals. In 2 Timothy 4: 13, Paul or one of his followers asked his fellow-teacher Timothy to bring 'the cloak that I left with Carpus at Troas, also the books (τὰ βιβλία) and especially the parchments' (μάλιστα τὰς μεμβράνας) when he comes. The parchment, μεμβράνα, is a transliteration of the Latin *membrana* (the term in Greek is διφθέρα), a word that means 'parchment notebook' made of skin.[49] It is uncertain what these books and notebooks actually contained, but it may well have been that selections of biblical passages were also included in them.[50]

The practice of excerpting biblical passages was not confined to the *vade mecum* of the missionary and traveller either, but is also found in a liturgical context. In Luke 4: 16–19, on the Sabbath Jesus stood up in the synagogue in Nazareth; he was given a βιβλίον of the prophet Isaiah; he unrolled (ἀναπτύξας; or the variant: ανοιξας) τὸ βιβλίον, found the place where it was written and read a composite biblical passage from Isaiah 61: 1 and 58: 6.

The Greek word τὸ βιβλίον, a diminutive of ἡ βίβλος, can mean roll or document (cf. Matt. 19: 7 and Mark 10: 4) and is also the word used in 2 Timothy 4: 13. Most commentators and translators

---

[49] C. H. Roberts, 'Books in the Graeco-Roman World and in the New Testament', in *CHB* i. 53.
[50] Ibid. 53–5.

have understood this word to mean 'the scroll' of Isaiah and the reading to be the section of the prophets in the synagogue service (called the *haptarah*), but this view presupposes that the corresponding portion of the Torah was also read, something which is nowhere mentioned in Luke.[51] There is conflicting evidence about the sequence and selection of readings in the synagogue service of this period (cf. Acts 13: 27 and Philo, *Quod omnis probus liber sit* 81–6), but what is important here is that the portion of scripture that Jesus read out is a composite citation, with selections from Isaiah 61: 1, 58: 6, and possibly Leviticus 25: 10, in that order.[52] It is, of course, true that post-Qumran perspective allows for a greater textual diversity, but no known scroll of Isaiah reverses the order of these verses (some three chapters removed from each other in the MT) and combines them into a composite citation. On the other hand, the citation of these verses in non-biblical scrolls is found at Qumran (e.g. 11QMelch[53]). It is possible that Jesus read the verses of chapters 61 and 58 not from a biblical text of Isaiah but from a collection of excerpts used in liturgy.

On the strength of the Qumran excerpts and the above passages, it may be supposed that prior to the writing of the Pauline letters there existed a number of biblical anthologies which circulated in Jewish and Christian circles. They were produced by Jewish and/or Christian communities in order to bring together important and favourite biblical passages to bear upon various topics. These collections were used for liturgical and devotional purposes as well as for controversy and debate and would constitute selections from either Hebrew bible manuscripts, Greek translations, or Aramaic targumim. They were written on single or multiple sheets, rather than on a codex or book, but in any case they must have been short enough to serve as handy collections. The biblical passages in these collections were quoted with short introductory formulae and brief comments or were simply juxtaposed to each other. A self-evident theme may unite the anthologies or the biblical passages may lack an obvious cohesion. The textual type of the biblical texts may follow the central witnesses of the LXX, or one of

[51] Cf. Joseph A. Fitzmyer, *Gospel According to Luke I–IX* (Garden City, NY: Doubleday & Co., 1979), 530–4.

[52] Noteworthy is the first mention of βίβλιον in the indefinite. Luke was describing a document rather than the scroll of the prophet Isaiah. The second definite τὸ βίβλιον simply refers to the document that was given to Jesus.

[53] See my '11QMelch, Luke 4 and the Dying Messiah', *JJS* 43 (1992), 90–2.

its recensions, the proto-Masoretic text, the Samaritan Pentateuch, some combination of the above, or none of them.

These anthologies were, moreover, diverse in nature, corresponding to the wide variety of Second Temple exegeses, but some of them did overlap in their selection of biblical passages. Leander Keck, in an interesting article,[54] has observed that the scriptural chain embedded in the Damascus Document 5. 13-17 may be compared to the biblical texts of Romans 3: 10-18. Both collections of passages are aimed at the indictment of sinners. CD cites, with intervening comments, Isaiah 50: 11; 59: 5; 27: 11; and Deuteronomy 32: 28, the second passage of which (Isa. 59) is also found in Romans 3: 15 (although the latter cited v. 5 instead of v. 7). Keck's study points in the right direction. Unfortunately, the comparative material that he adduces does not actually overlap, the closest being the citation of verses from the same fifty-ninth chapter of Isaiah.

A better example of this common selection is to be found in 4QFlor and 2 Corinthians 6: 14-7: 1, where both 'embedded' *excerpta* cite 2 Samuel 7: 14. 4QFlor (4Q174) is an eschatological interpretation of festival texts that is centred on 2 Samuel 7: 10-14 and Psalms 1: 1 and 2: 1. Recently it has been argued that 4QFlor is one of two copies of a text called 'eschatological Midrash', even though the texts do not overlap and there is no join between them.[55] As it is plausibly reconstructed by Annette Steudel, 4Q174 and 4Q177 have as their unifying theme the concept of 'the last days' (אחרית הימים).

When the biblical texts of 4QFlor are compared to those of 2 Corinthians 6: 14-7: 1, it appears that one of these verses, 2 Samuel 7: 14, is cited by both.

καί ἔσομαι ὑμῖν εἰς πατέρα καὶ ὑμεῖς ἔσεσθέ μοι εἰς υἱοὺς καὶ θυγατέρας, λέγει κύριος παντοκράτωρ   (2 Cor. 6: 18)

And I shall be to you as father and you will be to me as sons and daughters, says the Lord almighty.

אני אהיה לוא לאב והוא יהיה לי לבן   (4Q174 col. 3, frs. 1, 21, 2)

I shall be to him as father and he will be to me as son.

---

[54] Leander E. Keck, 'The Function of Rom. 3: 10-18. Observations and Suggestions', in J. Jervel and W. A. Meeks (eds.), *God's Christ and His People: Studies in Honour of Nils Alstrup Dahl* (Oslo: Universitetsforlaget, 1977), 141-57. I am indebted to John Ashton for bringing Keck's article to my attention.

[55] Steudel, *Der Midrasch zur Eschatologie*, 161 ff.

The Pauline quotation includes 'says the Lord almighty', which is not found in the uniform tradition of 4Q174, MT, and LXX.[56] This phrase occurs several times in the LXX and Samuel, the closest being in the preceding verse 8. Furthermore the quotation has additionally 'and daughters', a variant which was probably influenced by Isaiah 43: 6[57] and the second plural 'you' (cf. Lev. 26: 12) for the third singular 'he'.

It is perhaps going too far to propose, as some have done, that this is an Essene fragment interpolated into the text of 2 Corinthians 6: 13 and 7: 2, but it is nevertheless striking to find similar Qumranian themes in the opposition of righteousness and iniquity, light and darkness, Beliar (and Christ), believer and unbeliever, and the temple and idols, as well as the notion that the community is the temple of the living God. Interesting intertextual echoes also resonate in Revelation 21: 7 ('I will be his God and he shall be my son').[58]

Tolerance for Textual Diversity

Paul's tolerance for textual diversity can partially be accounted for by the method with which he studied scripture and drew out of it those passages of greatest interest and relevance. An example where Paul cites two different versions of the same biblical verse will be instructive. In the MT, Isaiah 40: 13 reads as follows:

מי תכן את רוח יהוה ואיש עצתו יודיענו

Who has estimated the spirit of the Lord
and as his adviser (lit: man of his counsel) will instruct him?

The LXX interprets and translates accordingly:

τίς ἔγνω νοῦν κυρίου,
καὶ τίς σύμβουλος αὐτοῦ ἐγένετο, ὃς συμβιβᾷ αὐτόν

who has known the mind of the Lord,
and who has become his counsellor, so as to instruct him?

In 1 Corinthians 2: 16, Paul asks the rhetorical question, 'Who among the wise know the mind of the Lord?', the expected answer

---

[56] Also not found is the independent pronoun 'I'.

[57] Victor Furnish, *II Corinthians* (New York: Doubleday, 1984), 364.

[58] There are several biblical passages that express this relationship (e.g. Ezek. 38: 27 and Lev. 26: 12). 2 Sam. 7: 14 is seen as the source text by virtue of its verbal proximity.

being the Corinthian Christians and Paul. Absent[59] from the lemma
is the phrase, 'who has become his counsellor'.

> τίς γὰρ ἔγνω νοῦν κυρίου
> ὃς συμβιβάσει αὐτόν

> for who has known the mind of the Lord
> so as to instruct him?

When he cites this same biblical verse in Romans 11: 34, however, it is the phrase about his instruction that is absent.

> τίς γὰρ ἔγνω νοῦν κυρίου
> ἢ τίς σύμβουλος αὐτοῦ ἐγένετο

> for who has known the mind of the Lord
> or who has become his counsellor?

Clearly, Paul is tolerant of two slightly different versions of Isaiah
40: 13. But has he simply modified his text for his own purposes,
omitting the phrase 'who has become his counsellor' in the one
and 'so as to instruct him' in the other?

Romans 11: 34 belongs to a doxology that serves as a fitting
conclusion to chapters 9-11. Here, the inscrutable wisdom and
knowledge of God, which he describes as a mystery in 11: 25, are
reiterated in the form of a rhetorical question, the implied answer
to which is that no one has known the mind of the Lord or been
his counsellor. The emphasis is placed upon the absence of anyone
who can penetrate the mind of God. The same question is posed in
1 Corinthians 2: 16 and Paul himself answers by declaring that
'we have the mind of Christ'.

What is interesting is that in 1QIsaᵃ there are also two versions
of Isa 40: 13. The original scribe wrote:

> מיא תכן את רוח יהוה ועצתו יודיענה

> (lit.) who has estimated the spirit of the Lord
> and made his counsel known

Here, the antecedent of the third feminine singular pronominal
suffix[60] of יודיענה ('made it known') is his counsel (עצתו).[61] A corrector added 'man' (איש) above עצתו, changing the sense from 'his

---

[59] There are also minor differences in 'for' and the future rather than the sub-
junctive of συμβιβάζω of the LXX.

[60] See Elisha Qimron, *The Hebrew of the Dead Sea Scrolls* (Atlanta: Scholars Press,
1986), sect. 322.

[61] So also, J. D. W. Watts, *Isaiah 34-66* (Waco, Tex.: Word Books, 1987), 86 n.
13d.

counsel' to 'a man of his counsel' or 'his counsellor'.[62] The original reading of 1QIsaᵃ agrees with the Corinthians quotation in leaving out 'his counsellor', whereas the same passage in Romans 11 agrees with the corrected reading, LXX, and MT.

The absence of the phrase 'so as to instruct him' in Romans 11 may be accounted for if it is recognized that verses 33-6 constitute a pre-Pauline doxology, begining with 'O depth and riches of the wisdom and knowledge of God' and ending with 'to him be the glory for ever, amen'. Within this source are two biblical excerpts from Isaiah 40: 13 and Job 41: 3. Only the first two phrases are cited in the former, perhaps with the rhetorical consideration of linking the thrice repeated τί, whereas the latter quotation of Job appears to be a revision of the Septuagint.[63]

CONCLUSIONS

Paul lived at a time when the biblical text remained fluid. Textual variety and pluriformity characterized the scriptural scrolls that he consulted. He could quote from them or from one of the biblical excerpts that he presumably had before him. Sometimes, as in Galatians 3: 15, he insisted on a literal reading of the biblical passage, while on other occasions he could freely adapt his source text (e.g. Deut. 30 in Rom. 10). Still other times, it is thought that he produced a biblical proof-text from memory, the misremembering of which could account for variants and discrepancies. This latter suggestion, though plausible, is difficult to prove or even analyse, since the incorrect attribution of the biblical source can otherwise be explained by the existence of anthologies. In any case, the postulate of pre-Pauline biblical excerpts does help in explaining some of the procedures which he was likely to have used.

---

[62] Without, however, changing the gender of the pronominal suffix to masculine.

[63] Berndt Schaller, 'Zum Textcharakter der Hiobzitate im paulinischen Schriftum', ZNW 71 (1980), 26, argues that προδιδόναι is closer in meaning to הקדים than ἀντίσταμαι.

10

Paul as Exegete

Having offered a descriptive analysis of his biblical quotations, it is appropriate to follow it up with an examination of possible reasons why Paul tolerated textual variety and even adapted his biblical texts. To begin with, it is important to draw out the significance of his multicultural and multilingual background. Despite the frequent mention in scholarship of his upbringing, it is sometimes assumed that Paul operated in only one linguistic mode, namely Hellenistic Greek.

SCRIPTURAL WORD AND MEANING

More serious attention should be paid to his credentials as a 'Hebrew of Hebrews' (Phil. 3: 5) in the Graeco-Roman world and the implications of growing up and living in a linguistically and culturally pluralistic world, for once it is recognized that Paul could speak, read, and write in two or three languages, then his emphasis upon the message over the form of the biblical texts becomes all the more understandable. It is in this context that a better understanding of Pauline hermeneutics, based upon the experience and revelation of Jesus Christ, may be achieved.

Linguistic Background

By his own self-description, Paul was a Jew whose zeal for the 'traditions of his fathers' was beyond that of his contemporaries (Gal. 1: 14). His training, whether primarily in Tarsus or Jerusalem,[1] would have included elementary forms of Greek rhetoric[2] as well as the traditional Jewish education of his day. In Jerusalem, he sat at the feet of no less a teacher than Rabban

---

[1] See W. C. van Unnik, 'Tarsus or Jerusalem, the City of Paul's Youth', and 'Once Again: Tarsus or Jerusalem', in *Sparsa Collecta*, pt. 1 (Leiden: E. J. Brill, 1973), 259–320 and 321–7.

[2] See my 'Not in Persuasive Words of Wisdom, but in the Demonstration of the Spirit and Power', *NovT* 29 (1987), 137–49.

Gamaliel, grandson of Hillel (cf. *m. 'Abot* 1. 16), and was educated according to the strict discipline of the law (Acts 22: 3).

Linguistically, he is reported by Luke to have been conversant in Greek and 'in the Hebrew dialect' (Acts 21: 37–22: 21). His request to be allowed to speak prompted the surprised tribune to ask, 'Do you know Greek?' (ἑλληνιστὶ γινώσκεις). While it may be doubted that events occurred exactly as they are described in Acts,[3] it is nevertheless too sceptical to dismiss the historical validity of this entire episode,[4] since some of the details of the account correspond well to the cultural linguistic situation of Jews in first-century Palestine.[5] To be sure, the speeches in Acts have been adapted for Luke's literary purpose,[6] but such sources are likely to have reflected the situation of the day and may even have been based upon some identifiable event.

Having asked the tribune in Greek and been granted permission to speak, Paul turned to the people and addressed them (lit.) 'in the Hebrew dialect'. Now the referent of τῇ Ἑβραΐδι διαλέκτῳ is disputed: does it refer to the Aramaic or Hebrew language? In Daniel 2: 4, ארמית is translated by the Septuagint and Theodotion as συριστί, but this evidence is not decisive for rendering Acts 21: 40 as the Hebrew language. The phrase τῇ Ἑβραΐδι διαλέκτῳ occurs twice more in the New Testament, Acts 22: 2 being in the same account of Paul's speech to the Jerusalemites incited by the charges of Asian Jews and Acts 26: 14 a reference to the language in which the visionary Jesus speaks to Saul. The cognate adverb ἑβραϊστί occurs seven times in the New Testament (John 5: 2; 19: 13, 17, 20; 20: 16; Rev. 9: 11 and 16: 16) and of those four are

[3] Ernst Haenchen, *The Acts of the Apostles*, Eng. trans. (Oxford: Basil Blackwell, 1971), 619–22, asks how someone who has been mobbed could have made such a speech.

[4] Richard Longenecker, *Acts* (Grand Rapids, Mich.: Zondervan, 1981), 524, offers an alternative reconstruction to Haenchen's.

[5] On the subject of languages, see among many others *HJP* ii. sect. 22; Saul Lieberman, *Greek in Jewish Palestine* (New York: JTS, 1942); Joseph A. Fitzmyer, 'Languages of Palestine in the First Century A.D.' in *A Wandering Aramean: Collected Aramaic Essays* (Chico, Calif.: Scholars Press, 1979), 29–56; Martin Hengel, *The Hellenization of Judaea in the First Century after Christ*, Eng. trans. (London: SCM Press, 1989), 19–29; J. N. Sevenster, *Do You Know Greek?* (Leiden: E. J. Brill, 1968); E. M. Meyers and J. F. Strange, *Archaeology, the Rabbis & Early Christianity* (Nashville, Tenn.: Abingdon, 1981), ch. 4.

[6] So already H. J. Cadbury, *The Book of Acts in History* (London: Adam & Charles Black, 1955), 46–57. The 'Areopagus speech', for example, would have been implausibly short (Acts 17: 22–31).

commonly believed to be qualifying Aramaic words ($\beta\eta\theta\zeta\alpha\theta\acute{\alpha}$, $\Gamma\alpha\beta\beta\alpha\theta\hat{\alpha}$, $\Gamma o\lambda\gamma o\theta\hat{\alpha}$, and $\dot{\rho}\alpha\beta\beta ouv\acute{\iota}$) and two other Hebrew names ($\mathcal{A}\beta\alpha\delta\delta\acute{\omega}\nu$ and $\mathcal{A}\rho\mu\alpha\gamma\epsilon\delta\acute{\omega}\nu$).[7] Evidently, $\dot{\epsilon}\beta\rho\alpha\ddot{\iota}\sigma\tau\acute{\iota}$ can qualify either Hebrew or Aramaic toponyms and words.[8]

Hebrew, it was previously thought, ceased to be a spoken language of the Jews when it was replaced by Aramaic.[9] While this view remains, supported as it is by Aramaic expressions recorded in the New Testament, 4QMMT does appear to attest to a spoken form of the language that contains elements of both biblical and mishnaic Hebrew. It cannot be ruled out as a possibility that in certain circles, like the Qumran community, Jews in this period continued to converse in Hebrew.[10]

The greater proportion of Qumran texts written in Hebrew over those penned in Aramaic is also an indicator that *lingua Hebraea* continued to flourish in the centuries around the turning of the era. Not only were biblical texts written in the 'holy language' (לשון הקודש[11]) but also sectarian and other documents were composed in Hebrew.

Paul spoke Greek and most probably Aramaic. Given his Jewish upbringing and pharisaic training under Gamaliel, it is likely that he could also read biblical texts in the original Hebrew and possibly even speak in that language. The implication of this poly-lingual background is that Paul would have been well aware of the difficulties in translating scripture from Hebrew to Greek. As the grandson of Sira eloquently testified centuries before in his Prologue: 'For what was expressed in the original Hebrew ($\dot{\epsilon}\nu$ $\dot{\epsilon}\alpha\nu\tauo\hat{\iota}s$ $E\beta\rho\alpha\ddot{\iota}\sigma\tau\acute{\iota}$) does not have the equivalent sense ($o\dot{\nu}$ $\dot{\iota}\sigma o\delta\nu\nu\alpha\mu\epsilon\hat{\iota}$)

---

[7] F. F. Bruce, *Commentary on the Book of Acts* (Grand Rapids, Mich.: Eerdmans, 1981), 437 n. 55.

[8] '$\dot{P}\alpha\beta\beta ouv\acute{\iota}$ can also be a transliteration of the mishnaic Hebrew term רבוני (Michael Sokoloff, *A Dictionary of Jewish Palestinian Aramaic of the Byzantine Period* (Ramat-Gan: Bar Ilan University Press, 1990), 513.

[9] Cf. the rise of Aramaic as an international language is evident in the biblical texts: the account concerning Rabshakeh in 2 Kgs. 18: 19-28 and the decline of Hebrew by the people being given the sense of the reading from the law in Neh. 8: 8.

[10] Elisha Qimron in *DJD* x. 64-108, points to a number of linguistic features that reflect the spoken Hebrew at Qumran (e.g. בשל).

[11] The phrase 'the holy language' as a description of the Hebrew language is now found in a fragmentary text, 4Q464 fr. 3, col. 1, l. 9. Similar to the 'Pesher on the Period' (4Q180), it is a text that seems to refer to the belief that the fracturing of human language at Babel will be reversed in the eschaton (so Esther Eshel and Michael Stone, 'לשון הקודש באחרית הימים לאור קטע קטע מקומראן', *Tarbiz*, 62 (1993), 170.

when translated ($\mu\epsilon\tau\alpha\chi\theta\hat{\eta}$) into another language ($\epsilon\dot{\iota}s$ $\dot{\epsilon}\tau\dot{\epsilon}\rho\alpha\nu$ $\gamma\lambda\hat{\omega}\sigma\sigma\alpha\nu$).' The other language he refers to here, of course, is Greek and the work is the wisdom of his grandfather Jesus. The translational difficulty of representing linguistic equivalents between languages, he further observes, is not confined to this work, but is also to be found in Greek translations of the Hebrew of the law ($\dot{o}$ $\nu\dot{o}\mu os$), prophecies ($\alpha\dot{\iota}$ $\pi\rho o\phi\eta\tau\epsilon\hat{\iota}\alpha\iota$), and remaining books ($\tau\dot{\alpha}$ $\lambda o\iota\pi\dot{\alpha}$ $\tau\hat{\omega}\nu$ $\beta\iota\beta\lambda\dot{\iota}\omega\nu$), a tripartite division that is often seen as evidence of the closing of the canon. These translations of the biblical books differ not a little from their original expressions in Hebrew ($o\dot{v}$ $\mu\iota\kappa\rho\dot{\alpha}\nu$ $\ddot{\epsilon}\chi\epsilon\iota$ $\tau\dot{\eta}\nu$ $\delta\iota\alpha\phi o\rho\dot{\alpha}\nu$ $\dot{\epsilon}\nu$ $\dot{\epsilon}\alpha\upsilon\tauο\hat{\iota}s$ $\lambda\epsilon\gamma\dot{o}\mu\epsilon\nu\alpha$).

Paul, like Ben Sira, would have been all too aware of translational difficulties in reading Hebrew biblical texts and excerpts and quoting them in his letters to Greek readers. He would have been uneasy with an over-reliance upon the words of his Greek biblical quotations. It is the meaning of the biblical passage, rather than its formulation that is important.[12]

Exegetical Training

Paul's Jewish education would have given him a thorough grounding in bible study and contemporary exegetical practices. It has long been recognized that rabbinic techniques of scriptural interpretation are detectable in Paul's writings. There is no need to rehearse these here.[13]

What is germane and largely unnoticed is the practice of citing abbreviated quotations, a technique that has biblical precedents and contemporary corroboration. In Ezra 3: 2–5, for instance, the returnees to Jerusalem built an altar to the God of Israel and offered burnt offerings upon it 'according to what is written in the torah of Moses (ככתוב בתורת משה), man of God'. They kept Sukkot, the feast of booths, as it is written (ככתוב), and offered the holocaust, according to the ordinance for daily ritual (כמשפט דבר יום ביומו).

Notable here are the terms ככתוב ('as it is written') and כמשפט ('according to the judgement') which the Septuagint translates respectively as $\kappa\alpha\tau\dot{\alpha}$ $\tau\dot{\alpha}$ $\gamma\epsilon\gamma\rho\alpha\mu\mu\dot{\epsilon}\nu\alpha$, $\kappa\alpha\tau\dot{\alpha}$ $\tau\dot{o}$ $\gamma\epsilon\gamma\rho\alpha\mu\mu\dot{\epsilon}\nu o\nu$ and $\dot{\omega}s$ $\dot{\eta}$ $\kappa\rho\dot{\iota}\sigma\iota s$. Literally, these Hebrew and Greek terms refer to what has

---

[12] Did Paul consider his Hebrew scriptures holy, but not his Greek translations? This is a possibility worth considering.

[13] See e.g. J. Bonsirven, *Exégèse rabbinique et exégèse paulinienne* (Paris: Beauchesne et ses Fils, 1939), and Henry St John Thackeray, *The Relation of St. Paul to Contemporary Jewish Thought* (London: Macmillan, 1900), 181–5.

been written, but here it is not the actual words of the law that are being cited. It is the content, rather than the verbal formulation, of the law of Numbers 29: 12-38. The force of this shorthand reference is that the returnees from Exile performed their sacrifice in conformity with the written rules.[14] In Nehemiah 10: 35, moreover, the law on wood offering is nowhere found in the Pentateuch, despite being described 'as written in the law' (ככתוב בתורה; ὡς γέγραπται ἐν τῷ νόμῳ).[15]

The same phenomenon is evident in 4QMMT.[16] For example, B 66-7 state: 'and also it is written that (ואף כתוב) after he (i.e. the leper) shaves and washes he should dwell outside his tent seven days'. This is not a verbatim quotation, but a paraphrase of Leviticus 14: 8. Or again, the formula והדבר כתוב (lit. 'and the matter is written') is appended to the ruling concerning the slaughter and eating of pregnant animals (עברה), but nowhere is this law stipulated in the Torah (cf. Leviticus 22: 28; 11QTS 52. 6-7).

The recognition that Paul too may have used this shorthand form of citation would go some way to resolve one of the central exegetical problems in Galatians. In Galatians 3: 13, he supports the contention that Christ has redeemed believers from the curse of the law by what appears to be a citation from Deuteronomy 21: 23: ὅτι γέγραπται ἐπικατάρατος πᾶς ὁ κρεμάμενος ἐπὶ ξύλου ('as it is written, cursed is everyone who hangs upon a tree'). The MT and LXX read respectively: כי קללת אלהים תלוי ('for cursed of God is the one who is hanged'), and ὅτι κεκατηραμένος ὑπὸ θεοῦ πᾶς κρεμάμενος ἐπὶ ξύλου. ('for cursed by God is everyone who hangs upon a tree'). By comparison, the Pauline quotation differs from the MT and LXX in reading ἐπικατάρατος for 'cursed by God'. On the literary level this variant repeats the initial 'cursed' of Deuteronomy 27: 26, cited two verses earlier, a rhetorical technique known as *anaphora* (e.g. the triple ἐγώ of 1 Cor. 1: 12b).[17] In

---

[14] A discussion of this technique is found in Michael Fishbane, *Biblical Interpretation in Ancient Israel* (Oxford: Clarendon Press, 1985), 209-16. Additionally, see Yigael Yadin, *The Temple Scroll*, Eng. trans. (Jerusalem: Israel Exploration Society, 1983), i. 128-31, for the extra-biblical sources of the festival of wood offering that appears in 11Q19 cols. 23-5. 2.

[15] Fishbane, *Biblical Interpretation*, 213.

[16] Qimron and John Strugnell, *DJD* x. 140-1.

[17] For a discussion of rhetorical techniques in 1 and 2 Cor., see my 'Not in Persuasive Words of Wisdom'.

doing so, he brings closer together the compatible (at least to his mind) ideas of the fate of those under the law and the scandal of Jesus' crucifixion. Moreover, it agrees with the LXX in making explicit what is implied in the MT, namely that the man who hangs 'upon a tree' is accursed.

In its original context, Deuteronomy 21: 22–3 was a law on the impalement of the corpse of a man killed because he has committed a crime punishable by death. The procedures are clearly laid down: after he is put to death his body must be hung on a tree, but it must be taken down before the night is done, since a corpse so treated is accursed and would defile the land which the Lord God has given as an inheritance. The passage does not stipulate what these transgressions were (חטא) and leaves ambiguous the exact crimes covered by משפט מות, 'judgement of crimes punishable by death', but in advocating the disrespectful display of the dead body it is following an ancient tradition of inflicting *post mortem* shame on the transgressor or enemy.[18] Thus, for instance, after Joshua had put to death the five kings who attacked Gibeon, his new ally, he hung them (ויתלם) on five trees, but took their corpses down at sunset and threw them into the same cave in which they had been hiding (Josh. 10: 26–7; cf. Num. 25: 4, 2 Sam. 4: 12; 21: 6–9).

Later tradition would understand the Deuteronomic impalement as a form of hanging, putting someone to death rather than simply impaling a corpse on a pole for humiliation. Thus, in 4QpNah the furious young lion, commonly thought to be Alexander Jannaeus, hanged men alive (יתלה אנשים חיים, frs. 3–4, col. i, l. 7). Here, the reference most probably refers to the 'seekers-of-smooth things', who may plausibly be identified with the Pharisees and other rebels (Jos. *BJ* 1. 4. 4–6 (90–8) and *AJ* 13. 13. 5–14. 2 (372–83)). The following fragmentary line makes explicit that the hanging did not involve corpses, but victims who were still alive: העץ בישראל מלפנים כי לתלוי חי על ('in Israel of the past, for one hanged alive upon the tree . . .'). The Temple Scroll, moreover, indicates that the form of punishment known among the writings of the Qumran community was one where hanging was intended to put the man to death (col. 64. 6–13). The word order of Deuteronomy 21: 23 (quoted in l. 9) is significant as it is reversed in line 10 (also l. 8): העץ וימות ותליתמה גם

---

[18] Roland de Vaux, *Ancient Israel: Its Life and Institutions*, Eng. trans. (London: Darton, Longman & Todd, 1961), 157–60.

אותו על ('and you shall hang him also upon the tree and he shall die'). That is to say, hanging puts the man to death.[19] In the Temple Scroll, the crimes deserving the punishment of death by hanging are specified to be those of treachery and defection. Whether this form of hanging is the same as crucifixion remains in doubt; it may well be a form of hanging at the end of a rope.[20]

Both the Temple Scroll and Pesher Nahum bridge the gap between Deuteronomy 21: 23 and its exegetical application by Paul in Galatians. Evidently, the Deuteronomic procedure of impalement was later understood to be a punishment of death by hanging. From contemporary Qumran evidence, it is now understandable how Paul could use Deuteronomy as proof-text for the crucifixion of Jesus. Even though ancient methods varied, there is no doubt that crucifixion also involved hanging as a means of killing the victim.

There remains, however, the further matter of the introductory formula ὅτι γέγραπται. In the Pauline letters, 'as it is written' or a similar formula regularly marks out a verbatim citation. If this formula were similarly understood here, then Paul would apparently be citing verbatim the curse which results from the impalement of a corpse. This prevalent view is possible, but it does not resolve the difficulty that the biblical text quoted contains notable variants unattested elsewhere.[21]

A better explanation may be achieved if the introductory formula is understood to be a marker for citing the content of Deuteronomy 21: 22-3 rather than the words of one phrase of verse 23. In conformity with מות משפט, 'judgement of crimes punishable by death', Jesus Christ is cursed because he hangs upon a tree. But this cursed state, Paul understands is paradoxically an act of redemption for sins of all men, Jews and Greeks alike. The better sense of Galatians 3: 13 would then be: Christ redeemed men from the curse of the law by himself becoming a curse on their behalf and in conformity with that which is written in the law, namely that everyone who hangs upon a tree is accursed.

[19] Following Yadin, *The Temple Scroll*, i. 373-9.

[20] Joseph Baumgarten, 'Does TLH in the Temple Scroll Refer to Crucifixion?', *JBL* 91 (1972), 472-81.

[21] Hans Dieter Betz, *Galatians: A Commentary on Paul's Letter to the Churches in Galatia* (Philadelphia: Fortress Press, 1979), 152, states: 'The problem is far from clear. Whatever the origin, the passage proves for Paul that Christ's death on the cross fulfilled Scripture.'

The citation of the content rather than the words of the law would explain away the textual variants. On the other hand, the verbal correspondences and affinities between Galatians 3: 13 and Deuteronomy 21: 23 are not unexpected and wholly natural. The law in view is indeed the one found in Deuteronomy 21: 22-3, as interpreted by later tradition and Paul, but 'cursed is everyone who hangs upon a tree' encapsulates, rather than cites, the crimes covered by the judgement deserving death, the form of punishment involved, and the status of the victim in the eyes of God.[22]

Indirect support for Paul's abbreviated reference may also be found in Galatians 3: 10. In this verse, Paul argues that all who are 'of the law' are under a curse and supports this statement with what appears to be a quotation from Deuteronomy 27: 26. Deuteronomy 27, of course, is part of the cultic ceremony, performed significantly on Mount Ebal, that dramatizes Israel's covenantal responsibilities by pronouncing curses upon those who transgress the commandments. At the end of this list of curses on specific transgressions, verse 26 summarizes the intention generally by affirming that all who so do are cursed.

If Galatians 3: 10 be considered a quotation, then it is one that reflects a number of significant variants against the MT[23] and the LXX[24] when it reads 'cursed is everyone who does not remain in that which is written in the book of the torah to do them'. In fact, the phrase 'that which is written in the book of the torah'[25] has verbal echoes with a number of other passages in the blessings and curses section of Deuteronomy, chapters 28-30 (e.g. 28: 58; 29: 20, and 30: 10). Here again, it may be that what Paul has in mind were the admonitions in the final chapters of Deuteronomy to obey all the words of the torah. The similarities between Galatians 3: 10 and Deuteronomy 27: 27 are coincidental and its verbal affinities due to the summarizing nature of both texts.

---

[22] It is interesting that Symmachus relates Deut. 21: 23 to the 'blasphemy of God' (see Max Wilcox, '"Upon the Tree"—Deut 21: 22-3 in the New Testament', *JBL* 96 (1977), 87), a charge not unlike that levelled at Jesus (Mark 14: 64 and par.).

[23] 'Cursed is he who confirms not the words of this torah to do them.'

[24] The variants include πᾶς, ὅς, τοῖς γεγραμμένοις ἐν τῷ βιβλίῳ τοῦ νόμου.

[25] It is noteworthy that in the 'Statutes of the King', the Temple Scroll reads 'this torah, upon a book' (11QTSᵃ 56. 21) where Deut. 17: 18 has 'this repeated law' (מנשה התורה הואה).

PAULINE HERMENEUTICS

Paul uses a variety of exegetical and argumentative techniques in his letters. If Galatians 3: 13 is indeed an abbreviated reference to Deuteronomy 21: 22–3, then it stands alongside his insistence upon the strict verbal meaning of 'seed'. As discussed above, the singular 'seed' is central to the argument that the Abrahamic promise is fulfilled in Jesus. Is there consistency in Paul's interpretation of scripture when he now reads the biblical text literalistically and at other times for its intended meaning and sense? How could this emphasis upon content be reconciled with Paul's appeal to the word of the biblical text in the same chapter of Galatians?

Letter and Spirit

It will be recalled that the apparent dichotomy between letter and spirit was introduced by Paul himself. In 2 Corinthians 3: 6, he states that God 'has qualified us to become ministers of a new covenant, not of the letter (γράμματος), but of the spirit (πνεύματος), for the letter (τὸ γράμμα) kills, but the spirit (πνεῦμα) gives life'. His language is pointed and the condemnation of the Mosaic commandments explicit when he further describes in verse 7 that that which was carved (ἐντετυπωμένη) in letters (ἐν γράμμασιν) on stone (λίθοις) to be a service of death (ἡ διακονία τοῦ θανάτου). It appears to be the letter of the law that is being attacked, the external and formal in contrast to the internal and spiritual.

Based on the remarkable passage in Jeremiah 31: 31–4 (LXX: 38: 31–4), in which Yahweh is said to have established a new covenant (ברית חדשה; διαθήκην καινήν) with the house of Israel and Judah, Paul contrasts the ministry of the old covenant[26] with that of the new. There are two particular features of the Jeremian passage that are given Pauline twists. First, the internalizing of the Mosaic law is formulated in the rhetorically effective juxtaposition between 'tables of stone' and 'tables of the fleshy heart'. In Jeremiah, Yahweh declares that 'I will put my law within them (נתתי את תורתי בקרבם; δώσω νόμους μου εἰς τὴν διάνοιαν αὐτῶν ('their minds')) and write it upon their heart (ועל לבם אכתבנה; καὶ ἐπὶ

---

[26] Although not explicitly formulated thus, there is no doubt that that is what is meant (cf. vv. 7 and 14). Jeremiah does not use the term 'old covenant', but the covenant established formerly with the fathers (31 (LXX 38): 32).

καρδίας αὐτῶν γράψω αὐτούς; v. 33). The 'tables of stone' (ἐν πλαξίν λιθίναις) in 2 Corinthians 3: 3 are a clear reference to the tables given to Moses on Mt. Sinai (Exod. 34: 1, שְׁנֵי לֻחֹת אֲבָנִים; δύο πλάκας λιθίνας), implied in the Jeremian critique of the law. The contrasting 'tables of the fleshy heart', (ἐν πλαξίν καρδίαις σαρκίναις), however, are a Pauline formulation, drawing out the significance of laws placed in the hearts and minds. The added qualification of 'fleshy', signifying no doubt 'human', is possibly influenced by the 'heart of flesh' (לֵב בָּשָׂר; καρδίαν σαρκίνην) of Ezekiel 36: 26.[27]

Second, the nullification of the teaching of the law is the basis for Paul's own Christological hermeneutics. In Jeremiah, a corollary of the internalized law of the heart and mind is the setting aside of the instruction commonly associated with it: 'And they shall no longer teach, each man his neighbour and each man his brother, saying 'Know the Lord, for they shall know me (יֵדְעוּ אוֹתִי; εἰδήσουσίν με), from their smallest to their greatest' (31: 34). Knowledge of God is no longer mediated through the external instructions of the laws, but direct and universal. Paul qualifies Jeremiah's new hermeneutics by showing that it is only through Christ that direct knowledge of God may be attained.

Like the pesherite interpretation of scripture, Paul's exegesis is based upon the revelation of God and how that divine disclosure functions in exegesis can also be compared. In verses 12–18 of 2 Corinthians 3, Paul argues that only through Christ (ἐν χριστῷ) is the veil (τὸ κάλυμμα) that remains upon the dulled minds (ἐπωρώθη τὰ νοήματα αὐτῶν) of his fellow Jews removed (καταργεῖται). This veil lies over their hearts during the public reading of the old covenant (ἐπὶ τῇ ἀναγνώσει τῆς παλαιᾶς διαθήκης), but is taken away when someone turns to the Lord. This latter phrase echoes Exodus 34: 34 where Moses himself removes the veil (הַמַּסְוֶה/τὸ κάλυμμα) from his face when he enters to speak with Yahweh and replaces it when he comes out. When Paul himself uses the word κύριος, rather than when it occurs in a biblical quotation, he generally refers to Christ. It has been suggested therefore that here, too, Christ is meant when someone 'turns to the Lord'.[28]

[27] So Richard B. Hays, *The Faith of Jesus Christ: An Investigation of the Narrative Substructure of Galatians 3: 1–4: 11* (Chico, Calif.: Scholars Press, 1983), 128–31. Hays usefully distinguishes between 'script' (*gramma*) and 'scripture' (*graphe*), but his suggestion that, for Paul, the Spirit is outward and external is difficult to accept.

[28] See Victor P. Furnish, *II Corinthians* (New York: Doubleday, 1984), 211, for a survey of the debate on this topic.

Given that Exodus 34: 34 is in view, however, there are good reasons to think that Yahweh (יהוה/κύριος), and not Christ, is the referent: 2 Corinthians 3: 18 states that those with unveiled faces behold 'the glory of the Lord', a clear allusion to Moses' first encounter with God on Mt. Sinai (Exod. 24: 17, כבוד יהוה/τῆς δόξης κυρίου). Moreover, it is significant that Paul uses the verb ἐπιστρέφω ('to turn, change course') in connection with the unveiling of the face. In Exodus 34: 34, Moses simply enters into the presence of Yahweh, but the notion of turning to God or away from errant ways is very often formulated in reference to the moral norms that have been set out (e.g. Deut. 4: 30, Hos. 3: 5, 11: 5; Isa. 6: 10). Paul, too, uses this verb when he explicitly refers to the Thessalonians' reported turning from idols to God (ἐπεστρέψατε πρὸς τὸν θεὸν ἀπὸ τῶν εἰδώλων δουλεύειν θεῷ ζῶντι καὶ ἀληθινῷ, 1 Thess. 1: 9).

Christ is the key to Pauline hermeneutics. The instrumental dative[29] of ἐν χριστῷ (v. 14) indicates that true understanding of 'the old covenant', metaphorically expressed by the removal of Moses' veil in the reading of scripture, is achieved only through Christ. Figuratively expressed, Christ (the implied agent of the passive περιαιρεῖται in v. 16) removes the veil that prevents one from beholding the glory of the Lord. The two procedures, one of reading scripture and the other of encountering the divine, are inextricably intertwined. To understand the true meaning of scripture is to read the texts from this Christological perspective. It is in the significance of the crucifixion, death, and resurrection of Jesus that Paul understands the holy writ of biblical Israel, a hermeneutical principle that distinguishes him from the pesherists and their understanding of the Teacher of Righteousness.

Added to the Christological hermeneutics of Paul is a spiritual dimension when he states in 2 Corinthians 3: 17–18 that those with unveiled faces not only behold the glory of the Lord, but that they are themselves being changed into his likeness, a reconformation to the image of God (cf. Gen. 1: 27) and a kind of return to Paradise. This latter procedure is apparently 'from the Lord, (namely) the spirit' (ἀπὸ κυρίου πνεύματος, 3: 18), probably meaning that the source is from God who is further equated with his spirit.

---

[29] C. K. Barrett, *A Commentary on the Second Epistle to the Corinthians* (London: Adam & Charles Black, 1973), 120–1.

At the heart of Paul's hermeneutics is his own and fellow believers' experience of Christ.[30] The Gospel message was not handed down to Paul from human intermediaries, but was received directly from a revelation of Jesus Christ (δι' ἀποκαλύψεως Ἰησοῦ Χριστοῦ, Gal. 1: 12). How many of these revelations Paul experienced altogether is debated, depending upon the way the details of Acts and the letters are read.[31] What is more important is that Paul himself describes his ministry as being characterized by 'the extraordinary character of the revelations' (τῇ ὑπερβολῇ τῶν ἀποκαλύψεων, 2 Cor. 12: 7). It was for this reason that a thorn was given in his flesh (ἐδόθη μοι σκόλοψ τῇ σαρκί), lest he become over-elated (ὑπεραίρωμαι). When he sought to have this thorn, an angel of Satan, removed, the Lord spoke directly to him and declared that paradoxically divine power is made perfect in weakness. The message of the folly of the cross and Paul's boasting in the wisdom of God have their source in divine revelation.

INSPIRED MESSAGE

Paul's hermeneutics are anchored in the revelation of God through the belief that Jesus, the Messiah, was crucified, died, was buried, and resurrected. Through his own experience on the Damascus Road and subsequent, trance-like, ecstatic encounters with the visionary Christ, he has come to interpret scripture not according to the traditions of the fathers, but in the new light of this revelation. The hermeneutical shift involved the reading of scripture around this basic belief that 'in Christ', a formula for the significance of the Christ-event, the intended will of God can be ascertained, and he used all the techniques known to him as exegete to argue for its biblical indications.

---

[30] Similarly Morna Hooker's *From Adam to Christ: Essays on Paul* (Cambridge: Cambridge University Press, 1990), ch. 9. For a wide-ranging discussion of the interaction between revelation and mystery, see Markus N. A. Bockmuehl, *Revelation and Mystery in Ancient Judaism and Pauline Christianity* (Tübingen: J. C. B. Mohr (Paul Siebeck), 1990).

[31] See recently, Christopher Morray-Jones, 'Paradise Revisited (2 Cor. 12: 12): The Jewish Mystical Background of Paul's Apostolate', pts. 1, 'The Jewish Sources', and 2, 'Paul's Heavenly Ascent and its Significance', *HTR* 86/2 (1993), 177–217 and 265–92, who argues that Paul's ascent into the third heaven (2 Cor. 12) occurred on his first visit to Jerusalem as recorded in Acts 21–2.

Power in Weakness

Illustrative of Pauline hermeneutics and exegesis is the view that paradoxically divine power is made manifest in weakness. As an argument, it is unflinching in tackling head-on the apparent nonsense of a divine Messiah whose shameful display on the cross is seen to be the will of God. This *theologia crucis*, Paul recognizes, is foolishness when assessed by the wisdom of the world. To circumvent this problem, he argues that contrary to expectations God has enacted his salvific and redemptive plan in the death of Jesus. God has paradoxically made his power evident in this apparent and shameful defeat.

More explicitly than any other Pauline passage, 1 Corinthians 1: 18–2: 5 expresses this paradox of the cross. The word or message of the cross is moronic (μωρία, 'folly') to those who abide by the wisdom of the world, whom Paul polemically describes as 'those who are dying' (τοῖς ἀπολλυμένοις; v. 18). For Jews, crucifixion is a scandal (σκάνδαλον), and for Gentiles foolishness (μωρίαν), but to those who are called, whether Jews or Gentiles, Christ is the power of God (θεοῦ δύναμιν) and the wisdom of God (θεοῦ σοφίαν). According to Paul, then, the standards of the world do not apply when evaluating the significance of Jesus's death on the cross and human wisdom will only mislead one to reject the Gospel. Only to those who are called (τοῖς κλητοῖς, v. 23) is the mysterious (ἐν μυστηρίῳ) and hidden wisdom (τὴν ἀποκεκρυμμένην), predetermined (προώρισεν) before the ages, revealed (2: 7).

The entire argument is framed by two quotations from Isaiah 29: 14 and Jeremiah 9: 23, neither of which prima facie can be construed to support a theology that turns human expectation on its head. The Isaianic passage quoted in 1: 19 is a critique of the wisdom and understanding of those who consider themselves clever,[32] while Jeremiah 9: 23 in 1: 31 simply admonishes the one who wishes to boast to do so in the Lord. In Jeremiah 9: 23–4, Yahweh declares that the wise, mighty, and rich should not glory in their wisdom, might, and riches respectively, but in this (בזאת, ἐν τούτῳ), namely in pondering (השכל, συνίειν) and knowing (ידע, γίνωσκειν) him who practises mercy, justice, and righteousness in

---

[32] The Pauline variant ἀθετήσω 'I shall set aside' may be due to the influence of Ps. 32: 10, the use of a different text or the mistaken derivation of תסתתר (from סתר 'to hide, conceal') from סור 'to turn aside' (cf. Isa. 31: 2 where הסיר is translated as ἀθετηθῇ).

the land. As found in 1 Corinthians 1: 31, the quotation differs verbally, but not in intent, from Jeremiah 9: 23–4. It reads: ὁ καυχώμενος ἐν κυρίῳ καυχάσθω ('let him who boasts boast in the Lord'). The Pauline verse appears to resemble a summary statement of Jeremiah 9: 23–4 more than a quotation of one of its phrases: 'in the Lord' captures the essence of what is meant by knowing the Lord; here, no doubt it refers to Christ rather than Yahweh. Could this be another instance of the shorthand form of reference already discussed?

Against such a view is the prophetic source of the indirect quotation. The abbreviated references discussed above were of laws found in the Pentateuch or extra-biblical laws, not of sayings or teachings from prophetic texts. The complicating factor is that on occasion Paul does treat prophecies under the generalized category of 'law'.[33] In 1 Corinthians 14: 21, for instance, Paul introduces the prophetic text of Isaiah 28: 11 with the introductory formula ἐν τῷ νόμῳ γέγραπται ὅτι ('in the law it is written that'). It may well be going too far to suggest that Paul likewise regarded Jeremiah 9: 23–4, but to do so would explain away the apparent verbal discrepancies.

Alternatively, Paul may simply be using the same shorthand technique, which is most commonly associated with legal texts, in alluding to the teaching of Jeremiah. In either case, reading 1 Corinthians 1: 31 as a shorthand form of reference would yield a better sense: should the Corinthian brothers wish to boast, they should do so in conformity with the teaching that boasting should be in the Lord.

Jeremiah 9: 23–4 undergirds the entire opening section of 1 Corinthians. In these chapters, Paul refers to Greek wisdom and rhetoric (1 Cor. 2: 4[34]), but also to the signs of the Jews. The categories of the wise (σοφοί), powerful (δυνατοί/τὰ ἰσχυρά), and well-born (εὐγενεῖς; esp. vv. 26–9) enumerated by Paul resemble not a little the three groups of the σοφός, ἰσχυρός, and πλούσιος of the biblical text.[35] What remains problematic is the exegetical leap from Jeremiah's boasting in the Lord to the paradox of the cross,

[33] Similarly in Gal. 4: 22, the formula 'it is written' is used to refer to the story of Abraham rather than cite the words of its narrative.

[34] 'Not in Persuasive Words of Wisdom.'

[35] So Gordon Fee, *The First Epistle to the Corinthians* (Grand Rapids, Mich.: Wm. B. Eerdmans, 1987), 80, and esp. Gail O'Day, 'Jeremiah 9: 22–23 and 1 Corinthians 1: 26–31: A Study in Intertextuality', *JBL* 109/2 (1990), 259–67.

a gap that Paul fills by advancing the argument about the mysterious ways of God. Did Paul hit upon the notion that God moves in unexpected and even counter-rational ways simply by meditating on Jeremiah 9: 23-4?

Maybe he did so, but according to his own account in 2 Corinthians 10-13 it was the Lord who revealed to him that 'my grace is sufficient for you, for my power is made perfect in weakness' (12: 9). The affinities between 2 Corinthians 10-13 and 1 Corinthians 1-2 are evident not only in the view that God's ways run counter to human expectations, but also explicitly in the citation of Jeremiah 9: 23. In 2 Corinthians 10: 17, Paul quotes Jeremiah 9: 23-4 as a proof-text for his argument that unlike his competitors, whom he derides as 'false apostles' and 'deceitful workmen' (11: 13) or sarcastically as 'super-apostles' (11: 5), he does not boast beyond his limit, but confines himself to what is done in the Lord (10: 17). Verbally, the shorthand reference to Jeremiah 9: 23-4 in 2 Corinthians 10: 17 is all but identical with that which is found in 1 Corinthians 1: 31.

As it is reported in 1 Corinthians 12, it was during his ascent to the third heaven, a mystical journey that confirmed his apostolic commission, that the Lord had reassured him that his power is made perfect (τελεῖται) in weakness (ἐν ἀσθενείᾳ). Paul was harassed by 'a messenger of Satan', whom he figuratively describes as 'a thorn in the flesh', was persecuted, and suffered various kinds of physical and psychological hardships. Yet when he appealed to the Lord for help, it was revealed to him that God's grace is sufficient for him, for his power is paradoxically brought to completion in his weaknesses. When applied to his own difficult situation then, Paul states that precisely when he is weak, is he strong (12: 10).

The paradox of power in weakness bridges the exegetical gap between Jeremiah 9 and the theology of the cross. By advocating a view that overturns human expectations, Paul successfully brings together Jeremiah's boasting in the Lord and the victory of God's will in the apparent defeat and death of Jesus.

CONCLUSIONS

Central to Paul's hermeneutics is his own experience of Jesus and understanding of the significance of the cross. On this basis, all his exegetical techniques and scriptural interpretation depended. He could argue from the literalistic meaning of a biblical word or he may underscore the thrust of the message; he could use interpretative traditions or play on the ambiguities of scripture. Whatever he may do exegetically, there is a theological agenda around which the biblical texts had to be conformed. The variety of biblical texts would not have disturbed him, for his belief in Jesus as the Christ did not result from a study of the Torah, but in an experiential encounter with the divine. To be sure the authoritative writings of Israel constituted the framework in which he worked, but his hermeneutics and exegetical endeavours have their source beyond these boundaries.

PART V
Summary

11

Attitudes to Holy Scripture

The oft-repeated juxtaposition between 'biblical writings' and 'post-biblical exegeses' is in need of reconsideration. In so far as this dichotomy describes how the ancients viewed the sacredness of scripture, the distinction between authoritative texts that are biblical and those that are exegetical is overdrawn.

Neither the Qumran pesherists nor Paul considered their biblical texts to be the inviolable word of God. They did not see themselves simply as 'post-biblical' exegetes who interpreted, but never added to or subtracted anything from, a recognized body of authoritative texts. The writings that together make up 'holy scripture' are sacred not because they have been formalized and fixed in stone (so to speak), but because in them it is thought that the divine will of God can be found. Whether in stories about the children of Israel, say of the giving of the Torah to Moses on Mt. Sinai, or in prophetic oracles that are thought to conceal a true meaning, the intention of God is so perceived and understood.

Using interpretative techniques that either overlap with the modern scholarly understanding of exegesis or are better described as a 'reading in' of a sense unintended by the original author, the pesherists and Paul explained the meaning within the context of life and experience. Their exposition of scripture was not a purely academic exercise of the ivory tower kind, but was rooted in situations that had historical and practical referrents. The conviction that God is uncovering his will within the communities of faith transforms the ancient's understanding of his own role from interpreter to what can only be described as author.

On the face of it, the citation of a biblical text is an act that conspicuously appeals to an authority that is external to the interpreter. Had the ancient exegete simply reproduced the text he had before him, then it could be said that he had drawn a line between that which is authoritative and that which is interpretative. Such a line fades away, however, once it is recognized that the interpretation also involved the adaptation of the biblical texts.

What is perceived as the correct way of interpreting texts has at its heart elements that are both foreign and familiar. It is familiar, because some modern literary interpretations, too, do away with authorial intention. The reader's response to a text, his engagement with it on cognitive and emotive levels, is the hermeneutical key of some modern biblical interpretations. It is foreign, since these exegetical adaptations occur precisely at the point where fidelity to the authoritative texts would be expected. In quoting a text verbatim, the implication seems to be that the source of an interpretation is being brought forward and its actual words and meaning are open to independent scrutiny by the reader or audience. Yet, the surprise is that this act of quoting a text verbatim is also the process by which the ancient interpreter passes on his own understanding of the texts. The text, suitably modified, is the basis for what is being claimed as the correct understanding. That such an exegetical sleight-of-hand runs counter to modern sentiments of fair play cannot be denied.

Surely one of the deductions to be drawn from these exegetical adaptations is that ancient interpreters felt the need for changes, because the literal sense of the words does not correspond to what they wish to say. Now the pesherists and Paul do not have to construe the words in this manner. Within their writings are displayed exegetical techniques that range from the literalistic to the figurative and allegorical. Why they chose the path of exegetical adaptation rather than an alternative one that leaves the biblical texts intact remains unclear. There seems to be no consistency or generalized principle that could explain why the literalistic reading should be used here and the figurative there.

Obscure though the choice of exegetical techniques be, the hermeneutical centre of their scriptural interpretations no doubt lies in the revelation of God. For the pesherists, God in his holy spirit has revealed his will to the members of the community through the words of various leaders, the most important of whom is the Teacher of Righteousness. It was to this priest that God made known all the mysteries of the biblical prophets, the events of which apparently concern the destinies of the pious and wicked men during the end-time. Paul too relied on the revelation of God in Jesus Christ. Not unlike the Teacher of Righteousness, Jesus, who is the Spirit, removes the veil that obscures men's vision of the glory of God. The new covenant of God, written on tables of the human heart, is founded on a Christological and spiritual reading of the biblical texts.

The similarities, however, should not be overemphasized. Exegetically, the Qumran pesherists were locked into the structure of the biblical prophecies that were being interpreted. There is a greater degree of order and regularity than that which is evident in Paul's exposition. The interpretation of scripture in the Pauline letters depended more upon the practical problems that he was addressing than any systematic commentary on larger and smaller portions of the biblical texts. Themes arise from real issues facing the Churches and these are supported and defended by proof-texts or illustrated by biblical precedents and patterns.

Significant, too, for Paul's hermeneutics is the centrality of the person and work of Jesus Christ. The pesharim do not invest the same kind of importance to the role of the Teacher of Righteousness. Nowhere in the Qumran pesharim is there any indication that the suffering of the Teacher at the hands of the Wicked Priest in his house of exile was understood to have a similar type of salvific efficacy that was attributed to Jesus' crucifixion. Despite the recent claims of some, the Teacher of Righteousness remained a teacher of scripture for the Qumran community, inspired to be sure, but not elevated to the position of Son of God and Lord. The pesherists' faith was in him as an authoritative interpreter of the law and of the divine will.

SELECT BIBLIOGRAPHY

TEXTS AND EDITIONS

Hebrew Bible

Biblia Hebraica Stuttgartensia, ed. K. Elliger, W. Rudolph, *et al.* (Stuttgart: Deutsche Bibelgesellschaft, 1966–7)

The Hebrew University Bible: The Book of Isaiah, ed. M. H. Goshen-Gottstein (Jerusalem: Magnes Press, 1975, 1981, 1993), i–iii.

LXX

The Old Testament in Greek According to the Septuagint, ed. H. W. Sweet (Cambridge: Cambridge University Press, 1894–6), i–iii.

The Old Testament in Greek, ed. Alan England Brooke and Norman McLean (Cambridge: Cambridge University Press), i. *Octateuch* (1906–11); ii. *Later Historical Books* (1927–32); iii. *Esther, Judith, Tobit* (1940).

Septuaginta: id est Vetus Testamentum graece iuxta LXX interpres, ed. A. Rahlfs (Stuttgart: Deutsche Bibelgesellschaft, 1935), i–ii.

Septuaginta: Vetus Testamentum Graecum Academiae Litterarum Gottingensis Editum (Göttingen: Vandenhoeck & Ruprecht), i. *Genesis*, ed. J. W. Wevers (1974);. ii. 2. *Leviticus*, ed. J. W. Wevers and U. Quast (1986); iii. 1 *Numeri*, ed. J. W. Wevers (1982); iii. 2 *Deuteronomium*, ed. J. W. Wevers (1974); x. *Psalmi cum Odis*, ed. A. Rahlfs (1979); xi. 4 *Job*, ed. J. Ziegler (1982); xiii. *Duodecim prophetae*, ed. J. Ziegler (1943); xiv. *Isaias*, ed. J. Ziegler (1939); xv. *Ieremias, Baruch, Threni, Epistula Ieremiae*, ed. J. Ziegler (1957).

Vulgate

Biblia Sacra iuxta Vulgatam Versionem: Editio Minor, ed. B. Fischer, J. Gribomont, H. F. D. Sparks, R. Weber, *et al.* (Stuttgart: Deutsche Bibelgesellschaft, 1984).

New Testament

The New Testament in the Original Greek, ed. B. F. Westcott and F. J. A. Hort, 2nd edn. (Cambridge and London: Macmillan, 1896), i–ii.

Novum Testamentum Graece, ed. Ebehard Nestle, Erwin Nestle, Kurt Aland, Barbara Aland, *et al.* 26th edn. (Stuttgart: Deutsche Bibelstiftung, 1979).

Novum Testamentum Graece ad antiquissimos testes denuo recensuit apparatum

Select Bibliography

criticum apposuit, ed. Constantin von Tischendorf, 8th edn. (Lipsiae: J. C. Hinrichs), i. (1869); ii. (1872); iii. (1894).

Qumran

DJD i. *Qumran Cave I,* ed. D. Barthélemy, J. T. Milik, *et al.* (1955).

DJD ii. *Les Grottes de Murabba'ât,* ed. P. Benoit, J. T. Milik, R. de Vaux, *et al.* (1961).

DJD iii. *Les 'Petites Grottes' de Qumrân: Exploration de la falaise. Les Grottes 2Q, 3Q, 5Q, 6Q, 7Q à 10Q. Le rouleau de cuivre,* ed. M. Baillet, J. T. Milik and R. de Vaux (1962).

DJD iv. *The Psalms Scroll of Qumrân Cave 11 (11QPsª),* ed. J. A. Sanders (1965).

DJD v. *Qumrân Cave 4. I (4Q158-4Q186),* ed. J. M. Allegro and A. A. Anderson (1968).

DJD vi. *Qumrân Grotte 4. II. 1 Archéologie,* ed. Roland de Vaux, *et al.* II. 2 *Tefillin, Mezuzot et Targums (4Q128-4Q157),* ed. J. T. Milik (1977).

DJD vii. *Qumrân Grotte 4. III (4Q482-4Q520),* ed. Maurice Baillet (1982).

DJD viii. *The Greek Minor Prophets Scroll from Nahal Hever (8HevXIIgr) (The Seiyâl Collection I),* ed. Emanuel Tov, Robert Kraft, and P. J. Parsons (1990).

DJD ix. *Qumran Cave 4. IV. Palaeo-Hebrew and Greek Biblical Manuscripts,* ed. Patrick W. Skehan, Eugene Ulrich, Judith E. Sanderson, and P. J. Parsons.

DJD x. *Qumran Cave 4. V. Miqsat Ma'aseh Ha-Torah,* ed. Elisha Qimron and John Strugnell (1994).

DJD xii. *Qumran Cave 4. VII. Genesis to Numbers,* ed. Eugene Ulrich, Frank Moore Cross, James R. Davila, Nathan Jastram, Judith E. Sanderson, and Emanuel Tov (1994).

DJD xiii. *Qumran Cave 4. VIII. Parabiblical Texts Part I,* ed. Harold Attridge, Torleif Elgvin, Jozef Milik, Saul Olyan, John Strugnell, Emanuel Tov, James VanderKam, and Sidnie White (1994).

Other

Broshi, Magen, *The Damascus Document Reconsidered* (Jerusalem: Israel Exploration Society, 1992).

Burrows, Millar, Trever, John C., and Brownlee, William H., *The Dead Sea Scrolls of St. Mark's Monastery,* i. *The Isaiah Manuscript and the Habakkuk Commentary;* ii. *The Manual of Discipline* (New Haven: American Schools of Oriental Research, 1950, 1951).

Charlesworth, James H., *Rule of the Community* (Tübingen: J. C. B. Mohr (Paul Siebeck), 1994).

——*Damascus Document, War Scroll and Related Documents* (Tübingen: J. C. B. Mohr (Paul Siebeck), 1995).

EISENMAN, ROBERT H., and ROBINSON, JAMES M., *A Facsimile Edition of the Dead Sea Scrolls* (Washington: Biblical Archaeology Society, 1991), i and ii.

SANDERS, JAMES A., *The Dead Sea Psalms Scroll* (New York: Cornell University Press, 1967).

SCHULLER, EILEEN M., *Non-Canonical Psalms from Qumran: A Pseudepigraphic Collection* (Atlanta: Scholars Press, 1986).

TOV, EMANUEL, with PFANN, STEPHEN, *The Dead Sea Scrolls on Microfiche. Companion Volume and Inventory List of Photographs* (Leiden: E. J. Brill, 1993).

VAN DER PLOEG, J. P. M., VAN DER WOUDE, A. S., and JONGELING, B. (eds.) *Le Targum de Job de la grotte XI de Qumran* (Leiden: E. J. Brill, 1971).

WACHOLDER, BEN ZION, and ABEGG, MARTIN G., *A Preliminary Edition of the Unpublished Dead Sea Scrolls: Fascicles 1 and 2* (Washington: Biblical Archaeology Society, 1991, 1992).

YADIN, YIGAEL, *The Temple Scroll*, Eng. trans. (Jerusalem: Israel Exploration Society, 1983), i–iii, and Suppl.

GRAMMARS, LEXICA, CONCORDANCES, AND OTHER TOOLS

ALAND, KURT, *Vollständige Konkordanz zum griechischen Neuen Testament: Unter Zugrundelegung aller kritischer Textausgaben und des Textus Receptus* (2 vols; Berlin and New York: de Gruyter, 1975, 1978).

Bible Windows, 4.08 beta, CD ROM, version 3.0 (Silver Mountain Software, Cedar Hills, Texas).

BLASS, F., DEBRUNNER, A., and FUNK, ROBERT W., *A Greek Grammar of the New Testament and Other Early Christian Literature* (Chicago: University of Chicago Press, 1961).

BROCK, SEBASTIAN P., FRITSCH, C. T., and JELLICOE, S., *A Classified Bibliography of the Septuagint* (Leiden: E. J. Brill, 1973).

CHARLESWORTH, JAMES H., *Graphic Concordance to the Dead Sea Scrolls* (Tübingen: J. C. B. Mohr (Paul Siebeck), 1991).

COGGINS, R. J., and HOULDON, J. L. (eds.), *Dictionary of Biblical Interpretation* (London: SCM Press, 1990),

DE ROSSI, JOHANNES BERNARDUS, *Variae Lectiones Veteris Testamenti* (Parmae: Regio Typographeo, 1784, 1785, 1788), i–iii.

FITZMYER, J. A., *The Dead Sea Scrolls: Major Publications and Tools for Study*, rev. edn. (Atlanta: Scholars Press, 1990).

GIBSON, J. C. L., *Davidson's Introductory Hebrew Grammar-Syntax* (Edinburgh: T. & T. Clark, 1994).

HATCH, EDWIN, and REDPATH, HENRY A., *A Concordance to the Septuagint and the other Greek Versions of the Old Testament* (3 vols; Oxford:

Select Bibliography

Clarendon Press, 1940). *An Expanded Hebrew Index for the Hatch–Redpath Concordance to the Septuagint* (Jerusalem: 1973).

KUHN, KARL GEORG, *et al. Konkordanz zu den Qumrantexten* (Göttingen: Vandenhoeck & Ruprecht, 1960).

LIDDELL, H. G., SCOTT, R., and JONES, H. S., *A Greek-English Lexicon.* (Oxford: Clarendon Press, 1968), i–ii, and Suppl.

LIM, TIMOTHY H., *in consultation with* PHILIP S. ALEXANDER, *The Dead Sea Scrolls Electronic Reference Library,* Vol. I (Oxford/Leiden: Oxford University Press/Brill Academic Publishers, 1997).

MANDELKERN, SOLOMON, *Veteris Testamenti Concordantiae Hebraicae atque Chaldaicae* (Leipzig: Veit, 1906).

MARTONE, CORRADO, 'A Concordance to the Newly Published Qumran Texts', *Henoch*, 15 (1993), 155–206.

A Preliminary Concordance to the Hebrew and Aramaic Fragments from Qumrân Caves II–X (Göttingen: private pub., 1988), i–iv.

QIMRON, ELISHA, *The Hebrew of the Dead Sea Scrolls,* Harvard Semitic Studies (Atlanta: Scholars Press, 1986).

REED, STEPHEN, *The Dead Sea Scrolls Catalogue: Documents, Photographs and Museum Inventory Numbers,* rev. Marilyn J. Lundberg (Atlanta: Scholars Press, 1994).

SEGAL, M. H., *A Grammar of Mishnaic Hebrew* (Oxford: Clarendon Press, 1927).

SOKOLOFF, MICHAEL, *A Dictionary of Jewish Palestinian Aramaic of the Byzantine Period* (Ramat-Gan: Bar Ilan University Press, 1990).

THACKERAY, H. ST JOHN, *A Grammar of the Old Testament in Greek According to the Septuagint.* i. *Introduction, Orthography and Accidence* (Cambridge: Cambridge University Press, 1909).

STUDIES

AAGESON, J. W., 'Paul's Use of Scripture: A Comparative Study of Biblical Interpretation in Early Palestinian Judaism and the New Testament with Special Reference to Romans 9–11', D.Phil., University of Oxford, 1983.

—— 'Scripture and Structure in the Development of the Argument in Romans 9–11', *CBQ* 48 (1986), 268–89.

—— 'Typology, Correspondence, and the Application of Scripture in Romans 9–11', *JSNT* 31 (1987), 51–72.

AEJMELAEUS, ANNELI, 'What Can We Know About the Hebrew Vorlage of the Septuagint?', *ZAW* 99 (1987), 58–9.

ALAND, KURT, and ALAND, BARBARA, *The Text of the New Testament* (Leiden: E. J. Brill, 1987).

Select Bibliography

ALBREKTSON, BERTIL, *Reflections on the Emergence of a Standard Text of the Hebrew Bible*, in VTS 29 (Leiden: E. J. Brill, 1978), 49–65.

—— 'Difficilior Lectio Probabilior: A Rule of Textual Criticism and its Use in Old Testament Studies', *OS* 21 (1981), 5–18.

ALBRIGHT, W. F., 'A Catalogue of Early Hebrew Lyric Poems (Psalm LXVIII)', *HUCA* 23 (1950–1), 1–39.

—— 'New Light on Early Recensions of the Hebrew Bible', *BASOR* 140 (1955), 27–33.

ALEXANDER, P. S., 'Rabbinic Judaism and the New Testament', *ZNW* 74 (1983), 237–46.

—— 'Midrash and the Gospels', in C. M. Tuckett (ed.), *Synoptic Studies: The Ampleforth Conferences of 1982 and 1983* (Sheffield: JSOT Press, 1984), 1–18.

—— 'Rabbinic Biography and the Biography of Jesus: A Survey of the Evidence', in C. M. Tuckett (ed.), *Synoptic Studies: The Ampleforth Conferences of 1982 and 1983*, (Sheffield: JSOT Press, 1984), 19–50.

—— 'Midrash and Pesher', in Speaker's Lecture Series, 'Midrash and the New Testament: The Interpretation of Scripture in the Synagogue and in the Early Church', University of Oxford, 10 November 1987.

—— 'Retelling the Old Testament', in D. A. Carson and H. G. M. Williamson (eds.), *It is Written: Scripture Citing Scripture: Essays in Honour of Barnabas Lindars* (Cambridge: Cambridge University Press, 1988), 99–121.

—— 'Jewish Aramaic Translation of Hebrew Scriptures', in *Mikra*, 217–53.

ALLEGRO, JOHN MARCO, 'A Newly Discovered Fragment of a Commentary on Psalm XXXVII from Qumrân', *PEQ* 86 (1954), 69–75.

—— 'Further Messianic References in Qumran Literature', *JBL* 75 (1956), 174–87.

—— 'A Recently Discovered Fragment of a Commentary on Hosea from Qumran's Fourth Cave' *JBL* 78 (1959), 142–7.

ALLO, E.-B., *Saint Paul: Première Épitre aux Corinthiens* (Paris: J. Gabalda, 1956).

—— *Saint Paul: Seconde Épitre aux Corinthiens* (Paris: J. Gabalda, 1956).

AMOUSINE, JOSEPH D., 'Observatiunculae qumraneae', *RQ* 7 (1969–70), 533–5.

AMSLER, SAMUEL, *L'Ancien Testament dans L'Église* (Neuchatel: Delachaux & Niestlé, 1960).

ANDERSON, FRANK, and FORBES, DEAN A., 'What Did the Scribes Count?', in D. N. Freedman, Frank Anderson, and A. Dean Forbes (eds.), *Studies in Hebrew and Aramaic Orthography* (Winona Lake, Ind.: Eisenbrauns, 1992), 297–318.

ATTRIDGE, H. W., *Interpretation of Biblical History in the Antiquitates Judaicae of Flavius Josephus* (Missoula, Mont.: Scholars Press, 1976).

Select Bibliography

ATTRIDGE, H. W., *Hebrews* (Philadelphia: Fortress Press, 1989).

AULD, A. GRAEME, *Kings without Privilege: David and Moses in the Story of the Bible's Kings* (Edinburgh: T. & T. Clark, 1994).

AVIGAD, NACHMAN, 'The Paleography of the Dead Sea Scrolls and Related Documents', *Scripta Hierosolymitana 4*, ed. C. Rabin and Y. Yadin (Jerusalem: Magnes Press, 1958), 56–87.

BACHER, WILHELM, *Die Agada der Tannaiten: von Akiba's Tod bis zum Abschluß der Mischna* (Strasburg: Karl J. Trübner, 1890), i–ii.

——*Die exegetische Terminologie der jüdischen Traditionsliteratur*, i. *Die bibel-exegetische Terminologie der Tannaiten* (Leipzig: J. C. Hinrichs, 1899, repr. 1905).

BAMMEL, ERNST, 'Gottes *ΔΙΑΘΗΚΗ* (Gal. III. 15–17) und das Jüdische Rechtsdenken', *NTS* 6 (1960), 313–19.

BANKS, ROBERT, *Jesus and the Law in the Synoptic Tradition* (Cambridge: Cambridge University Press, 1975).

BARR, JAMES, *Judaism—Its Continuity with the Bible*, Seventh Montefiore Memorial Lecture, University of Southampton (Southampton: Camelot Press, 1968).

——'Le Judaïsme postbiblique et la théologie de l'Ancien Testament', *RTP* 18 (1968), 209–17.

——*The Typology of Literalism in Ancient Biblical Translations*, Mitteilungen des Septuaginta-Unternehmens (MSU), 15 (Göttingen: Vandenhoeck & Ruprecht, 1979).

——*Old and New in Interpretation* (London: SCM Press, 1982).

——*Holy Scripture. Canon, Authority, Criticism* (Oxford: Clarendon Press, 1983).

——*The Variable Spellings of the Hebrew Bible* (Oxford: Oxford University Press, 1989).

——'Paul and the LXX: A Note on Some Recent Work', *JTS* 45/2 (1994), 593–601.

BARRETT, CHARLES KINGSLEY, *A Commentary on the Epistle to the Romans* (London: Adam & Charles Black, 1957).

——*A Commentary on the First Epistle to the Corinthians* (New York: Harper & Row, 1968).

——*A Commentary on the Second Epistle to the Corinthians* (London: Adam & Charles Black, 1973).

——'The Interpretation of the Old Testament in the New', in *CHB* i. 377–411.

BARTHÉLEMY, DOMINIQUE, 'Redécouverte d'un chaînon manquant de l'Histoire de la Septante', *RB* 60 (1953), 18–29. Repr. *QHBT*, 127–39.

——*Les Devanciers d'Aquila: Première publication intégrale du texte des fragments du Dodécaprophéton trouvés dans le Désert de Juda, précédée d'une étude sur les traductions et recensions grecques de la Bible réalisées au premier siècle de notre ère sous l'influence du rabbinat palestinien*, VTS 10 (Leiden: E. J. Brill, 1963).

BARTHÉLEMY, DOMINIQUE, *Les Tiqquné Sopherim et la critique textuelle de l'Ancien Testament*, VTS 9 (Leiden: E. J. Brill, 1963), 285-304.

—— 'Text, Hebrew, History of', *IDBS*, 878-84.

BARTON, JOHN, *Oracles of God: Perceptions of Ancient Prophecy in Israel after the Exile* (London: Darton, Longman & Todd, 1986).

—— , *People of the Book? The Authority of the Bible in Christianity* (London: SPCK, 1988).

—— 'Canon', in R. J. Coggins and J. L. Houlden (eds.), *Dictionary of Biblical Interpretation* (London: SCM Press, 1990), 101-5.

BASSER, H. W., 'Pesher Hadavar: The Truth of the Matter', *RQ* 49-52 (1988), 389-406.

BAUMGARTEN, JOSEPH M., 'Does TLH in the Temple Scroll Refer to Crucifixion?', *JBL* 91 (1972), 472-81.

—— *Studies in Qumran Law* (Leiden: E. J. Brill, 1977).

—— 'A "Scriptural" Citation in 4QFragments of the Damascus Document', *JJS* 43 (1992), 95-8.

—— 'A New Qumran Substitute for the Divine Name and Mishnah Sukkah 45', *JQR* 88 (1992), 1-6.

—— 'The Disqualification of Priest in 4Q Fragments of the ⟨⟨Damascus Document⟩⟩, a Specimen of the Recovery of Pre-Rabbinic Halakha', in *Madrid*, ii. 503-14.

BEALL, TODD S., *Josephus' Description of the Essenes Illustrated by the Dead Sea Scrolls* (Cambridge: Cambridge University Press, 1988).

BECKWITH, ROGER, *The Old Testament Canon of the New Testament Church and its Background in Early Judaism* (London: SPCK, 1985).

BERNSTEIN, MOSHE, 'Introductory Formulas for Citation and Re-citation of Biblical Verses in the Qumran Pesharim', *DSD* 1 (1994), 30-70.

BETZ, HANS DIETER, *Galatians: A Commentary on Paul's Letter to the Churches in Galatia* (Philadelphia: Fortress Press, 1979).

BETZ, OTTO, *Offenbarung und Schriftforschung in der Qumransekte*, WUNT (Tübingen: J. C. B. Mohr, 1960).

BIRNBAUM, S. A., *The Hebrew Script*, i. *The Texts* (Leiden: E. J. Brill, 1957); ii. *The Plates* (London: Paleographia, 1957).

BLACK, MATTHEW, 'The Christological Use of the Old Testament in the New Testament', *NTS* 18 (1971), 1-14.

—— 'The Theological Appropriation of the Old Testament in the New' *SJT* 39 (1986) 1-17.

BLENKINSOPP, JOSEPH, *A History of Prophecy in Israel: From the Settlement in the Land to the Hellenistic Period* (Philadelphia: Westminster Press, 1983).

BLIGH, J., *Galatians: A Discussion of St. Paul's Epistle* (London: St Paul, 1969).

BLOCH, RENÉE, 'Midrash' in *SDB*, v. 1263–81.

BOCK, DARRELL L., 'Evangelicals and the Use of the Old Testament in the New', *BSac* 142 (1985), 209–23 and 306–19.

BOCKMUEHL, MARKUS N. A., *Revelation and Mystery in Ancient Judaism and Pauline Christianity* (Tübingen: J. C. B. Mohr (Paul Siebeck), 1990).

BONANI, G., *et al.* 'Radiocarbon Dating of the Dead Sea Scrolls', *'Atiqot*, 20 (1991), 27–32.

BONSIRVEN, J., *Exégèse rabbinique et exégèse paulinienne* (Paris: Beauchesne et ses Fils, 1939).

BRAUN, HERBERT, *Qumran und das Neue Testament* (Tübingen: J. C. B. Mohr, 1966), i–ii.

BREWER, DAVID INSTONE, *Techniques and Assumptions in Jewish Exegesis before 70 C.E.* (Tübingen: J. C. B. Mohr, 1992).

BRIGHT, JOHN, *Jeremiah* (Garden City, NY: Doubleday, 1965).

BROCK, SEBASTIAN P., 'The Recensions of the Septuagint Version of 1 Samuel', D.Phil., Oxford, 1966.

——'Lucian *redivivus*: Some Reflections on Barthélemy's *Les Devanciers d'Aquila*', *SE* 5 (1968), 176–81.

——'Origen's Aims as a Textual Critic of the Old Testament', *SP* 10 (1970), 215–18.

——'The Phenomenon of the Septuagint', *OS* 17 (1972), 11–36.

——'Bibelhandschriften I. Altes Testament', *TR* 6: 109–14.

——'Bibelübersetzungen I' *TR* 6: 161, 163–72.

——'To Revise or not to Revise: Attitudes to Jewish Biblical Translation', in *SSCW*, 301–38.

——'some Aspects of Translation Technique in Antiquity', in *Syriac Perspectives on Late Antiquity* (London: Variorum Reprints, 1984), ii and iv.

BROOKE, GEORGE J., 'Qumran Pesher: Towards the Redefinition of a Genre', *RQ* 40 (1981), 483–503.

——*Exegesis at Qumran: 4QFlorilegium in its Jewish Context* (Sheffield: JSOT Press, 1985).

——'The Biblical Texts in the Qumran Commentaries: Scribal Errors or Exegetical Variants?', in Craig A. Evans and William F. Stinespring (eds.), *Early Jewish and Christian Exegesis: Studies in Memory of William Hugh Brownlee* (Atlanta: Scholars Press, 1987), 85–100.

——'The Thematic Content of 4Q252', *JQR* 85 (1994), 33–59.

BROWNLEE, WILLIAM HUGH, 'Bible Interpretation among the Sectaries of the Dead Sea Scrolls', *BA* 19 (1951), 54–76.

——'The Habakkuk Midrash and the Targum of Jonathan', *JSS* 7 (1955), 169–86.

——*The Text of Habakkuk in the Ancient Commentary from Qumran*. JBL

Monograph Series, 11 (Philadelphia: Society for Biblical Literature and Exegesis, 1959).

BROWNLEE, WILLIAM HUGH, 'The Background of Biblical Interpretation at Qumrân', in M. Delcor (ed.), *Qumrân: Sa piété, sa théologie et son milieu* (Leuven: Leuven University Press, 1978), 183–94.

——*The Midrash Pesher of Habakkuk* (Missoula, Mont.: Scholars Press, 1979).

BRUCE, F. F., *Biblical Exegesis in the Qumran Texts* (The Hague: Vitgeverij van Keulen N.V., 1959).

BRUCE, F. F., *The New Testament Development of Old Testament Themes* (Exeter: Paternoster Press, 1968).

——*The Epistle of Paul to the Galatians: A Commentary on the Greek Text* (Exeter: Paternoster Press, 1972).

——*Commentary on the Book of Acts* (Grand Rapids: Eerdmans, 1981).

——'Biblical Exposition at Qumran', in R. T. France and D. Wenham (eds.), *Gospel Perspectives: Studies in Midrash and Historiography* (Sheffield: JSOT Press, 1983), iii. 77–98.

——and RUPP, E. G. (eds.), *Holy Book and Holy Tradition* (Manchester: Manchester University Press, 1968).

BURKITT, F. C., *The Gospel History and its Transmission* (Edinburgh: T. & T. Clark, 1907).

BURROWS, MILLAR, 'The Meaning of 'šr 'mr in DSH', *VT* 2 (1952), 255–60.

BURTON, ERNEST DE WITT, *The Epistle to the Galatians* (Edinburgh: T. & T. Clark, 1921).

CADBURY, H. J., *The Book of Acts in History* (London: Adam & Charles Black, 1955).

CAIRD, G.B., *A Commentary on the Revelation of St. John the Divine* (New York: Harper & Row, 1966).

CARMIGNAC, JEAN, 'Notes sur les Peshârîm', *RQ* 3 (1961–2), 505–38.

——'Le Document de Qumrân sur Melkisédeq', *RQ* 7 (1969–71), 342–78.

——COTHENET, É., and H. LIGNÉE, *Les Textes de Qumran: Traduits et Annotés* (Paris: Éditions Letouzey et Ané, 1963), ii.

CARPOZ, J. G., *A Defence of the Hebrew Bible, in Answer to the Charge of Corruption Brought Against it by Mr. Whiston . . .* (London, 1729).

CASSUTO, M. D. U., *The Prophet Hosea and the Books of the Pentateuch in Biblical and Oriental Studies*, Eng. trans. (Jerusalem: Magnes Press, 1973), 79–100.

CHARLESWORTH, JAMES H. (gen. ed.), *Rule of the Community and Related Documents* (Tübingen: J. C. B. Mohr (Paul Siebeck), 1994).

CHAZON, ESTHER, 'Is Divrei ha-me'orot a Sectarian Prayer?', in *FYR* 3–17.

CHESTER, ANDREW, 'Citing the Old Testament', in D. A. Carson and

H. G. M. Williamson (eds.), *It is Written: Scripture Citing Scripture: Essays in Honour of Barnabas Lindars* (Cambridge: Cambridge University Press, 1988), 141-69.

CHIESA, BRUNO, 'Textual History and Textual Criticism of the Hebrew Old Testament', in *Madrid*, i. 257-72.

CHILDS, BREVARD, *Introduction to the Old Testament as Scripture* (London: SCM Press, 1979).

CHILTON, B. D., 'Commenting on the Old Testament (with Particular Reference to the Pesharim, Philo and the Mekilta)', in D. A. Carson and H. G. M. Williamson (eds.), *It is Written: Scripture Citing Scripture: Essays in Honour of Barnabas Lindars* (Cambridge: Cambridge University Press, 1988), 122-40.

COHEN, SHAYE, *Josephus in Galilee and Rome: His Vita and Development as a Historian* (Leiden: E. J. Brill, 1979).

—— 'The Modern Study of Ancient Judaism', in Shaye J. D. Cohen and Edward L. Greenstein (eds.), *The State of Jewish Studies* (Detroit: Wayne State University, 1990), 55-74.

COLLIN, MATTHIEU, 'Recherches sur l'histoire textuelle du Prophète Michee', *VT* 21 (1971), 281-97.

COLLINS, JOHN J., 'Jewish Apocalyptic against its Hellenistic Near Eastern Environment', *BASOR* 220 (1975), 27-36.

—— 'Was the Dead Sea Sect an Apocalyptic Movement?', in Lawrence H. Schiffman (ed.), *Archaeology and History in the Dead Sea Scrolls* (Sheffield: Sheffield Academic Press, 1990), 25-52.

—— *Daniel* (Minneapolis: Fortress, 1993).

—— *The Scepter and the Star: The Messiahs of the Dead Sea Scrolls and Other Ancient Literature* (New York: Doubleday, 1995).

CRANFIELD, C. E. B., *A Critical and Exegetical Commentary on the Epistle to the Romans* (Edinburgh: T. & T. Clark Ltd., 1975), i-ii.

CROSS, FRANK MOORE, 'A New Qumran Biblical Fragment Related to the Original Hebrew Underlying the Septuagint', *BASOR* 132 (1953), 15-26.

—— 'The Oldest Manuscripts from Qumran', in *QHBT*, 147-76.

—— 'The Development of the Jewish Scripts', in G. E. Wright (ed.), *The Bible and the Ancient Near East: Essays in Honor of W. F. Albright* (New York: Doubleday, 1961), 144-202.

—— 'The History of the Biblical Text in the Light of Discoveries in the Judaean Desert', *QHBT* 177-95.

—— 'The Contribution of the Qumran Discoveries to the Study of the Biblical Text', *QHBT* 278-92.

—— 'The Evolution of a Theory of Local Texts', *QHBT* 306-20.

—— 'Problems of Method in the Textual Criticism of the Hebrew Bible', in Wendy Doniger O'Flaherty (ed.), *The Critical Study of Sacred Texts*,

Berkeley Religious Studies Series, 2 (Berkeley: Graduate Theological Union, 1979), 31–54.

CROSS, FRANK MOORE, 'The Ammonite Oppression of the Tribes of Gad and Reuben: Missing Verses from 1 Samuel 11 found in 4QSamuel[a]', in H. Tadmor and M. Weinfeld (eds.), *History, Historiography and Interpretation* (Jerusalem: Magnes Press, 1983), 148–58.

—— 'Some Notes on a Generation of Qumran Studies', in *Madrid*, i. 1–14.

—— *The Ancient Library of Qumran*, 3rd edn. (Sheffield: Sheffield Academic Press, 1995).

DAUBE, DAVID, 'Rabbinic Methods of Interpretation and Hellenistic Rhetoric', *HUCA* 22 (1949), 239–64.

—— *The New Testament and Rabbinic Judaism* (London: Athlone Press, 1956).

DAVIES, P. R., *The Damascus Covenant: An Interpretation of the 'Damascus Document'* (Sheffield: JSOT Press, 1983).

DAVIES, W. D., *Paul and Rabbinic Judaism: Some Rabbinic Elements in Pauline Theology* (London: SPCK, 1948).

—— *The Setting of the Sermon on the Mount* (Cambridge: Cambridge University Press, 1964).

—— 'Reflections about the Use of the Old Testament in the New in its Historical Context', *JQR* 74 (1983), 105–36.

—— *Jewish and Pauline Studies* (London: SPCK, 1984).

—— and ALLISON, D. C., *The Gospel According to Saint Matthew* (Edinburgh: T. & T. Clark Ltd., 1988).

DE JONGE, MARTINUS, and VAN DER WOUDE, A. S., '11QMelchizedek and the New Testament', *NTS* 12 (1966), 301–26.

DE VAUX, ROLAND, *Ancient Israel: Its Life and Institutions*, Eng. trans. (London: Darton, Longman & Todd, 1961).

DE WAARD, J., *A Comparative Study of the Old Testament Text in the Dead Sea Scrolls and in the New Testament* (Leiden: E. J. Brill, 1966).

DIMANT, DEVORAH, 'The Pesher on the Periods (4Q180) and 4Q181', *IOS* 9 (1979), 77–102.

—— 'Qumran Sectarian Literature', in *JWSTP*, 483–550.

—— 'Pesharim, Qumran', in *ABD*, v. 244–51.

DITTMAR, W., *Vetus Testamentum in Novo: Die alttestamentlichen Parallelen des Neuen Testaments in Wortlaut der Urtexte und der Septuaginta* (Göttingen: Vandenhoeck & Ruprecht, 1899–1903).

DODD, C. H., *The Epistle of Paul to the Romans* (London: Hodder & Stoughton, 1932).

—— *According to the Scriptures: The Sub-Structure of New Testament Theology* (London: Nisbet, 1952).

DOEVE, J. W., *Jewish Hermeneutics in the Synoptic Gospels and Acts* (Assen: Koninklijke van Gorcum, 1954).

DORVALL, GILLES, HARL, MARGUERITE, and MUNNICH, OLIVIER, *La Bible* grecque des Septante du judaïsme hellénistique au christianisme ancien (Paris: Éditions du CERF/CNRS, 1988).

DRIVER, S. R. Deuteronomy (Edinburgh: T. & T. Clark, 1895).

DUBARLE, A. M., 'Note conjointe sur l'inspiration de la Septante', RSPT 49 (1965), 221–9.

DUNCAN, JULIE ANN, 'Consideration of 4QDt^j in light of the 'All Souls Deuteronomy' and Cave 4 Phylactery Texts', in Madrid, i. 199–216.

DUNN, JAMES D. G., The Epistle to the Galatians (London: A. & C. Black, 1993).

DUPONT-SOMMER, ANDRÉ, 'Le "Commentaire d'Habacuc" découvert près de la Mer Morte: Traduction et notes', RHR 137 (1950), 129–71.

——The Essene Writings from Qumran, trans. G. Vermes (Oxford: Blackwells, 1961).

EDGAR, S. L., 'Respect for Context in Quotations from the Old Testament', NTS 9 (1962–3), 55–62.

EISENMAN, ROBERT, and WISE, MICHAEL, The Dead Sea Scrolls Uncovered (Longmead: Element Press, 1992).

ELLIGER, KARL, Studien zum Habakuk-Kommentar vom Toten Meer (Tübingen: J. C. B. Mohr (Paul Siebeck), 1953), plus insert 'Der Hebräische Text des Habakkuk-Commentars vom Toten Meer (DSH) in Umschrift'.

ELLIS, E. EARLE, Paul's Use of the Old Testament (London: Oliver & Boyd, 1957).

——'Midrash, Targum and New Testament'. in E. Earle Ellis and Max Wilcox (eds.), Neotestamentica et Semitica: Studies in Honour of Matthew Black (Edinburgh: T. & T. Clark, 1969), 61–9.

——Prophecy and Hermeneutics in Early Christianity: New Testament Essays (Tübingen: J. C. B. Mohr, 1978).

——'Biblical Interpretation in the New Testament Church', in Mikra, 691–726.

EPP, ELDON JAY, 'Textual Criticism, NT', IDBS, 891–5.

——'New Testament Textual Criticism. Past, Present and Future: Reflections on the Alands' Text of the New Testament', HTR 82/2 (1989), 213–29.

——'The New Testament Papyrus Manuscripts in Historical Perspective', in Maurya P. Horgan and Paul J. Kobelski (eds.), To Touch the Text: Biblical and Related Studies in Honor of Joseph A. Fitzmyer, S.J. (New York: Crossroad, 1989), 261–88.

——'Textual Criticism' in E. J. Epp and G. W. MacRae (eds.), The New Testament and its Modern Interpreters (Atlanta: Scholars Press, 1989), 75–126.

ESHEL, ESTHER, and STONE, MICHAEL, 'לשון הקודש באחרית הימים לאור קטע מקומראן', Tarbiz, 62 (1993), 169–78.

EVANS, CRAIG A., and SANDERS, JAMES A., *Paul and the Scriptures of Israel* (Sheffield: Sheffield Academic Press, 1993).

FEE, GORDON, *The First Epistle to the Corinthians* (Grand Rapids, Mich.: Wm. B. Eerdmans, 1987).

FELDMAN, LOUIS H., 'Hellenization in Josephus' Potrayal of Man's Decline', in J. Neusner (ed.), *Religions in Antiquity: Essays in Memory of E. R. Goodenough* (Leiden: E. J. Brill, 1968), 336–53.

——'Use, Authority and Exegesis of Mikra in the Writings of Josephus', in *Mikra*, 455–518.

FELTES, H., *Die Gattung des Habakukkommentars von Qumran (1QpHab): Eine Studie zum frühen Jüdischen Midrasch* (Würzburg: Echter Verlag, 1986).

FIELD, F., *Origenis Hexaplorum* (Oxford: Clarendon Press, 1875), i–ii.

FINKEL, ASHER, 'The Pesher of Dreams and Scriptures', *RQ* 4 (1963–4), 357–70.

FISHBANE, MICHAEL, 'The Qumran Pesher and Traits of Ancient Hermeneutics', in *Proceedings of the Sixth World Congress of Jewish Studies held at the Hebrew University of Jerusalem, 13–19 August 1973* (Jerusalem: World Union of Jewish Studies, 1977), i. 97–114.

——'Revelation and Tradition: Aspects of Inner-Biblical Exegesis', *JBL* 99 (1980), 343–61.

——*Biblical Interpretation in Ancient Israel* (Oxford: Clarendon Press, 1985).

——'Inner Biblical Exegesis: Types and Strategies of Interpretation in Ancient Israel', in Geoffrey H. Hartman and Sanford Budick (eds.), *Midrash and Literature* (New Haven: Yale University Press, 1986), 19–40.

——'Use, Authority and Interpretation of Mikra at Qumran', in *Mikra*, 339–78.

FITZMYER, JOSEPH A., 'Crucifixion in Ancient Palestine, Qumran Literature, and the NT', *CBQ* 40 (1978), 493–513.

——*A Wandering Aramean: Collected Aramaic Essays* (Chico, Calif.: Scholars Press, 1979).

——*The Gospel According to Luke I–IX* (Garden City, NY: Doubleday, 1979).

——'The Qumran Scrolls and the New Testament After Forty Years', *RQ* 49–52 (1988), 609–20.

——*Romans* (Garden City, NY: Doubleday, 1992).

——Preliminary Publication of pap4QTob[a] ar, Fragment 2', *Bib.* 75/2 (1994), 220–4.

FLUSSER, DAVID, 'The Dead Sea Sect and Pre-Pauline Christianity', in C. Rabin and Y. Yadin (eds.), *Scripta Hierosolymitana 4* (Jerusalem: Magnes Press, 1958), 215–66.

FOX, MICHAEL V., 'The Identification of Quotations in Biblical Literature', *ZAW* 93 (1981), 416–31.

FRAADE, STEVEN D., 'Interpretive Authority in the Studying Community at Qumran', *JJS* 44 (1993), 46-69.

FREEDMAN, D. N., 'The "House of Absalom" in the Habakkuk Scroll', *BASOR* 114 (1949), 11-12.

FRÖHLICH, IDA, 'Le Genre Littéraire des Pesharim de Qumrân', *RQ* 47 (1986), 383-98.

—— 'Pesher, Apocalyptic Literature and Qumran', in *Madrid*, i. 295-306.

FULLER, RUSSELL EARL, 'Textual Traditions in the Book of Hosea and the Minor Prophets', in *Madrid*, i. 247-56.

FURNISH, VICTOR PAUL, *II Corinthians* (New York: Doubleday, 1984).

GABRION, HERVÉ, 'L'Interprétation de l'Écriture dans les littératures de Qumrân', *ANRW* 19/1 (1979), 779-848.

GALLING, KURT, 'Das Rätsel der Zeit im Urteil Kohelets (Koh. 3, 1-15)', *ZTK* 58 (1961), 1-15.

GARCÍA MARTÍNEZ, FLORENTINO, 'El pesher: interpretación profética de la Escritura', *Salmanticensis*, 26 (1979), 125-39.

—— 'Qumran Origins and Early History: A Groningen Hypothesis', *Folia Orientalia*, 25 (1988), 113-36.

—— 'Lista de MSS procedentes de Qumran', *Henoch*, 11 (1989), 149-232.

—— 'Traditions communes dans le *IVe Esdras* et dans les MSS de Qumrân', *RQ* 15 (1991), 287-301.

—— *Textos de Qumrán* (Madrid: Editorial Trotta, 1992); Eng. trans. and rev. edn., *The Dead Sea Scrolls Translated: The Qumran Texts in English* (Leiden: E. J. Brill, 1994).

—— and VAN DER WOUDE, A. S., 'A "Groningen" Hypothesis of Qumran Origins and Early History', *RQ* 14 (1990), 521-42.

GÄRTNER, BERTIL, 'The Habakkuk Commentary (DSH) and the Gospel of Matthew', *ST* 8 (1954), 1-24.

GERHARDSSON, BIRGER, *Memory and Manuscript: Oral Tradition and Written Transmission in Rabbinic Judaism and Early Christianity* (Lund: Gleerup, 1961).

—— *Tradition and Transmission in Early Christianity* (Lund: Gleerup, 1964).

—— *The Origins of the Gospel Traditions*, Eng. trans. (Philadelphia: Fortress Press, 1979).

GERTNER, M., 'Midrashim in the New Testament', *JSS* 7 (1962), 267-92.

—— 'Terms of Scriptural Interpretation: A Study in Hebrew Semantics', *BSOAS* 25 (1962), 1-27.

GINSBURG, CHRISTIAN D., *Introduction to the Massoretico-Critical Edition of the Hebrew Bible*, repr. with a Prolegomenon by Harry M. Orlinsky (New York: KTAV, 1966).

GOODING, D. W., 'Aristeas and the Septuagint Origins: A Review of Recent Studies', *VT* 13 (1963), 357-79.

GOODING, D. W., 'An Appeal for a Stricter Terminology in the Textual Criticism of the Old Testament', *JSS* 21 (1976), 15–25.

——*Relics of Ancient Exegesis: A Study of the Miscellanies in 3 Reigns 2* (Cambridge: Cambridge University Press, 1976).

GOODMAN, MARTIN D., *Mission and Conversion: Proselytizing in the Religious History of the Roman Empire* (Oxford: Clarendon Press, 1994).

GORDON, ROBERT P., 'The Interpretation of "Lebanon" and 4Q285', *JJS* 43 (1992), 92–4.

——'The Targum to the Minor Prophets and the Dead Sea Texts: Textual and Exegetical Notes', *RQ* 8 (1974), 425–9.

GOSHEN-GOTTSTEIN, M. H., *The Book of Isaiah: Sample Edition with Introduction* (Jerusalem: Magnes Press, 1965).

——'Hebrew Syntax and the History of the Bible Text: A Pesher in the MT of Isaiah', *Textus*, 8 (1973), 100–6.

——'The Textual Criticism of the Old Testament: Rise, Decline, Rebirth', *JBL* 102 (1983), 365–99

——'Scriptural Authority (Judaism)', *ABD* v. 1017–21.

GREENBERG, MOSHE, 'The Stabilization of the Text of the Hebrew Bible', *JAOS* 76 (1956), 157–67.

GREENFIELD, J., 'The Words of Levi Son of Jacob in Damascus Document IV, 15–19', *RQ* 13 (1988), 319–22.

GREENSPOON, LEONARD, 'The Use and Abuse of the Term "LXX" and Related Terminology in Recent Scholarship', *BIOSCS* 20 (1987), 21–9.

GREER, ROWAN, and KUGEL, JAMES L., *Early Biblical Interpretation* (Philadelphia: Westminster Press, 1986).

HAAK, ROBERT D., *Habakkuk*, VTS 44 (Leiden: E. J. Brill, 1992).

HADAS, MOSES, *Aristeas to Philocrates* (*Letter of Aristeas*), Jewish Apocrypha Literature of Dropsie College (New York: Harper & Bros., 1951).

HAENCHEN, ERNST, *The Acts of the Apostles*, Eng. trans. (Oxford: Basil Blackwell, 1971).

HALPERIN, D. L., 'Crucifixion, the Nahum Pesher and the Rabbinic Penalty of Strangulation', *JJS* 32 (1981), 32–46.

HANHART, ROBERT, 'Das Neue Testament und die griechische Überlieferung des Judentums', in *Überlieferungsgeschichtliche Untersuchungen*, 121 (1981), 293–303.

——'Die Bedeutung der Septuaginta in neutestamentlichen Zeit', *ZNW* 81 (1984), 395–416.

——'Zum gegenwärtigen Stand der Septuagintaforschung', in A. Pietersma and C Cox (eds.), *De Septuaginta: Studies in Honour of John William Wevers on his Sixty-Fifth Birthday* (Mississauga: Benben Publications, 1984), 3–18.

——'The Translation of the Septuagint in Light of Earlier Tradition and Subsequent Influences', in *SSCW*, 339–79.

HANSON, A. T., *Studies in Paul's Technique and Theology* (London: SPCK, 1965).

——*The New Testament Interpretation of Scripture* (London: SPCK, 1980).

HARL, M., 'Un groupe de mots grecs dans le judaïsme hellénistique dans le Psaume 37,8 de la Septante', in E. Lucchesi and H. D. Saffrey (eds.), *Mémorial André-Jean Festugière: Antiquité païenne et chrétienne* (1984), 89-105.

——'La Septante et la pluralité textuelle des écritures: Le témoignage des pères grecs', in *Naissance de la méthode critique: Colloque du centenaire de l'École biblique et archéologique française de Jérusalem* (Paris: Cerf, 1992), 231-43.

HARNACK, A., *A History of Dogma*, Eng. trans. (New York: Russell & Russell, 1958).

HARRIS, J. RENDEL, *Testimonies I-II* (Cambridge: Cambridge University Press, 1916, 1920).

HATCH, EDWIN, *Essays in Biblical Greek* (Oxford: Clarendon Press, 1889).

HAYS, RICHARD B., *The Faith of Jesus Christ: An Investigation of the Narrative Substructure of Galatians 3: 1-4: 11* (Chico, Calif.: Scholars Press, 1983).

——*Echoes of Scripture in the Letters of Paul* (New Haven: Yale University Press, 1989).

HENGEL, MARTIN, *Judaism and Hellenism: Studies in their Encounter in Palestine during the Early Hellenistic Period*, Eng. trans. (London: SCM Press Limited, 1974), i-ii.

——*Crucifixion: In the Ancient World and the Folly of the Message of the Cross* (Philadelphia: Fortress Press, 1977).

——*The Hellenization of Judaea in the First Century after Christ*, Eng. trans. (London: SCM Press, 1989).

——*The History of the Jewish People in the Age of Jesus Christ (175 B.C.-A.D. 135)*, by Emil Schürer, ed. and rev. by Geza Vermes, Fergus Millar, Martin Goodman, *et al.* (Edinburgh: T. & T. Clark, 1973, 1979, 1986, 1987), i, ii, iii. 1, iii. 2.

HODGSON, ROBERT, 'The Testimony Hypothesis', *JBL* 98 (1979), 361-78.

HOOKER, M. D., *From Adam to Christ: Essays on Paul* (Cambridge: Cambridge University Press, 1990).

HORGAN, MAURYA P., *Pesharim: Qumran Interpretations of Biblical Books* (Washington: Catholic Biblical Association of America, 1979).

——'The Bible Explained (Prophecies)', in Robert A. Kraft and George W. E. Nickelsburg (eds.), *Early Judaism and its Modern Interpreters* (Philadelphia: Fortress Press, 1986), 247-53.

HORTON, F. L., 'Formulas of Introduction in the Qumran Literature', *RQ* 7 (1969-71), 505-14.

HOUSMAN, A. E., 'The Application of Thought to Textual Criticism', in J. Diggle and F. R. D. Goodyear (eds.), *The Classical Papers of*

A. E. *Housman* (Cambridge: Cambridge University Press, 1972), iii. 1058-69.

HOWARD, GEORGE, 'Revision Towards the Hebrew in the Septuagint Text of Amos', *EI* 16 (1982), 125-33.

HUBY, JOSEPH, *Saint Paul: Épitre aux Romans* (Paris: Beauchesne, 1940).

HUMBERT, PAUL, *Problèmes du Livre D'Habacuc* (Neuchâtel: Université de Neuchâtel, 1944).

JAUBERT, ANNIE, *La Date de la cène* (Paris: J. Gabalda, 1957).

JACOBSEN, HOWARD, '4Q252: Addenda', *JJS* 44 (1993), 118-20.

JASTRAM, NATHAN RAY, 'The Text of 4QNum^b', in *Madrid*, i. 177-98.

JELLICOE, SIDNEY, *The Septuagint and Modern Study* (Oxford: Clarendon Press, 1968).

——(ed.), *Studies in the Septuagint: Origins, Recensions, and Interpretations* (New York: KTAV Publishing, 1974).

JEREMIAS, GERT, *Der Lehrer der Gerechtigkeit* (Göttingen: Vandenhoeck & Ruprecht, 1963).

JUCCI, ELIO, 'Il Pesher, un Ponte tra il Passato', *Henoch*, 7 (1986), 321-38.

KAHLE, PAUL, *The Cairo Genizah*, 2nd edn. (Oxford: Basil Blackwell, 1959).

KATZ, PETER [also under PETER WALTERS], 'Septuagintal Studies in the Mid-Century', in W. D. Davies and D. Daube (eds.), *The Background of the New Testament and its Eschatology* (Cambridge: Cambridge University Press, 1956).

KATZOFF, RANON, 'פפירוס ידין 19: שטר מתנה ממדבר יהודה והתפתחות דיני הצוואה בישראל' in *Proceedings of the Tenth World Congress of Jewish Studies, Jerusalem, August 16-24, 1989* (Jerusalem: World Union of Jewish Studies, 1990), 1-8.

KAUTZSCH, E. F., *De veteris testamenti locis a Paulo apostolo allegatis* (Leizpig: Metzger and Wittig, 1869).

KECK, L. E., 'The Function of Rom. 3: 10-18: Observations and Suggestions', in J. Jervel and W. A. Meeks (eds.), *God's Christ and His People: Studies in Honour of Nils Alstrup Dahl* (Oslo: Universitetsforlaget 1977), 141-57.

KENNICOTT, BENJAMIN, *Vetus Testamentum Hebraicum cum variis lectionibus* (Oxford: Clarendon Press, 1780).

KISTER, MENAHEM, 'Biblical Phrases and Hidden Biblical Interpretations and Pesharim', in *FYR*, 27-39.

KLEIN, RALPH W., *Textual Criticism of the Old Testament: The Septuagint after Qumran* (Philadelphia: Fortress Press, 1974).

KNIBB, M. A., 'Apocalyptic and Wisdom in 4 Ezra', *JSJ* 13 (1982), 56-74.

——*The Qumran Community* (Cambridge: Cambridge University Press, 1987).

KOCH, DIETRICH-ALEX, 'Beobachtungen zum christologischen Schrift-gebrauch in den vorpaulinischen Gemeinde', *ZNW* 71 (1980), 174-91.

——'Der Text von Hab. 2: 4, in der Septuaginta und im Neuen Testament', *ZNW* 76 (1985), 68-85.

——*Die Schrift als Zeuge des Evangeliums: Untersuchungen zur Verwendung und zum Verständnis der Schrift bei Paulus* (Tübingen: J. C. B. Mohr (Paul Siebeck), 1986).

KRAFT, R. A., 'Barnabas' Isaiah Text and the "Testimony Book" Hypothesis', *JBL* 79 (1960), 336-50.

——'Septuagint: B. Earliest Greek Versions ("Old Greek")', *IDBS*, 811-15.

KUGEL, JAMES L., and GREER, ROWAN A., *Early Biblical Interpretation* (Philadelphia: Westminster Press, 1986).

KUHL, CURT, 'Die "Wideraufnahme"—ein literarisches Prinzip?', *ZAW* 64 (1952), 1-11.

KUTSCHER, E. Y., *The Language and Linguistic Background of the Isaiah Scroll (1QIsa A)*, Eng. trans. (Leiden: E. J. Brill, 1974).

LAGRANGE, M.-J., *Saint Paul: Épitre aux Galates* (Paris: J. Gabalda, 1950).

LEIMAN, SID Z., *The Canonization of Hebrew Scripture: The Talmudic and Midrashic Evidence*. Transaction, Connecticut Academy of Arts and Science, 47 (Hamden, 1976).

——'Josephus and the Canon of the Bible' in L. H. Feldman and G. Hata (eds.), *Josephus, the Bible, and History* (Detroit: Wayne State University Press, 1989), 50-8.

LEIPOLDT, J. and MORENZ, S., *Heilige Schriften* (Leipzig: Harrosowitz, 1953).

LEWIS, NAPTHALI, YADIN, Y., and GREENFIELD, J. C., *The Documents from the Bar Kokhba Period in the Cave of Letters: Greek Papyri, Aramaic and Nabatean Signatures and Subscriptions* (Jerusalem: Israel Exploration Society, 1989).

LIEBERMAN, S., *Greek in Jewish Palestine* (New York: Jewish Theological Seminary of America, 1942).

LIFSHITZ, B., 'The Greek Documents from the Cave of Horrors', *IEJ* 12 (1962), 201-7.

LIGHTFOOT, J. B., *St. Paul's Epistle to the Galatians*, 5th edn. (London: Macmillan, 1876).

——*Notes on Epistles of St. Paul*, ed. J. R. Harmer; repr. (Grand Rapids, Mich.: Baker Book House, 1980).

LIM, TIMOTHY H., 'Not in Persuasive Words of Wisdom, but in the Demonstration of the Spirit and Power', *NovT* 29 (1987), 137-49.

——'Eschatological Orientation and the Alteration of Scripture in the Habakkuk Pesher', *JNES* 49 (1990), 185-94.

——'Attitudes to Holy Scripture in the Qumran Pesharim and Pauline Letters', D.Phil., University of Oxford, 1991.

——'11QMelch, Luke 4 and the Dying Messiah', *JJS* 43 (1992), 90-2.

LIM, TIMOTHY H., 'The Chronology of the Flood Story in a Qumran Text (4Q252)', *JJS* 43 (1992), 288-98.

—— 'The Qumran Scrolls: Two Hypotheses', *SR* 21 (1992), 455-66.

—— 'Notes on 4Q252 fr. 1, cols. i-ii', *JJS* 44 (1993), 121-6.

—— Review of Joseph Naveh's *On Sherd and Papyrus* in *IOUDAIOS Review*, 3.010 (available from IOUDAIOS @YORKVMI.BITNET).

—— 'The "Psalms of Joshua" (4Q379 fr. 22 col. 2): A Reconsideration of its Text', *JJS* 44 (1993), 309-12.

—— Review of Christopher D. Stanley, *Paul and the Language of Scripture*, in *JJS* 44 (1993), 143-4.

LIM, TIMOTHY H., 'The Wicked Priests of the Groningen Hypothesis', *JBL* 112 (1993), 415-25.

LINDARS, BARNABAS, *New Testament Apologetic: The Doctrinal Significance of the Old Testament Quotations* (London: SCM Press, 1961).

—— and BORGEN, PEDER, 'The Place of the Old Testament in the Formation of New Testament Theology', *NTS* 23 (1976-7), 59-66.

LOEWE, RAPHAEL, 'The "Plain" Meaning of Scripture in Early Jewish Exegesis', *Papers of the Institute for Jewish Studies, London* 1 (1964), 140-85.

LOHSE, EDUARD, *Die Texte aus Qumran: Hebräisch und Deutsch mit masoretischer Punktation: Übersetzung, Einführung und Anmerkungen*, 2nd edn. (Munich: Kösel-Verlag, 1971).

LOWY, S., *Principles of Samaritan Exegesis* (Leiden: E. J. Brill, 1977).

LOHFINK, NORBERT, *Das Deuteronomium: Entstehung, Gestalt und Botschaft*, BETL 68 (Leuven: Peeters, 1985).

LONGENECKER RICHARD, *Biblical Exegesis in the Apostolic Period* (Grand Rapids, Mich.: Eerdmans, 1975).

—— *Acts*, The Expositor's Bible Commentary (Grand Rapids, Mich.: Zondervan, 1981).

—— *Galatians* (Dallas: Word Books, 1990).

LYONNET, STANISLAV, 'Saint Paul et l'exégèse juive de son temps: A propos de Rom., 10: 6-8', in *Mélanges Robert* (Paris: Bloud de Gay, 1957), 494-506.

MAAS, PAUL, 'Textual Criticism', in M. Cary *et al.* (eds.), *Oxford Classical Dictionary* (Oxford: Clarendon Press, 1949), 888-9.

McCARTER, P. KYLE, *1 Samuel* (Garden City, NY: Doubleday, 1980).

—— *Textual Criticism: Recovering the Text of the Hebrew Bible* (Philadelphia: Fortress Press, 1986).

McCARTHY, CARMEL, *The Tiqqune Sopherim and other Theological Corrections in the Masoretic Text of the Old Testament* (Göttingen: Vandenhoeck & Ruprecht, 1981).

McNAMARA, MARTIN, *Palestinian Judaism and the New Testament* (Wilmington, Del.: Michael Glazier, 1983).

Select Bibliography

MAIER, JOHANN, *Die Texte vom Totem Meer* (Munich and Basle: Ernst Reinhardt Verlag, 1960), i–ii.

—— *The Temple Scroll: An Introduction, Translation and Commentary*, Eng. trans. (Sheffield: JSOT Press, 1985).

—— 'Auslegungsgeschichtliche Beobachtungen zu Psalm 37, 1.7.8', *RQ* 13 (1988), 465–80.

MANNS, FREDERIC, *Le Midrash: Approche et Commentaire de l'Écriture* (Jerusalem: no pub., 1990).

MANSON, T. W., 'The Argument from Prophecy', *JTS* 46 (1945), 129–36.

MARSHALL, I. HOWARD, *New Testament Interpretation: Essays on Principle and Methods* (Exeter: Paternoster Press, 1977).

—— 'An Assessment of Recent Developments' in D. A. Carson and H. G. M. Williamson (eds.), *It is Written: Scripture Citing Scripture. Essays in Honour of Barnabas Lindars* (Cambridge: Cambridge University Press, 1988), 1–24.

MARTIN, MALACHI, *The Scribal Character of the Dead Sea Scrolls* (Louvain: Université de Louvain Institut Orientaliste, 1958).

MASS, F., 'Von den Ursprüngen der rabbinischen Schriftauslegung', *ZTK* 52 (1955), 153–4.

MEEKS, WAYNE A., '"And Rose Up to Play": Midrash and Paranaesis in 1 Corinthians 10.1–22', *JSNT* 16 (1982), 64–78.

METZGER, BRUCE, 'The Formulas Introducing Quotations of Scripture in the New Testament and the Mishna', *JBL* 70 (1951), 297–307.

—— *The Text of the New Testament: Its Transmission, Corruption, and Restoration*, 2nd edn. (Oxford: Clarendon Press, 1968).

—— *A Textual Commentary on the Greek New Testament* (London: United Bible Societies, 1971).

—— *The Early Versions of the New Testament: Their Origin, Transmission, and Limitations* (Oxford: Clarendon Press, 1977).

MEYERS, E. M., and STRANGE, J. F., *Archaeology, the Rabbis & Early Christianity* (Nashville: Abingdon, 1981).

MICHEL, OTTO, *Der Brief an die Römer*, 10th edn. (Göttingen: Vandenhoeck & Ruprecht, 1955).

—— *Paulus und Seine Bibel* (Darmstadt: Wissenschaftliche Buchgesellschaft, 1929; repr. 1972).

MILIK, J. T., *Ten Years of Discovery in the Wilderness of Judaea*, trans. J. Strugnell (London: SCM Press, 1959).

—— 'Milkî-ṣedeq et Milkî-reša' dans les anciens écrits juifs et chrétiens', *JJS* 23 (1972), 95–144.

—— 'Les Modèles araméens du livre d'Esther dans la grotte 4 de Qumrân', *RQ* 15 (1992), 321–408.

MILLARD, ALAN R., 'In Praise of Ancient Scribes', *BA* 45/3 (1982), 143-54.

MILLER, M. P., 'The Function of Isa. 61.1-2 in 11QMelchizedek', *JBL* 88 (1969), 467-9.

——'Targum, Midrash and the Use of the Old Testament in the New Testament', *JSJ* 2 (1971), 29-82.

MOLIN, GEORG, 'Der Habakukkommentar von 'En Fešḥa in der alttesta-mentlichen Wissenschaft', *TZ* 8/5 (1952), 340-56.

MORGAN, ROBERT, with BARTON, JOHN, *Biblical Interpretation* (Oxford: Oxford University Press, 1988).

MORRAY-JONES, C. R. A., 'Paradise Revisited (2 Cor. 12: 12): The Jewish Mystical Background of Paul's Apostolate', ps. 1, 'The Jewish Sources', and 2, 'Paul's Heavenly Ascent and its Significance', *HTR* 86/2 (1993), 177-217 and 265-92.

MUILENBURG, JAMES, 'Fragments of Another Qumran Isaiah Scroll', *BASOR* 135 (1954), 28-32.

MÜLLER, K., *Anstoß und Gericht: Eine Studie zum jüdischen Hintergrund des paulinischen Skandalon-Begriffs* (Munich: Kösel-Verlag, 1969).

MUNNICH, OLIVIER, 'Contribution à l'étude de la première revision de la Septante', *ANRW* 20/1 (1987), 190-220.

MURPHY-O'CONNOR, J., 'The Essenes and their History', *RB* 81 (1974), 215-44.

NAEH, SHLOMO, אין אם למסורת או :האם דרשו התנאים את כתיב התורה שלא כקריאתו המקובלת? *Tarbiz*, 61 (1992), 401-48.

NAVEH, JOSEPH, על חרס וגומא (Jerusalem: Magnes Press, 1992).

NEILL, STEPHEN, and WRIGHT, TOM, *The Interpretation of the New Testament 1861-1986*, 2nd edn. (Oxford: Oxford University Press, 1988).

NEUSNER, JACOB, *The Rabbinic Traditions about the Pharisees before 70. I-III* (Leiden: E. J. Brill, 1971).

——'Types and Forms in Ancient Jewish Literature: Some Comparisons', *HR* 11 (1971-2), 354-90.

——*What is Midrash?* (Philadelphia: Fortress Press, 1987).

The New Jerome Biblical Commentary, ed. Raymond E. Brown, Joseph A. Fitzmyer, and Roland E. Murphy (London: Geoffrey Chapman, 1989).

NEWSOM, CAROL, 'The "Psalms of Joshua" from Cave 4', *JJS* 39 (1988), 56-73.

NIEHOFF, MAREN, 'A Dream Which is not Interpreted is Like a Letter Which is not Read', *JJS* 43 (1992), 58-84.

NITZAN, BILHA, (1QpHab) מגילת פשר חבקוק ממגילות מדבר יהודה (Jerusalem: Bialik, 1986).

NOTH, MARTIN, 'The "Re-Presentation" of the Old Testament in Proclamation' in C. Westermann (ed.), *Essays on Old Testament Interpretation* (London: SCM Press, 1963), 76-88.

NYBERG, H. S., *Studien zum Hoseabuche: Zugleich ein Beitrag zur Klärung des Problems der alttestamentlichen Textkritik* (Uppsala: Lundequistska Bokhandeln, 1935).

O'DAY, GAIL, 'Jeremiah 9: 22–23 and 1 Corinthians 1: 26–31: A Study in Intertextuality', *JBL* 109/2 (1990), 259–67.

OESCH, JOSEF M., *Petucha und Setuma: Untersuchungen zu einer überlieferten Gliederung im hebräischen Text des Alten Testaments* (Göttingen: Vandenhoeck & Ruprecht, 1979).

O'NEILL, J. C., *Paul's Letter to the Romans* (Harmondsworth: Penguin, 1975).

——'The Lost Written Records of Jesus' Words and Deeds behind our Records', *JTS* 42 (1991), 483–504.

——*Who Did Jesus Think He Was?* (Leiden: E. J. Brill, 1995).

OPPENHEIM, A. L., 'The Interpretation of Dreams', *TAPA* 46 (1956), 179–355.

OUELLETTE, JEAN, 'Variantes Qumrâniennes du livres des Psaumes', *RQ* 7 (1969), 105–23.

PARDEE, DENNIS, 'A Restudy of the Commentary on Psalms 37 from Qumran Cave 4 (Discoveries in the Judean Desert of Jordan, vol. V no. 171)', *RQ* 8 (1973), 163–94.

PATTE, DANIEL, *Early Jewish Hermeneutic in Palestine*, SBL and Scholars Press Dissertation Series, 22 (1975).

PFANN, STEPHEN, 'The Aramaic Text and Language of Daniel and Ezra in the Light of some Manuscripts from Qumran', *Textus*, 16 (1991), 127–37.

POLAK, FRANK H., 'Statistics and Textual Filiation: The Case of 4QSam^a/LXX (with a Note on the Text of the Pentateuch', in *SSCW*, 215–76.

QIMRON, ELISHA, *Indices and Corrections*, (Leiden: E. J. Brill, 1979).

——'Observations on the History of Early Hebrew (1000 B.C.E.–200 C.E.) in the Light of the Dead Sea Documents', in *FYR*, 349–62.

RABIN, CHAIM, 'Notes on the Habakkuk Scroll and the Zadokite Documents', *VT* 5 (1955), 148–62.

——'The Dead Sea Scrolls and the History of the Old Testament Text', *JTS* 6 (1955), 174–82.

RABINOWITZ, ISAAC, 'Pēsher/Pittāron: Its Biblical Meaning and its Significance in the Qumran Literature', *RQ* 8 (1973), 219–32.

REYNOLDS, L. D., and WILSON, N. G., *Scribes & Scholars: A Guide to the Transmission of Greek and Latin Literature*, 2nd edn. (Oxford: Clarendon Press, 1974).

ROBERTS, BLEDDYN J., *The Old Testament Text and Versions: The Hebrew Text in Transmission and the History of the Ancient Versions* (Cardiff: University of Wales Press, 1951).

ROBERTS, BLEDDYN J., 'The Dead Sea Scrolls and Old Testament Scriptures', *BJRL* 36 (1953-4), 75-96.

——'Bible Exegesis and Fulfilment in Qumran' in P. R. Ackroyd and B. Lindars (eds.), *Words and Meanings: Essays Presented to D. W. Thomas*, (Cambridge: Cambridge University Press, 1968), 195-207.

ROBERTS, C. H., 'Books in the Graeco-Roman World and in the New Testament', in *CHB*, i. 48-66.

ROBERTS, J. J. M., *Nahum, Habakkuk, and Zephaniah* (Louisville, Ky.: Westminster/John Knox Press, 1991).

ROSENZWEIG, A., 'Die Al-Tikri-Deutungen: Ein Beitrag zur talmudischen Schriftdeutung' in M. Brann and J. Elbogen (eds.), *Festschrift zu Israel Lewy* (Breslau: M. & H. Marcus Verlag, 1911), 204-53.

ROWLAND, CHRISTOPHER, *Revelation* (London: Epworth Press, 1993).

SANDERS, E. P., *Paul and Palestinian Judaism: A Comparison of Patterns of Religion* (Philadelphia: Fortress Press, 1977).

——*Paul, the Law and the Jewish People* (Philadelphia: Fortress Press, 1983).

——*Paul* (New York: Oxford University Press, 1991).

——*Judaism: Practice and Belief 63 BCE-66 CE* (London: SCM Press, 1992).

SANDERS, J. A., 'Dissenting Deities and Philippians 2 1-11', *JBL* 88 (1969), 279-90.

——*Torah and Canon* (Philadelphia: Fortress Press, 1972).

——'Habakkuk in Qumran, Paul and the Old Testament', rev. edn. in Craig A. Evans and James A. Sanders (eds.), *Paul and the Scriptures of Israel* (Sheffield: Sheffield Academic Press, 1993), 98-117.

SANDMEL, SAMUEL, 'The Haggada within Scripture', *JBL* 80 (1981), 105-22.

SARNA, NAHUM, 'Ps. 89: A Study of Inner Biblical Exegesis', in A. Altmann (ed.), *Biblical and Other Studies* (Cambridge, Mass.: Harvard University Press, 1963), 29-46.

——'The Authority and Interpretation of Scripture in Jewish Tradition', in C. Thoma and M. Wyschogrod (eds.), *Understanding Scripture: Explorations of Jewish and Christian Traditions of Interpretation* (New York: Paulist Press, 1987), 9-20.

SCANLIN, HAROLD, *The Dead Sea Scrolls & Modern Translations of the Old Testament* (Wheaton, Ill.: Tyndale House Publishers, 1993).

SCHALLER, BERNDT, 'Zum Textcharakter der Hiobzitate im paulinischen Schriftum', *ZNW* 71 (1980), 21-6.

——'Ἥξει ἐκ Σιων ὁ ρυομενος: Zur Textgestalt von Jes 59.20f in Röm 11.26f.' in A. Pietersma and C. Cox (eds.), *De Septuaginta: Studies in Honour of John William Wevers on his Sixty-Fifth Birthday* (Mississauga: Benben Publications, 1984), 201-8.

Select Bibliography

SCHIFFMAN, LAWRENCE H. (ed.), 'The LXX and the Temple Scroll: Shared "Halakhic" Variants', in *SSCW*, 277–97.

—— 'The Temple Scroll and the Systems of Jewish Law of the Second Temple Period' in George J. Brooke (ed.), *Temple Scroll Studies* (Sheffield: Sheffield Academic Press, 1989), 239–56.

—— *Archaeology and History in the Dead Sea Scrolls: The New York University Conference in Memory of Yigael Yadin* (Sheffield: JSOT Press, 1990).

—— 'Miqsat Ma'aseh Ha-Torah and the *Temple Scroll*', *RQ* 14 (1990), 435–57.

—— *Reclaiming the Dead Sea Scrolls* (Philadelphia: Jewish Publication Society, 1994).

SCHOLEM, GERSHOM, 'Revelation and Tradition as Religious Categories in Judaism', in *The Messianic Idea in Judaism and Other Essays on Jewish Spirituality*, trans. M. A. Meyer *et al.* (New York: Schocken, 1974).

SEELIGMAN, I. L., *The Septuagint Version of Isaiah: A Discussion of its Problems* (Leiden: E. J. Brill, 1948).

—— 'Indications of Editorial Alteration and Adaptation in the MT and LXX', *VT* 11 (1961), 201–21.

SEGAL, M. H., 'The Promulgation of the Authoritative Text of the Hebrew Bible', *JBL* 72 (1953), 35–47.

SEGERT, STANISLAV, 'Zur Habakuk-Rolle aus dem Funde vom Toten Meer I–IV', *AO* 21 (1953), 218–39; 22 (1954), 99–113, 444–59; 23 (1955), 178–83, 364–73, 575–619.

SELWYN, E. G., *The First Epistle of St Peter*, 2nd edn. (London: Macmillan, 1947).

SEVENSTER, J. N., *Do You Know Greek?* (Leiden: E. J. Brill, 1968).

SIEGEL, JONATHAN P., 'The Employment of Palaeo-Hebrew Characters for the Divine Names at Qumran in the Light of Tannaitic Sources', *HUCA* 42 (1971), 159–72.

SILBERMAN, LOU H., 'Unriddling the Riddle: A Study in the Structure and Language of the Habakkuk Pesher', *RQ* 3 (1961), 323–64.

SILVA, M., 'Old Testament in Paul', in G. F. Hawthorne and R. P. Martin (eds.), *Dictionary of Paul and his Letters* (Leicester: InterVarsity Press, 1993), 630–42.

SINCLAIR, LAWRENCE A., 'A Qumran Biblical Fragment: Hosea 4QXV[d] (Hos 1.7–2.5)', *BASOR* 239 (1981), 61–5.

—— 'Hebrew Text of the Qumran Micah Pesher and Textual Traditions of the Minor Prophets', *RQ* 11 (1983), 253–63.

SKARSAUNE, Oskar, *The Proof from Prophecy* (Leiden: E. J. Brill, 1987).

SKEAT, T. C., 'Early Christian Book-Production: Papyri and Manuscripts', in *CHB*, ii. 54–79.

SKEHAN, PATRICK W., 'Exodus in the Samaritan Recension from Qumran', *JBL* 74 (1955), 182–7.

SKEHAN, PATRICK W., *The Qumran Manuscripts and Textual Criticism*, VTS 4 (Leiden: Brill, 1957) 148–69.

——'The Period of the Biblical Texts from Khirbet Qumrân', *CBQ* 19 (1957), 435–40.

——'Qumran and the Present State of Old Testament Text Studies: The Massoretic Text', *JBL* 78 (1959), 21–5.

——'The Scrolls of the Old Testament Text', in David Noel Freedman and Jonas C. Greenfield (eds.), *New Directions in Biblical Archaeology* (Garden City, NY: Doubleday, 1971), 99–112.

——'The Biblical Scrolls from Qumran and the Text of the Old Testament', in *QHBT*, 264–77.

——'The Qumran Manuscripts and Textual Criticism', in *QHBT*, 212–25.

——'4QLXX^Num: A Pre-Christian Reworking of the Septuagint', *HTR* 70 (1977), 39–50.

——'IV. Littérature de Qumran: A. Textes bibliques', *SDB*, 805–22.

SLOMOVIC, ELIESER, 'Toward an Understanding of the Exegesis of the Dead Sea Scrolls', *RQ* 9 (1969), 3–15.

SMITH, D. MOODY, 'The Use of the Old Testament in the New', in James M. Efird (ed.), *The Use of the Old Testament in the New and Other Essays: Studies in Honor of William Franklin Stinespring* (Durham, NC: Duke University Press, 1972), 3–65.

——'The Pauline Literature', in D. A. Carson and H. G. M. Williamson (eds.), *It is Written: Scripture Citing Scripture: Essays in Honour of Barnabas Lindars* (Cambridge: Cambridge University Press, 1988).

SMITH, JOHN MERLIN, WARD, WILLIAM HAYES, and BEWER, JULIUS A., *Micah, Zephaniah, Nahum, Habakkuk, Obadiah and Joel* (Edinburgh: T. & T. Clark, 1912).

SMITH, MORTON, 'A Comparison of Early Christian and Early Rabbinic Tradition', *JBL* 82 (1963), 169–76.

SOUTHWELL, P. J. M., 'A Note on Habakkuk ii.4', *JTS* 19 (1968), 614–17.

SPERBER, ALEXANDER, 'New Testament and Septuagint', *JBL* 59 (1940), 193–293.

——*The Bible in Aramaic: The Latter Prophets According to Targum Jonathan* (Leiden: E. J. Brill, 1962), iii.

SPICQ, C., *L'Épitre aux Hébreux*, 2 vols. (Paris: J. Gabalda, 1952–3).

STANLEY, CHRISTOPHER D., *Paul and the Language of Scripture: Citation Technique in the Pauline Epistles and Contemporary Literature* (Cambridge: Cambridge University Press, 1992).

STANTON, GRAHAM N., *The Gospels and Jesus* (Oxford: Oxford University Press, 1989).

STEGEMANN, HARMUT, 'Der Pešer Psalm 37 aus Höhle 4 von Qumran (4QpPs37)', *RQ* 4 (1963–4), 235–70.

STEGEMANN, HARMUT, 'Weitere Stücke von 4Qp Psalm 37, von 4 Q Patriarchal Blessings und Hinweis auf eine unedierte Handschrift aus Höhle 4Q mit Exzerpten aus dem Deuteronomium', *RQ* 6 (1967-9), 193-227.

——*The Origins of the Temple Scroll*, VTS 40 (Leiden: Brill, 1988), 235-56.

——'The Institutions of Israel in the *Temple Scroll*', in *FYR*, 156-85.

——'The Qumran Essenes—Local Members of the Main Jewish Union in the Late Second Temple Times', in *Madrid*, ii. 83-166.

——'Is the Temple Scroll a Sixth Book of the Torah—Lost for 2,500 Years?' in Hershel Shanks (ed.), *Understanding the Dead Sea Scrolls* (New York: Random House, 1992), 126-36.

STENDAHL, KRISTER, *The School of Matthew and its Use of the Old Testament* (Lund: C. W. K. Gleerup, 1954; 2nd edn. Philadelphia: Fortress Press, 1968).

STEUDEL, ANNETTE, *Der Midrasch zur Eschatologie aus der Qumrangemeinde (4QMidrEschat^(a.b)): Materielle Rekonstruktion, Textbestand, Gattung und traditionsgeschichtliche Einordnung des durch 4Q174 ('Florilegium') und 4Q177 ('Catena A') repräsentierten Werkes aus den Qumranfunden* (Leiden: E. J. Brill, 1994).

STRUGNELL, JOHN, 'Notes en marge du volume V des *Discoveries in the Judaean Desert of Jordan*', *RQ* 7 (1969-71), 163-276.

——'A Plea for Conjectural Emendation in the New Testament, with a Coda on 1 Cor 4: 6', *CBQ* 36 (1974), 139-47.

SUNDBERG, ALBERT C., *The Old Testament of the Early Church* (Cambridge, Mass.: Harvard University Press, 1964).

——'Reexamining the Formation of the Old Testament Canon' *Int.* 42 (1988), 78-82.

SUSSMAN, YAAKOV, 'חקר תולדות ההלכה מגילות מדבר יהודה: הרהורים תלמודיים ראשונים לאור מגילת "מקצת משעי התורה"', *Tarbiz*, 59/1-2 (1989-90), 11-76. An English version of this is found in *DJD* x. app. I.

SWEET, HENRY BARCLAY, *An Introduction to the Old Testament in Greek*, rev. Richard Rusden Ottley and H. St J. Thackeray (Cambridge: Cambridge University Press, 1900).

TALMON, SHEMARYAHU, 'The Old Testament Text', in *CHB*, i. 159-99.

——'The Textual Study of the Bible—A New Outlook', in *QHBT*, 321-400.

——'The Ancient Hebrew Alphabet and Biblical Text Criticism' in A. Caquot, S. Légasse, and M. Tardieu (eds.), *Mélanges bibliques et orientaux en l'honneur de M. Matthias Delcor* (Neukirchen-Vluyn: Neukirchener, 1985), 387-402.

——*The World of Qumran from Within* (Jerusalem: Magnes Press; Leiden: E. J. Brill, 1989).

TAYLOR, CHARLES, *Fragments of the Book of Kings according to the Translation of Aquila* (Cambridge: Cambridge University Press, 1879).

THACKERAY, HENRY ST JOHN, *The Relation of St. Paul to Contemporary Jewish Thought* (London: Macmillan, 1900).

——*The Septuagint and Jewish Worship* (London: H. Milford, 1923).

TOMSON, PETER J., *Paul and the Jewish Law: Halakha in the Letters of the Apostle to the Gentiles* (Assen and Maastricht: Van Gorcum, 1990).

TORCZYNER, N. H., 'אל תקרי' in ישראלית אנציקלופדיה אשכול, ii. (Berlin: Eshkol, 1932), 376-86.

TOV, EMANUEL, *The Septuagint Translation of Jeremiah and Baruch: A Discussion of an Early Revision of the LXX of Jeremiah 29-52 and Baruch 1: 1-3: 8* (Missoula, Mont.: Scholars Press, 1976).

TOV, EMANUEL, 'The Textual Character of 11QpaleoLev' (Heb.), *Shnaton*, 3 (1978-9), 238-44.

——'Determining the Relationship between the Qumran Scrolls and the LXX: Some Methodological Issues', in E. Tov (ed.), *The Hebrew and Greek Texts of Samuel* (Jerusalem: Academon, 1980), 45-68.

——*The Text-Critical Use of the Septuagint in Biblical Research* (Jerusalem: Simor, 1981).

——'Some Aspects of the Textual and Literary History of the Book of Jeremiah', in P.-M. Bogaert (ed.), *Le Livre de Jérémie* (Leuven, Leuven University Press, 1981), 145-65.

——'A Modern Textual Outlook Based on the Qumran Scrolls', *HUCA* 53 (1982), 11-27.

——'Criteria for Evaluating Textual Readings: The Limitations of Textual Rules', *HTR* 75 (1982), 429-48.

——'The "Temple Scroll" and Old Testament Textual Criticism' (Heb.), *EI* 16 (1982), 100-11.

——'Did the Septuagint Translators Always Understand their Hebrew Text', in *De Septuaginta: Studies in Honour of John William Wevers on his Sixty-Fifth Birthday* (Mississauga: Benben Publications, 1984), 53-82.

——'The Rabbinic Tradition Concerning the Alterations Inserted into the Greek Pentateuch and their Relation to the Original Text of the LXX', *JSJ* 15 (1984), 65-89.

——'The Nature and Background of Harmonizations in Biblical Manuscripts', *JSOT* 31 (1985), 3-29.

——'Jewish Greek Scriptures', in Robert A. Kraft and George W. E. Nickelsburg (eds.), *Early Judaism and its Modern Interpreters* (Philadelphia: Fortress Press, 1986), 223-37.

——'The Orthography and Language of the Hebrew Scrolls Found at Qumran and the Origin of these Scrolls', *Textus*, 13 (1986), 31-57.

——'The Nature and Study of the Translation Technique of the LXX in the Past and Present', in *VI Congress of the International Organization for*

Septuagint and Cognate Studies: Jerusalem, 1986 (Atlanta: Scholars Press, 1986), 337-59.

——'Die griechischen Bibelübersetzungen', in *ANRW*, ser. 2, 20/2: 121-89.

——'Hebrew Biblical Manuscripts from the Judaean Desert: Their Contribution to Textual Criticism', *JJS* 39 (1988), 5-37.

——'The Septuagint', in *Mikra*, 161-88.

——ביקורת נוסח המקרא (Jerusalem: Bialik, 1989), revised and trans. as *Textual Criticism of the Hebrew Bible* (Minneapolis: Fortress Press, 1992).

——'The Jeremiah Scrolls from Cave 4', *RQ* 14 (1989), 189-206.

——'The Contribution of the Qumran Scrolls to the Understanding of the LXX', in *SSCW*, 11-47.

——*The Original Shape of the Biblical Text*, in VTS (Leiden: Brill, 1991), 345-59.

——'Some Notes on a Generation of Qumran Studies (by Frank M. Cross). A Reply', in *Madrid*, i. 15-22.

——'4QLev^d (4Q26)', in F. García Martínez, A. Hilhorst, and C. J. Labuschagne (eds.), *The Scriptures and the Scrolls: Studies in Honour of A. S. van der Woude on the Occasion of his 65th Birthday* (Leiden: Brill, 1992), 1-5.

——'4QJosh B (preliminary publication with Photo)', in Z. Kapera (ed.), *Intertestamental Essays in Honour of Jósef Tadeusz Milik* (Cracow: Enigma Press, 1992), 205-12.

——Textual Status of 4Q364-367', in *Madrid*, i. 43-82.

——'Groups of Biblical Texts found at Qumran', in D. Dimant and L. H. Schiffman (eds.), *Time to Prepare the Way in the Wilderness: Papers on the Qumran Scrolls* (Leiden: E. J. Brill, 1995), 85-102.

TOWNER, S. SIBLEY, 'Hermeneutical Systems of Hillel and the Tannaim: A Fresh Look', *HUCA* 53 (1982), 101-35.

——'Halakhic Literary Patterns: Types, History and Affinities with New Testament Literature', *HUCA* 74 (1983), 46-60.

TOY, CRAWFORD H., *Quotations in the New Testament* (New York: Scribner, 1884).

TREBOLLE BARRERA, JULIO, 'A Preliminary Edition of 4QKings (4Q54)', in *Madrid*, i. 229-46.

——'Light from 4QJudg^a and 4QKgs on the Text of Judges and Kings', in *FYR*, 315-24.

TREMBLATH, KERN ROBERT, *Evangelical Theories of Biblical Inspiration: A Review and Proposal* (New York: Oxford University Press, 1987).

UBIGLI, L. ROSSO, 'Indice italiano-inglese dei testi di Qumran/Italian-English Index of Qumran Texts', *Henoch*, 11/2-3 (1989), 233-70.

ULLENDORFF, EDWARD, *Ethiopia and the Bible* (Oxford: Oxford University Press, 1967).

ULRICH, EUGENE C., *The Qumran Text of Samuel and Josephus* (Missoula, Mont.: Scholars Press, 1978).

—— '4QSam^c: A Fragmentary Manuscript of 2 Sam 14-15 from the Scribe of the Serek Hay-yaḥad (1QS)', *BASOR* (1979), 1-25.

—— 'Horizons of Old Testament Textual Research at the Thirtieth Anniversary of Qumran Cave 4', *CBQ* 46 (1984), 613-36.

—— 'The Greek Manuscripts of the Pentateuch from Qumrân, including Newly-Identified Fragments of Deuteronomy (4QLXXDeut)', in *De Septuaginta: Studies in Honour of John William Wevers on his Sixty-Fifth Birthday*. (Mississauga: Benben Publications, 1984), 71-82.

—— 'The Biblical Scrolls from Qumran Cave 4: A Progress Report of their Publication', *RQ* 14 (1989), 207-28.

—— 'Josephus' Biblical Text for the Books of Samuel', in L. H. Feldman and G. Hata (eds.), *Josephus, the Bible and History* (Detroit: Wayne State University Press, 1989), 81-96.

—— 'Pluriformity in the Biblical Text, Text Groups, and Question of Canon', in *Madrid*, i. 23-41.

—— 'The Canonical Process, Textual Criticism, and Latter Stages in the Composition of the Bible', in M. Fishbane and E. Tov with W. Fields (eds.), *Sha'arei Talmon: Studies in the Bible, Qumran, and the Ancient Near East Presented to Shemaryahu Talmon* (Winona Lake, Ind.: Eisenbrauns, 1992), 267-91.

VAGANAY, LÉON, and AMPHOUX, CHRISTIAN-BERNARD, *An Introduction to New Testament Textual Criticism* (Cambridge: Cambridge University Press, 1992).

VAN DER PLOEG, J., 'Le Rouleau d'Habacuc de la grotte de 'Ain Fešḥa' *BO* 8 (1951), 2-11.

VAN DER WOUDE, A. S., 'Melchisedech als himmlische Erlösergestalt in den neugefundenen eschatologischen Midraschim aus Qumran Höhle XI', *OS* 14 (1965), 354-73.

—— 'Fünfzehn Jahre Qumranforschung (1974-1988)', *TR* 54 (1989), 221-61.

—— 'Pluriformity and Uniformity: Reflections on the Transmission of the Text of the Old Testament', in J. N. Bremmer and F. García Martínez (eds.), *Sacred History and Sacred Texts in Early Judaism: A Symposium in Honour of A. S. van der Woude* (Kampen: Kok Pharos Publishing House, 1992), 151-69.

VAN UNNIK, W. C., 'De la régle μήτε προσθεῖναι μήτε ἀφελεῖν dans l'histoire du canon', *VC* 3 (1949), 1-36.

—— 'Tarsus or Jerusalem, the City of Paul's Youth', and 'Once Again: Tarsus or Jerusalem', in *Sparsa Collecta*, pt. 1 (Leiden: E. J. Brill, 1973), 259-320, 321-7.

Select Bibliography

VAN UNNIK, W. C., (ed.), *La Littérature Juive entre Tenach et Mischna* (Leiden: E. J. Brill, 1974).
——*Flavius Josephus als historischer Schriftsteller* (Heidelberg: Verlag Lambert Schneider, 1978).
VEGAS MONTANER, L., *Biblia del Mar Muerto: Profetas Menores: Edición crítica según manuscritos hebreos procedentes del Mar Muerto* (Madrid: Instituto 'Arias Montano', 1980).
——'Computer-Assisted Study on the Relation between 1QpHab and the Ancient (Mainly Greek) Biblical Versions', *RQ* 14 (1989), 307-23.
VERMES, GEZA, 'Le "Commentaire d'Habacuc" et le N.T.', *CS* 5 (1955), 342-3.
——'A propos des Commentaires bibliques découverts à Qumran', *RHPR* 35 (1955), 96-102.
——'Pre-Mishnaic Jewish Worship and the Phylacteries from the Dead Sea', *VT* 9 (1959), 5-72.
——*Scripture and Tradition in Judaism: Haggadic Studies* (Leiden: E. J. Brill, 1961).
——*Discovery in the Judean Desert* (New York: Desclée, 1965).
——'Bible and Midrash: Early Old Testament Exegesis', in *CHB* i. 199-231.
——*Post-Biblical Jewish Studies* (Leiden: E. J. Brill, 1975).
——'Interpretation, History of. B. At Qumran and in the Targums', in *IDBS*, 438-43.
——*The Dead Sea Scrolls: Qumran in Perspective*, 2nd edn. (London: SCM Press, 1982).
——'A Summary of the Law by Flavius Josephus', *NovT* 24 (1982), 289-303.
——'The Dead Sea Scrolls Forty Years On', Fourteenth Sacks Lecture. Oxford: Oxford Centre for Postgraduate Hebrew Studies, 1987.
——'Bible Interpretation at Qumran', *EI* 20 (1989), 184-91.
——'Biblical Proofs in Qumran Literature', *JSS* 34 (1989), 493-508.
——'Preliminary Remarks on Unpublished Fragments of the Community Rule from Qumran Cave 4', *JJS* 42 (1991), 250-5.
——'Oxford Forum for Qumran Research Seminar on the Rule of War from Cave 4 (4Q285)', *JJS* 43 (1992), 85-90.
——*The Religion of Jesus the Jew* (Minneapolis: Fortress Press, 1993).
——'4QS Manuscripts', unpublished plenary paper at the International Organization for Qumran Study, Cambridge, 16 July 1995 (forthcoming in M. Hengel (ed.), *Festschrift*).
——and GOODMAN, MARTIN D. (eds.), *The Essenes According to the Classical Sources*, Oxford Centre Textbook (Sheffield: JSOT Press, 1989).
VIELHAUER, P., 'Paulus und das Alte Testament', in G. Klein, *Oikodome: Aufsätze zum Neuen Testament* (Munich: Kaiser, 1979), 196-228.

VOLLMER, HANS, *Die Alttestamentlichen Citate bei Paulus: textkritisch und biblisch-theologisch gewürdigt nebst einem Anhang Über das Verhältnis des Apostels zu Philo* (Freiburg and Leipzig: J. C. B. Mohr (Paul Siebeck), 1895).

WACHOLDER, BEN ZION, *The Dawn of Qumran* (Cincinnati: Hebrew Union College Press, 1983).

——with ABEGG, MARTIN, 'The Fragmentary Remains of 11Q Torah (Temple Scroll)', *HUCA* 62 (1991), 1–116.

WALTERS, PETER [see also PETER KATZ]. 'Justin's Old Testament Quotations and the Greek Dodekapropheton Scroll', *SP* 1 (1957), 343–53.

WATTS, JOHN D. W., *Isaiah 1–33* (Waco, Tex.: Word Books, 1985).

——*Isaiah 34–66* (Waco, Tex.: Word Books, 1987).

WEINFELD, MOSHE, *Deuteronomy and the Deuteronomic School* (Oxford: Clarendon Press, 1972).

——*Deuteronomy 1–11* (New York: Doubleday, 1991).

——'Grace after Meals in Qumran', *JBL* 111 (1992), 427–40.

——'Prayer and Liturgical Practice in the Qumran Sect', in *FYR*, 241–58.

WEINGREEN, JACOB, *From Bible to Mishna* (Manchester: Manchester University Press, 1976).

WEISS, RAPHAEL, 'A Comparison between the Massoretic and the Qumran Texts of Nahum III, 1–11', *RQ* 4 (1963–4), 433–49.

——'Notes on the Additional Columns of the Pešer of Nahum' (Heb.), *BM* 2 (1962–3), 57–63.

——'K'wrh (Pesher Nahum 2.6)' (Heb.), *BM* 3 (1963–4), 156.

WEITZMAN, MICHAEL, 'The Analysis of Open Traditions', *Studies in Bibliography*, 38 (1985), 84–120.

WERNBERG-MÜLLER, PREBEN, *The Manual of Discipline* (Leiden: E. J. Brill, 1957).

WESTERHOLM, STEPHEN C., *Jesus and Scribal Authority* (Lund: C. W. K. Gleerup, 1978).

WEVERS, JOHN WM., 'Evidence of the Text of the John H. Scheide Papyri for the Translation of the Status Constructus of Ezekiel', *JBL* 70 (1951), 211–16.

——'Septuaginta-Forschungen seit 1954', *TR* 33 (1968), 18–76.

——'The Earliest Witness to the LXX Deuteronomy', *CBQ* 39 (1977), 240–4.

——'An Early Revision of the Septuagint of Numbers', *EI* 16 (1982), 235–9.

WHITE, SIDNIE ANN, '4QDt[n]: Biblical Manuscript or Excerpted Text?', in Harold W. Attridge, John J. Collins and Thomas H. Tobins (eds.), *Of Scribes and Scrolls* (New York: University Press of America, 1990), 13–20.

WHITE, SIDNIE ANN, 'The All Souls Deuteronomy and the Decalogue', *JBL* 109 (1990), 193-206.

——'Three Deuteronomy Manuscripts from Cave 4, Qumran', *JBL* 112 (1993), 23-42.

WILCOX, MAX, '"Upon the Tree"—Deut. 21: 22-23 in the New Testament', *JBL* 96 (1977), 85-99.

——'On Investigating the Use of the Old Testament in the New Testament', in E. Best and R. McL. Wilson (eds.), *Text and Interpretation: Studies in the New Testament Presented to Matthew Black* (Cambridge: Cambridge University Press, 1979), 231-50.

WILES, MAURICE F., 'Origen as Biblical Scholar', in *CHB*, i. 454-88.

WILLIAMSON, H. G. M., 'The Translation of 1QpHab V, 10', *RQ* 9 (1977-8), 263-5.

WISE, MICHAEL O., 'Accidents and Accidence: A Scribal View of Linguistic Dating of the Aramaic Scrolls from Qumran', in T. Muraoka (ed.), *Abr-Nahrain Supplement 3* (Louvain: Peeters Press, 1992), 124-67.

WRIGHT, N. T., *The Climax of the Covenant: Christ and the Law in Pauline Theology* (Edinburgh: T. & T. Clark, 1991).

WÜRTHWEIN, ERNST *The Text of the Old Testament*, Eng. trans. (London: SCM Press, 1980).

YADIN, YIGAEL, 'Pesher Nahum (4QpNahum) Reconsidered', *IEJ* 21 (1971), 1-12.

——*The Temple Scroll*, Eng. trans. (Jerusalem: Israel Exploration Society, 1983), i-iii.

YARON, REUVEN, *Gifts in Contemplation of Death in Jewish and Roman Law* (Oxford: Clarendon Press, 1960).

——'Acts of Last Will in Jewish Law', in *Actes à Cause de Mort*, Recueils de la Société Jean Bodin pour l'histoire comparative des institutions, 59 (Brussels: De Broeck Université, 1992), 29-45.

ZUNTZ, GUNTHER, *The Text of the Epistles: A Disquisition upon the Corpus Paulinum* (Oxford: Oxford University Press, 1953).

INDEX OF BIBLICAL
AND OTHER SOURCES

Index of Biblical and Other Sources

INDEX OF SUBJECT
AND AUTHOR

980122 B   75.00 (60.00)